John A. R MacDonald

The History of Blairgowrie

Town, Parish, and District

John A. R MacDonald

The History of Blairgowrie
Town, Parish, and District

ISBN/EAN: 9783337326135

Printed in Europe, USA, Canada, Australia, Japan

Cover: Foto ©ninafisch / pixelio.de

More available books at **www.hansebooks.com**

... THE ...

HISTORY OF BLAIRGOWRIE

(TOWN, PARISH, AND DISTRICT)

BEING AN ACCOUNT OF

The Origin and Progress of the Burgh from
the Earliest Period

WITH A DESCRIPTION OF THE

Antiquities, Topography, Civil History,
Ecclesiastical and Parochial Records, Institutions, Public Works,
Manufactures, Legends, Sports, Statistics, and
Biographical Sketches of Eminent
Persons, &c., &c.

... BY ...

JOHN A. R. MACDONALD,

C.E. and Architect

ILLUSTRATED

BLAIRGOWRIE:
PRINTED AT THE ADVERTISER OFFICE.
1899.

PREFACE.

"The Barony of Blairgowrie—a gift fit even for a Queen to bestow."—*Queen Mary to Ronald Græme.*

THE volume now published has been the work of my leisure for many months, but the collecting and compiling has been the labour of nearly fifteen years. During that period the MS. has been revised, condensed, and re-written five times. It was undertaken more from regard to the necessity of meeting a want long felt to exist than from any sense of fitness for the task. The Rev. James Johnstone's contribution to the Statistical Account of Scotland is very valuable, and is reproduced in its entirety, yet up to 1865, when Ireland's handbook was issued, no History of Blairgowrie existed. In supplying the want referred to, I have endeavoured to collect and compile, as far as possible, the historical facts, records, and traditions, in the hope that they will interest and gratify the sons and daughters of "Rest and be thankful," especially those scattered abroad, with the memories of the good old town.

I desire to express my obligations to those writers (a list of whom is given) of whose labours I have availed myself, and also to many townsmen who have kindly afforded me the use of materials in their possession, or communicated information tending to make the volume more complete:—To Rev. Robert Kemp, M.A., for the "Parochial Registers"; to Mr G. S. Duncan, F.S.A., Scot., for "Church Records"; to Mr William Davie, for "Notes on Blairgowrie"; to Mr A. Davidson Smith, C.A., Edinburgh, Secretary of Royal Caledonian Curling Club, for permission to reproduce the illustration, "Curlers of Blairgowrie"; to Messrs C. & R. Anderson, publishers of "North British Agriculturist," Edinburgh, for block of "John Panton"; to Mr John L. Ford, merchant, for blocks "At Blairgowrie," "The Square, Wellmeadow,"

"Keith Falls," and "Craighall"; to Mr J. E. Butchart, litho. artist, and Mr Robert Blackwood, lithographer, Dundee, for the excellent litho. portraits and sketches; and to Mr Alex. Allan, of the "Blairgowrie Advertiser," for all other blocks reproduced in the volume.

My thanks are specially due to Mr John Christie, of the "Blairgowrie Advertiser," for his valuable assistance in the correction of proof sheets, and in the supervision of the work while passing through the press.

I trust that the volume (imperfect as it may be) now submitted to the indulgent consideration of the public, will promote an intelligent and healthy interest in all that pertains to the Town, Parish, and District.

J. A. R. M.

16 NEWTON STREET,
BLAIRGOWRIE, *3rd March, 1899.*

CONTENTS.

CHAPTER I.

PAGE

Situation of the Town—Extent of the Parish—Topography—Latitude and Longitude—Etymology of Blairgowrie—Traditions—Description of the Town—Origin of Street Names—Soil—Geology—Quarries—Fossils—Wood—Arboriculture—Piscatorial—Zoology, - - - - - - 15

CHAPTER II.

Authentic Records—Roman Invasions—Suetonius Paulinus—Julius Agricola—Galdus—Mons Grampius—Site of the Battle—A Bone of Contention—Opinions of Eminent Men—Tacitus—Description of the Battle—A Disputed Victory—Sad Experience of the Romans—False Reports—Vespasian—Evidences of the Struggle—Tulina—Emperor Severus—Bridge of Lornty—St Ninian's Well—Invasion of Northmen—Kenneth M'Alpin—Regner Lodbrog—Inchtuthil—Battle of Stenton Craig—Bloody Inches—Church and Lands of Blair—Kinclaven Castle taken by Wallace—Robert the Bruce at Stormont Loch—Highland Caterans—Battle of Glasclune—Drummond Feud and Massacre—Queen Mary's Summons—Offers by Murderers—Their Trial and Execution—Bond of Manrent, - - - - - - 25

CHAPTER III.

King Charles I.—Charter of Burgh of Barony—Barony Court—Gallows Knowe—Montrose—Sacking of Newton Castle—Donald Cargill—John Erskine—The Ghost of Mause: Full Description—Prince Charlie and the Curlers' Dinner—Duke of Cumberland at Woodlands—Division of the Muir of Blair—Coble Pule—Boat Brae—Muckle Mill Erected—Purchase of Blairgowrie Estate—Military Service in Blairgowrie—Enrolment Returns, 1803—A Rifle Corps—A Distinguished Officer—Burgh Charters—Erection of Parish Church—Stage Coach—Introduction of Gas and Printing—Visits of the Queen—Auld Brig o' Blair—An Incident of the French Revolution—The First Newspaper—Introduction of the Railway Service—A Good Story—Burns Centenary Celebration—Inauguration of Volunteer Movement, 1859, - - 42

CHAPTER IV.

Founding of Public Hall—Earl Russell at Meikleour—Address from Inhabitants—Public Banquet—Address by Meikleour Tenantry—Earl Russell's Speech—Opinions of the Press—A French View—Introduction of Water Supply—Report and Analysis of Water—Drainage of Town—Erection of New Schools—Opening Up of Commercial Street—Planting Trees in Wellmeadow—Franchise Demonstration—County Council—Boundary Commission—Public Park: a Generous Gift—Burgh Seal—Macpherson Memorial Fountain—New Sewage Works—Visit of Lord Wolseley—The Bailies of Blair—Magistrates—Provosts, - - - - - 57

CHAPTER V.

Original Inhabitants of Scotland—Druids and Druidical Remains—Standing Stones—Haer Cairns—Tumuli—Store Mount—Blairs—Buzzard Dykes—Bloody Inches—Steed Stalls—Roman Relics—Local Antiquarian Collections—Relics in Scottish Antiquarian Museum—French Bell—Hirchen Hill—Agreements and Charters—Interesting Map—Seals of Families—Pedigree of Drummonds of Blair—Copy of Two Letters by King James the Seventh—Notes from Rental Book of Coupar Abbey—Cally—Murtoun—Blair—Old Parish Tokens, - - - - - - - - 76

CHAPTER VI.

Ecclesiastical State—Parish Church and Ministers—Associate Antiburgher Secession Church—Brown Street Chapel—St Mary's Church—First Free Church—Free South Church—St Catherine's Church—St Stephen's Church—Congregational Church—Extracts from Parochial Registers—Shearing on Sabbath—Selling Aile in time of Sermon—English Army in Scotland—Collection in Aid of Glasgow—No Session—Applicant for Schoolmaster—An Indigent Baronet—Act Anent Brydals—In the Jouggs—The Boatman of Blair—Administering the Lord's Supper—Irregularities—Sabbath Breach—Communion Cups—New Schoolhouse—Poor's Rates Established—Sunday Shooting Match for a Sow—Population—Schools and Schoolmasters—Parish School—James Street School—William Street School—New Public Schools—Episcopal School—Dames' Schools—Adventure Schools—St Stephen's R. C. School—Sextons of Parish of Blair, - - 91

CHAPTER VII.

Statistical Account of the Parish, 1796—Population and Statistical Table—Conditions and Professions—Births, &c.—Religious Persuasions — Stock, Rent. &c. — Population—Character—Origin—Extent, Surface, Situation, Soil, &c.—Cattle—Prices of Provisions and Labour—Bleachfield, Cloth, Stamp Office—Climate and Diseases—Rivers, Cascades, Fish, Birds, Scenery, &c.—Lakes, Islands, &c.—Minerals and Mineral Springs—Woods—Manufactures, Mills, &c.—Ecclesiastical State, Schools, &c. — Poor — Village and Markets—State of Property, Inclosures, &c.—Agriculture, Produce, &c.—Improvements, Farm Rents, &c.—Roads and Bridges—Gentlemen's Seats—Eminent Men—Antiquities—Disadvantages, - - - - - - - 114

CHAPTER VIII.

Castles and Mansions—Legends, Ballads, &c., - - - 129

CHAPTER IX.

Institutions, Societies, &c.—Banks—Barty Mortification—Blairgowrie and District Photographic Association—Choral Society—Constitutional Club—Dramatic Society—Dundee, Blairgowrie and District Association—Edinburgh Blairgowrie Club—Evening Classes—Free Masonry—Horticultural Society — Literary Societies — Mechanics' Institute — Post Office—Press—Shepherds—Volunteer Rifle Brigade, - - 147

CHAPTER X.

Manufactures—Lornty Mill—Brooklinn—Oakbank—The Meikle Mill—Ericht Linen Works—Greenbank Engineering Works—Millwright Works—Brewing—Ancient Trade—Recollections of the Past—A Merchant's Rhyme—The Whisky Roadie and its Associations—Duncan Watchie—Posty Reid—The Toon's Officers—The Guard House—The Bell o' Blair—Lily Harris—Matthew Harris—Tammy Mann—Daft Hary—John Couper—Quoit Club—Candy Betty—Smith Lamont—Voluntary Constables—Abram Low and the Welltown Brownies—Isaac Low, the Ingenious Blacksmith, - - 165

CHAPTER XI.

Sports, Pastimes, &c.—Angling—The Ericht as a Salmon River—Fishways on the Ericht—Fish Ladders for Loch Benachally—Ardle—Blackwater—Ericht—Lornty—Lunan—Tay—Isla—Drimmie Burn—Fyall Burn—Lochs Benachally, Butterstone, Clunie, Marlee, Loch o' the Lowes, Stormont, Rae, Fengus, White, &c.—Bowling—Cricket—Curling—Cycling—Fair o' Blair—The Fair o' Blair 50 Years ago—Football—Golf—Gymnastics, - - - - - - - - 183

CHAPTER XII.

Eminent Men, &c.—Drummond of Newton—George Drummond—May Drummond—Blair of Ardblair—Mercer of Meikleour—Admirable Crichton—Thomas Graham (Lord Lynedoch)—Rattray of Rattray and Craighall—Grimond of Lornty—Professor Adams—Rev. John Baxter—Macpherson of Blairgowrie—Allan Macpherson—Dr James Neilson—William Geddes—David C. Robb—John Bridie—Dr Robert Lunan—Thomas S. Bisset—John Panton, &c., &c., - - - 206

CHAPTER XIII.

Walks and Drives around Blairgowrie—To Lornty and the Heughs—Round Knock-ma-har—Round the Golf Course—Places of Interest near Blairgowrie—Distances from Blairgowrie—The Royal Route—Blairgowrie to Dunkeld—To Alyth—To Coupar Angus, - - - - - 233

CHAPTER XIV.

Curious, Interesting, and Amusing.—A Blairgowrie in America—A Curious Despatch from India—A Blair Chiel' Mayor of Dunedin—A Blair Highlander in Russia—Pennant's Description of Blair—Copy of a Burgess Circular—Waterloo Heroes connected with Blairgowrie—An Interesting Operation on the Ameer—Blairgowrie in 1800—Blairgowrie 50 Years Ago—Statistics of Death Rate—"Blair Watter Curlin' Stanes"—Blairgowrie Instrumental Band—The Hymn Tune, "Blairgowrie"—Forest of Clunie Farms—The Catty Mill—Carsie Scutching Mill—Baldornoch Slate—Merchants' Pic-Nic—St Fink—Benachally Monument—Parish Kirk Elders—Copy Letter from the Young Chevalier—The Bridge of Craighall—The Priest's House—The Ash Trees—Parish Church—Illuminated Clock—Athletics—An Inducement to Feuars on Blairgowrie Estate—Montrose Disbands his Army near Blairgowrie—Genealogy of the Family of Blair—Blairgowrie Volunteers in 1804—Interesting Despatches from India, 1858—A Local Violin Maker, &c., 244

ILLUSTRATIONS.

At Blairgowrie,
The Square, Wellmeadow,
The Beech Hedge,
Blairgowrie in 1860,
Meikleour Cross,
Burgh Seal,
Macpherson Memorial Fountain,
Churches—Established, St Catherine's, }
        First Free, South Free, }
Rev. William Fraser, M.A.,
St Mary's Parish Church,
Public School,
Clunie Loch and Castle,
Craighall,
Shepherds' Badge,
Volunteer Badge,
Curlers of Blairgowrie, 1888,
The Lansdowne Golf Course,
Admirable Crichton, Provost Drummond, }
   Thomas Graham, Hon. Mrs Graham, }
Dr James Neilson, Alexander Robertson, }
      William Geddes, }
Rev. John Baxter, D.D., Thomas S. Bisset, }
Allan Macpherson,
John Bridie, First Provost of Blairgowrie,
Robert Lunan, Surgeon,
John Panton,
Keith Falls,
Bridge of Cally,
Spittalfield,
Tron and Jouggs,
Church Tokens,

LIST OF AUTHORITIES.

Acts of the Parliaments of Scotland.
Advertiser, The Blairgowrie.
Advertiser, The Dundee.
Annals of Scotland, - - - - - - *Hailes*
Armorial Bearings.
Antiquities.
Ancient Criminal Trials, - - - - *R. Pitcairn*
A Tour in the Highlands, 1819.
Biographical Dictionary of Eminent Scotsmen, - *Rev. J. Thomson*
Burgh Records of Scotland.
Blairgowrie as a Pic-nic Resort, - - - - *J. Ferguson*
Blairgowrie Annual, The.
Blairgowrie News, The.
Caledonia, - - - - - - *Chalmers*
Cronykil, - - - - - - *Wyntoun*
Crests of Families of Scotland, - - - *J. Fairbairn*
Calendarium Genealogicum.
Coupar Angus Abbey Register, - - - *Dr C. Rogers*
Crail College Church Register, - - - *Do.*
Courier and Argus, The Dundee.
Domestic and Castellated Architecture of Scotland, *M'Gibbon and Ross*
Domestic Annals of Scotland, - - - *R. Chambers*
Drummonds of Blair-Drummond, - - - *W. Frazer*
Fasti Ecclesia Scoticanæ, - - - - *Dr Scott*
Gazetteer of Scotland, 1803.
Guide to Perthshire, - - - - - *T. Hunter*
Genealogy of Craighall Family, - - - *Balfour*
Historic Scenes in Perthshire, - - - *Dr Marshall*
History of the M'Combies, - - - *Wm. M'Combie Smith*
History of Dundee, - - - - *James Maclaren*
History of the Scottish Nation, - - - *W. Anderson*
Historical Castles and Mansions, - - - *A. H. Miller*
History of Scotland, - - - - - *J. H. Burton*
History of Scotland, - - - - - *Buchanan*
Industries of Scotland, - - - - - *Bremner*
Linen Trade, - - - - - - *Warden*
Linnæan Transactions, - - - - - *A. Bruce*
Mercurius Caledonicus.
New Statistical Account of Scotland.
Parochial Registers of Blairgowrie.
Prehistoric Annals of Scotland, - - - *Dr Wilson*
Reminiscences of Flax Spinning, - - - *Brown*
Strathmore, Past and Present, - - - *Dr M'Pherson*
Scots Magazine, 1773.
Sportsman's Guide, - - - - *J. Watson Lyall*
Statistical Account of Scotland, - - - *Sir J. Sinclair*

Seats of Scotland, ... *Maitland Club*
Transactions of Blairgowrie Angling Club.
Transactions of Blairgowrie Bowling Club.
Transactions of Blairgowrie Curling Club.
Transactions of Scottish Antiquarian Society.
Transactions of Perthshire Society of Natural Science.
Transactions of Royal Caledonian Curling Club.
Theatrum Scotiæ, ... *Slezer*
Tours in Scotland, ... *Pennant*
Topography of the Basin of the Tay, ... *Knox*
The Red Book of Menteith, ... *Wm. Frazer*
Wallace, Life of, ... *Blind Harry*

The History of Blairgowrie.

INTRODUCTION.

NO recreation is generally more delightful than that of viewing a stretch of country in which the large extent of its fertile lands and the number of its villages, cottages, villas, and homesteads bear ample witness to the skill and the industry, the wealth and contentment of human beings.

A large city, with its crowds, its commerce, its works of art, its exhibitions, and its splendour, dazzles and attracts many individuals, yet there is something more pleasing, more calm and sedative, in viewing from an elevated position a highly-cultivated district stretched out, as it were a map, to the gaze of the spectator.

How delightful and glorious the prospect of the luxurious and verdant valley of Strathmore, viewed from the summit of the slope of hills (the southern range of the Grampians) to the north of Blairgowrie, known as Knock-ma-har, locally termed "Knocky."

The quiet and peaceful town of Blairgowrie—"Rest and be Thankful"—lies at the foot of the slope, with its red-tiled and purple-slated roofs, the tall and pointed spires of the churches, and the dull red stalks of the public works; the whole beautifully interspersed with different specimens of trees — the hazel, the beech, and the poplar being predominant. Away beyond we gaze on fields crowned with plenty, the grand tract of country—the Howe of Strathmore—stretching between Forfar and Perth, clothed in the beautiful garb of autumn, the varied hues of the woods showing distinctly against the dark serried ridges of the Sidlaw Hills.

"We gaze upon the spreath unshorn
　In Autumn garb of tree and corn;
　Strathmore, that labour's arts adorn,
　　And plenty fills,
　And Ericht vale, where we were born,
　　'Atween the hills.

"The wilderness behind outgrew,
　Of moor and moss, where peesweeps flew
　And joyous screamed the slow curlew
　　The scene that crossed;
　On this we gaze, till 'wildered too
　　In thought, and lost.

"We gaze upon the delta sweet,
　Where Ericht and the Isla meet,
　That 'pretty carse' before our feet
　　To see, a joy;
　Where Xerxes' host, again complete,
　　Might free deploy.

"We gaze upon the rivers, three—
　The Ericht and Isla and the Tay—
　The Ardle kythes not to oor e'e
　　For banks between,
　Tho' weel we ken far it sud be,
　　Not sinnle seen.

"We gaze on towns not unrenowned,
　That held their ancient sites around,
　Seen, or by their tokens found
　　Of hoverin' reek,
　Frae Forfar east, twin steeple crowned
　　Wi' skyward peak.

"Tae Perth—fair city—on the green,
　By winding Tay, that sits serene;
　Scone, Stanley, Coupar, these between,
　　Burrelton and Woodside,
　Newtyle exposed, by Sidlaw seen,
　　An' Meigle hid.

"Dunkeld, proud Celtic city sma',
　Blairgowrie and the Rattrays twa,
　An' Alyth—by the Grampians a'
　　Sae snugly placed;
　An' Kirrie, tae complete the raw,
　　Far in the east.

"We gaze in venerative mood
　On classic spots, seen whence we stood;
　On Glamis, yet red wi' Duncan's blood,
　　Dunsinane Hill,
　And Birnam, and where dwelt the good,
　　Yea great, Cargill.

> "We gaze on many a cherished scene,
> Familiar, where our feet had been,
> On' mony auld-kent fairm o' frien'
>   Wi' memories showered—
> Wi' yearnin' heart an' lovin' e'en
>   On them we glowered.
>
> "We gaze on mills, and wish them weel,
> Of industry that tend the wheel,
> On kirks, an' Scottish fire did feel,
>   An' hoped the day
> We yet shall a' bend in one beil',
>   An' truth have sway.
>
> "Frae labour's piles in kirks an' mills
> We gaze upon the woods an' rills,
> Theme tender bard with rapture fills;
>   Frae these we turn
> An' kindlier gaze upon the hills
>   An' mony a cairn.
>
> "Mons Grampius near, full an' compac'
> That may be nae mountaineous trac',
> But just the hill of our Gormack
>   As 'twas away
> Far 'mid the scenes an' ages back
>   And is this day.
>
> "The Lomonds, Wallace' bow-shot famed,
> The Sidlaws and the Ochils named,
> On Ben-a-chally, stubborn framed
>   Wi' ribs of rock
> On Ben-y-ghloe, in Perthshire claimed
>   The highest block."

We gaze . . . on the Hatton Hill and Glower-ower-im, on Mount Blair and Kinpurnie, on the beautiful windings of the Ericht and the Tay; on the placid waters of Stormont Loch, White, Black, Fengus, Marlee, and Clunie; on

> "Deep waving fields an' pastures green,
> With gentle slopes and groves between."

All around there are spots dear to a patriotic breast as the scene of peaceful industry in these modern times, or of deeds of heroism and renown in those that have long gone by; and as we hear the splash of the wheel, the birr and clang of machinery, and the shrill piercing shrieks of the locomotive, we can in fancy picture to ourselves the scenes of the past. Here, where we stand, were marshalled the squadrons of Caledonia (Caoill daoin—the people of the woods) under Galgacus to oppose the

Roman legions under Julius Agricola encamped by Meiklcour and Delvine; and here our countrymen, the Caoill daoin, inflicted a heavy defeat on their enemies, though with terrible loss to themselves (A.D. 84).

Once more we hear in fancy the victorious shout of M'Alpin's warriors pursuing the fierce Norse Vikings at Inchtuthil on the Tay, A.D. 847; there, along the Howe, march the Highland host to free their country at Bannockburn, 1314; behind us, the pipe of the clansmen's slogan at the Battle of Glasclune, 1392; from the castles of Glasclune, Drumlochy, and Gormack, behold the murderous lairds and their retainers march to the Drummond Massacre at the "Peroche Kyrke," 1554; on the Haughs of Rattray, the great Montrose disband his army, 1646; Cromwell, the Protector of the English Commonwealth, at the sack of Newton Castle, 1650; the dragoons of Claverhouse pursue Donald Cargill, the Covenanter, who made his wonderful escape by leaping the cascade of the Keith, 16—; the young Laird Drummond of Newton (1700) (the future founder of the Royal Infirmary in Edinburgh) romp about; Prince Charlie and his Highlanders feast at the curlers' expense in Eppie Clark's ale-house at the Hill o' Blair, 1745; the "Butcher" Cumberland encamped on the Muir of Blair, 1746; the future hero of Barossa—Thomas Graham—engage at agricultural pursuits at Newton, 1786; Sir Walter Scott wander amid the wild sylvan grandeur of Tullyveolan (Craighall), 1793; the Royal entry of Her Majesty the Queen through the town in 1842 and 1857; the introduction of the railway, 1855; the banqueting of Earl Russell in 1863, with the tumults, bickerings, and excitement prevailing in these present times.

To the native of Blairgowrie and district wandering amid the llanos and prairies of America, the wilds of Africa, the jungle of India, the bush of Australia, the isles of the South, or the snows of the North, these old associations cling tenaciously and lead him to think of home, and he naturally carries with him the feeling so beautifully expressed by Sir Walter Scott:—

> "Breathes there a man with soul so dead
> Who never to himself hath said,
> This is my own, my native land?"

CHAPTER I.

Situation of the Town—Extent of the Parish—Topography—Latitude and Longitude—Etymology of Blairgowrie—Traditions—Description of the Town—Origin of Street Names—Soil—Geology—Quarries—Fossils—Wood—Arboriculture—Piscatorial—Zoology.

THE town of Blairgowrie is situated at the base of that part of the southern range of the Grampian Mountains cut by the River Ericht. On the left the valley and burn of Lornty give a double breast to the cut. The heights to the north are the Heughs of Mause, Knock-ma-har, and the Hill of Blair. On the east side of the river are the "Cennethy," or the Hatton Hill, and the higher one "Glower-ower-im," possibly so termed because the spectator from its summit can survey a huge tract of country. Behind Knock-ma-har is the valley of the Lornty, and away further north, on the heights beyond, the Muir of Cochrage and Forest of Clunie. Immediately to the south of Blairgowrie is the famous strath—the Howe of Strathmore—with its streams, and lakes, and woods, and pastures.

As regards beauty of situation and salubrity of climate the town enjoys peculiar advantages. Situated on the banks of a pure and rapid river, on the confines of the Highlands, it possesses the advantage of highly-picturesque and diversified scenery, both highland and lowland. Sheltered by the wooded heights to the north from the cold northern winds, snow seldom falls to any depth, and soon melts from the southern slope on which the town is situated, while its openness to the south, east, and west gives free circulation to the winds from these directions.

Blairgowrie is situated between north latitude 56 degs. 35 mins. 6 secs. and 56 degs. 35 mins. 44 secs., and between west longitude 3 degs. 20 mins. and 3 degs. 20 mins. 45 secs.

The extent of the parish of Blairgowrie is about eleven miles from north to south, and about eight miles east and west, irregular in figure, and frequently intersected by the parishes of Rattray, Kinloch, and Bendochy.

The town is situated at a good altitude from the mean sea level at Liverpool, according to the data of the Ordnance Survey of 1863. At the Beeches, west-end of town, the height in feet is 264·5; Greenbank Engineering Works, 258; Bankhead Toll, 229·75; Bridge of Blair, 197·75; foot of Allan Street, 216; Royal Hotel, 243; Bank of Scotland, 245; First Free Church, 279·75; Parish Church, 331·62; and Hill of Blair, 337·5.

Regarding the origin of Blairgowrie and the derivation of the name there have been suggested many definitions, but they are not very certain. The first half of the name may be traced from the Celtic "Blair," signifying a battlefield; the latter part, however, "Gowrie," is difficult to trace. One derivation, according to the following tradition, if not certain, is at least plausible. The great valley of Strathmore was, at one time, a vast forest in which the kings of Scotland were wont to hunt. At intervals here and there in the forest were considerable patches of ground or crofts cultivated by woodmen, in the pay of the sovereign, to raise the crops necessary for the Court. These woodmen had also, when called upon, to attend the King during the chase, and join his bodyguard in the event of war. We are not informed who this royal personage was, who, like the Gudeman o' Ballingeich, used to disguise himself in the chase so that he might better see the condition of his people. On one of these occasions alone, save with an attendant and a pack of hounds, the King had got separated from the rest of the party, and, drawing near to one of the clearings from which they saw a column of smoke ascend, heard the sound of music. A nearer approach revealed to their astonished gaze the sprightly trippings of a lovely maiden dancing a reel to the spirit-enlivening music of the pibroch played by an old piper. The maid, not the least shy when she discovered the stranger gazing at her, told him to "glower aye," and the old piper, removing the chanter from his mouth, invited him to join in. Nothing loath the stranger accepted the invitation, perhaps not unwilling to be recognised. At the finish he politely asked the maiden's name, and with a captivating smile she muttered, though scarcely audible, "Gow." Then the stranger, clasp-

WELLMEADOW.

ing her hand in his own, addressed the old piper:—"Thy name is 'Gow' and I am 'Righ,' and now

> "This muir shall be my huntingfield;
> This p'easant hen my queen shall be;
> Of twenty miles ye'll get the yield;
> An' be the laird of 'Gow-an-Righ.'"

Gow, a smith; *Righ*, a king—Blairgowrie, the field of the king's smith. Another derivation, however, may be the more correct one. *Blair*, a battlefield; and *Gowrie*, a hollow or between the hills—the battlefield in the hollow, probably so called from the Battle of Mons Grampius reputed to have been fought in the valley between Knock-ma-har and the ridge along by the Heughs of Mause.

The town in its present state takes the form of a square, and by its streets is formed into squares. The streets are of the ordinary breadth, with side footways paved with asphalte, granolithic, or gravel, and are kept very clean. In the north and western districts of the town a small plot of ground in front of the houses gives a healthy openness to the town, combined with seclusion.

In the disposition of its principal thoroughfares, the old roads which formed the means of communication with the neighbouring districts still form the main arteries of the burgh. Dividing it into two almost equal divisions, the old turnpike from Perth to Kirriemuir is still the main street, though termed in its different sections Allan Street, High Street, and Perth Street. From the south the turnpike from Coupar Angus intersects again, leading across towards the north over the Hill of Blair. Of the numerous streets running parallel south by west, the furthest south is Terminus Street. This has its end to the west running into the Coupar Angus Road, and terminating at the east in Welton Road. This street bounds the Gas Works on the south and the Railway Station on the north. The Station Buildings have within recent years been entirely remodelled and reconstructed, and present a very handsome appearance. Gas Brae bounds the Gas Works on the north, running from foot of Reform Street to Wellmeadow. Leslie Street, with continuation of Union Street lies to the west. On the south side of Leslie Street is the North of Scotland Bank, formerly

Bleaton House; on the south side of Union Street is the Volunteer Drill Hall, opened 1898. High Street runs westwards, with continuation of Perth Street and Perth Road. At the Cross—the site of the old Mercate Cross of Blair—is the Royal Hotel, built on the site of a house in which a former proprietor (Brown of Marlee) was born, as recorded by a tablet over the entrance door. In the High Street are the Queen's Hotel, immediately opposite which stood John Tyrie's brew-house; the Mechanics' Institute and Working Men's Club, erected in 1870 at a cost of £800; the Bank of Scotland. On the south side of the street, nearly opposite the Institute, stood a small house in which Prince Charlie is said to have passed a night on his way to the south, and which was known long afterwards as "The Palace."

George Street, in the same parallel, extends from Dunkeld Road on the west, alongside of the "Lochy," with access to Bowling Green, and terminating in James Street with a two-branch way, the left leading to the First Free Church and the right to Upper Allan Street, the Parish Church, Public Schools, and Hill of Blair.

Lochy Terrace, Emma Terrace, and Newton Terrace are in a way of being opened up.

From the east end of the Station the Welton Road, leading up the west side of the River Ericht, enters the "Tannage," now known as Tannage Street, a tan work at one time having been in operation there. Commercial Street, opened up in 1882 through what used to be the garden of the Station Hotel, leads from the front entrance of the Station Buildings to the Wellmeadow and heart of the town. The north side of the Meadow is bounded by a handsome block known as the "Bank Buildings," containing principally a branch of the Union Bank, and the Blairgowrie Arms and the Constitutional Club, erected on the site of what was formerly Jackson's Inn. Nearly opposite this building was St Ninian's Well, from which the square took its name—Wellmeadow—having its source in a spring, led some years ago into the town drainage. In former times this area was a marsh, and, having been improved and drained, was, within the memory of some of our old worthies, a public park where the nomadic drover and shepherd pastured their flocks.

DESCRIPTION OF THE TOWN.

The square presents rather an ornate appearance if only it was kept in better condition, a row of trees having been planted round it over a dozen years ago, and which are thriving luxuriantly. At the south-east corner is a memorial fountain, erected in 1893, to commemorate the life and work of the late Superior, Allan Macpherson, Esq. of Blairgowrie. The fountain is of red stone, beautifully carved and finished. On the south side of the Meadow are the Gas Works, erected in 1834; the Auction Mart and cattle sale stores; the Crown Inn and Railway Hotel—a very busy rendezvous for farmers and dealers on market days. On the east side are the Temperance Hotel and the Bridge of Blairgowrie; the Ogilvy Arms; Victoria Hotel, built on the site of an old hostelry; the Commercial Bank; and the intersection of Leslie and Allan Streets. The latter (Allan Street) leads from the Meadow to the "Cross," with continuation of Upper Allan Street to Hill of Blair. Immediately to the right are Blairgowrie Brewery, belonging to Messrs Ogilvy, and Upper Mill Street leading to the Meal Mill, Ericht Linen Works, the old Plash Mill, and to Oakbank up the river side; opposite is the Royal Bank, and Ericht Lane leading west to the Croft. On the left of this street is a handsome block of buildings which give some appearance. The site they occupy was in former years held by a block considered, in its day, the best in town, but burned down in 1890. Near by stood also a public-house, and a bye-path leading thereto was known as the "Whuskie Roadie." On the other side of the street, at "Davie's Pend," over 80 years ago stood the old "guard house" of Blair or jail for the retention of prisoners; adjoining the gable, strung up between two posts, was the "auld bell o' Blair," tolled on high days and market days. The Croft connects west end of Wellmeadow with Leslie Street and High Street, with continuation of Bank Street and David Street to Newton Terrace. From the west end of Gas Brae, Reform Street leads up to Perth Street and is set off on the left by the South Free Church, St Mary's Parish Church, Mission House, and "Advertiser" Office; an off-side continuation is John Street, leading to the Roman Catholic School, formerly the old Parochial School.

Further west is William Street, running from Bankhead

Toll to Perth Street, in which are South Free Church School and Congregational Church. Jessie Street leads from Emma Street to Perth Street. Side streets further west, but still unformed, are Castle Street, opposite Lochy Street, leading to the Lochy and Bowling Green; Athole Street, opposite the intersection of the Dunkeld Road with Perth Road. On the Dunkeld Road are the famous Agricultural Engineering Works of Messrs Bisset & Sons, Limited. The west-end of Blairgowrie, from Athole Street onwards out to Falcon House, is well laid out and enriched with cottages and villas of the upper class. East of Lochy Street and mid-way to John Street is Newton Street leading from Perth Street to Maryfield. In this street are, for the most part, many fashionable and desirable residences —The Parsonage, Viewfield, The Feu, and Newton Castle being most prominent. Newton Castle is an interesting historical pile, and is frequently mentioned in history. It was sacked by Oliver Cromwell and by Montrose; occupied by Royalist troops in 1745; was the birth-place of George Drummond, six times Lord Provost of Edinburgh, and founder of the Royal Infirmary (died 1766); and of Thomas Graham, the hero of Barossa and Vittoria (Lord Lynedoch), died 1843.

Newton Terrace extends from west-end of Gallowbank east to Upper Allan Street, and is for the most part unformed though rather a pleasant promenade in summer.

Upper Allan Street leads from the Cross, at Royal Hotel, northwards past the site of the earliest Parochial School—the Parish Manse—where it divides into two, that road to the right, the Little Hill, leading to the Parish Church and Parish Burying-Ground. The church was erected in 1824 on the public bowling green of a former generation, and where the laird of Newton was massacred by his neighbours in 1554. Almost adjoining are the Maltings of Mr William Panton, who carries on an extensive business in this line. The road to the left, the Hill, leads north, passing the Public Schools of Blairgowrie, erected in 1879 on part of the parish glebe, but used for many a year as "The toon's park."

This road joins on to the Little Hill at Stormont Lodge, and leads northward over the Bridge at the "Cuttle" ravine to the "Board of Health," Knoch-ma-har,

Lornty, and the Heughs of Mause.

* * * * * *

The names of a few of the principal streets throughout the town are derived thus:—" Allan Street," after Col. Allan Macpherson, Superior of the Burgh in 1800 ; "Brown Street" and "John Street," after John Brown of Marlee (born in a house on the site of which the Royal Hotel now stands); " Bank Street," formerly Constable Lane, changed when the Bank of Scotland was built; " Leslie Street," after James Leslie, proprietor of the Leslie Feus; "James Street," after James Geddes, mason ; "Keay Street," after Miss Keay, a feuar there; "Mitchell Square," after Thomas Mitchell of Greenfield ; " Newton Lane " and "Newton Street," as the lane and street leading to Newton Castle; " Chalmers Street," after Provost Chalmers ; "George Street," after George Drummond of Newton ; "Tannage Street," from a tannery which existed there ; "Terminus Street," the terminus of the railway system ; "Mill Street," as leading to the Mill, &c.

Soil.

The alluvium which covers the strata around Blairgowrie is a species of till of very irregular thickness and quality.

At a place known as the Heughs of Mause, a mile or so north of the town, it forms a precipice of a very singular and picturesque appearance, rising from the bed of the river to a height of over 200 feet.

To the north-west the grey wacke formation is covered with moss, forming the great moss of Cochrage, an extensive tract of barren moor covered with heath and marsh.

South of this, on the slopes of the ridges rising to the north of the town, the soil is a stiff brown clay of considerable fertility, and in the south of the parish, it is a strong black loam intervened by the Muir of Blair, a large extent of barren, unproductive, gravel, part under cultivation of strawberry and other fruits, part under plantation, and the remainder covered with whins and heather.

Geology.

All the rocks in the parish are of the conglomerate or sandstone formation.

About four miles north of the town there is a quarry, now discontinued, of clay slate. This formation seems to stretch across the parish in a south-westerly direction, but it is not visible at any other point till it reappears at Forneth. Its thickness is supposed to be about 40 feet.

A stratum of whinstone is found along the summit of the ridge at the back of the town known as Knock-ma-har. The strata is nearly horizontal, with a slight inclination to the north-west. All along the southern slope entending into the lower ground to the south and west, there is a very extensive stratum of coarse red sandstone of great thickness running in a north-westerly direction across the parish.

About a mile south-east of the town this red sandstone assumes a finer grain and darker colour, and forms a perpendicular cliff of a considerable height on the bank of the river.

Scarcely a mile south of this there is another very regular and beautiful stratum of fine grey sandstone of excellent quality for building, and apparently of great thickness.

On both sides of the bed of the Ericht, about half-a-mile north of the town, there is a fine dyke of columnar basalt in horizontal layers.

All the rocks which are of any height are of the conglomerate, the strata being intersected by occasional fissures at right angles to the planes of their stratification.

Quarries.

The only kinds of stone found in extensive beds in the parish, and which are at all adapted for building, are the coarse red sandstone and a species of whinstone of a very dark colour. This latter has been used only to a limited extent in building, owing to its sombre and gloomy colour, and its almost impracticable hardness. It is mostly used for macadamising the streets and roads in the neighbourhood.

There are two quarries of grey-wacke stone in the north-west of the parish, but the use of them has been discontinued owing to the hardness of the stone. There is a quarry of the coarse red sandstone, south of Altamont, in full working operation. This stone is of very coarse quality, not easily dressed, but is very durable. Another quarry of red sandstone of fine quality, but softer texture, was opened several years ago and worked on the grounds of Rosemount, in the face of an almost perpendicular cliff rising out of the bed of the river, but it has now been abandoned. There is also another quarry of fine grey sandstone at Parkhead, but it has not been worked to any considerable extent of late years.

Fossils.

The district around Blairgowrie is very interesting to geologists, as large and distinct specimens of fossil plants are to be found in the old quarries and rocks, particularly at Mayriggs, near Rosemount, and Gellyburn, Murthly.

Notices of the most frequent plants have been given by Dr Geekie in his famed "Text-book of Geology." Several of the more frequent finds are:—*Psilophyton princeps*, very abundant, represented by profusion of fragments of stems and branches, and more rarely by specimens of the rhizomata and of the sporocarps; *P. robustius*, by fragments of stems, less abundant; and *Arthrostigma gracile*, by some portions of stems. From the sandstone beds of Murthly, several specimens of rounded objects, referable to *Pachytheca*, have been found.

Wood.

In the southern division of the parish there are extensive plantations of Scotch fir, on ground which had previously been a barren moor covered with heather and broom. A great part of this moor still remains in a waste and unproductive state, although the soil seems congenial to the growth of larch and fir. The face of the country generally is embellished with clumps and belts of oak, elm, ash, and beech.

In the south-western part of the parish the wood has suffered much from being blown, and from rooting out for the purposes of fruit cultivation. The northern division is comparatively bare and destitute of trees, except the banks of the river, which are richly covered with wood, such as birch, hazel, alder, mountain ash, and oak coppice. There is reason, however, to believe that the face of the country had once been much more densely wooded than at present from the fact that the peasants, in excavating for peats, have frequently discovered fossil remains, chiefly of oak, in a perfect state of preservation.

ARBORICULTURE.

The species of trees most generally planted are larch and Scotch fir. Of the latter there are large plantations in the southern division of the parish. There are no plantations of hardwood to any great extent, but there is a considerable quantity of ash, elm, and beech, which appear to thrive well. The kinds which are indigenous are the alder, birch, hazel, and mountain ash. The first, especially, grows in considerable quantities along the banks of the rivers and burns in the parish.

PISCATORIAL.

The rivers are abundantly stocked with trout and salmon; the lochs with pike, perch, eels, &c., one of them containing a few large trout.

ZOOLOGY.

There are no rare kinds of the quadruped or feathered tribe in the parish, with the exception of the falcon, which breeds among the precipices of Craighall. The Stormont Loch, about 2 miles south of the town, is in summer frequented by immense flocks of gulls, which build their nests among the reeds and rushes.

These birds thrive well, and arrive from the sea coast about the beginning of March, and take their departure for the coast again in the end of autumn. Their eggs are highly prized, and are annually gathered for the benefit of the proprietors and tenants. The loch is also frequented by a large number of swans.

A species of the great northern bulldiver was shot several years ago on the Lochy.

The kingfisher is frequently to be seen on the lower reaches of the Ericht; pheasants, partridges, and waterfowl are abundant.

There are abundance of hares, rabbits, weasels, squirrels, &c., in the vicinity, but none of the larger animals, although the wild cat has been shot frequently in the northern part of the parish.

There are also large numbers of moles, which destroy the land with their numerous burrowing.

CHAPTER II.

Authentic Records — Roman Invasions — Suetonius Paulinus — Julius Agricola—Galdus—Mons Grampius—Site of the Battle—A Bone of Contention—Opinions of Eminent Men—Tacitus—Description of the Battle—A Disputed Victory—Sad Experience of the Romans—False Reports—Vespasian—Evidences of the Struggle—Tulina—Emperor Severus—Bridge of Lornty—St Ninian's Well—Invasion of Northmen—Kenneth M'Alpin—Regner Lodbrog—Inchtuthil—Battle of Stenton Craig—Bloody Inches—Church and Lands of Blair—Kinclaven Castle Taken by Wallace—Coupar Abbey—Robert the Bruce at Stormont Loch—Highland Caterans—Battle of Glasclune—Drummond Feud and Massacre—Queen Mary's Summons—Offers by Murderers—Their Trial and Execution—Bond of Manrent.

THERE are no authentic records to inform us whether Blairgowrie existed prior to the Christian era, but in the early days of the Roman invasions, when these ruthless foreign marauders waged war with our countrymen, we have the knowledge that Suetonius Paulinus, in command of the Roman legions about 61 A.D., finished his last expedition to Caledonia, choosing as the scene of his operations the valley of Strathmore. In this campaign he had but little success until, in progress of his march southwards through the provinces of Albin, he encountered a formidable force under Caractacus, a British King, who for nearly ten years had waged successful war against the Roman arms. After a long and bloody fight the Roman legions triumphed, and the British King, being betrayed, was carried to Rome.

In 84 A.D. Julius Agricola, one of Suetonius Paulinus' successors, and the last of the Roman Generals in Britain, entrenched his army to the east of the Tay in the Stormont, along that sward now known as the Haughs of Delvine. The country at this time, and for some years previous, was oppressed by Roman invaders, but an attempt was now to be made by the Caledonians, under Galdus (the Galgacus of Tacitus), to free their country and sweep their foes out of it. It has long been a bone of contention amongst antiquarians and historians to locate the site of this battle, "Mons Grampius," but the researches of eminent men, amongst others Lieutenant-Colonel Bayly, R.E., Superintendent of the Ordnance Survey, 1863, and Mr Knox, author of "The Map of the Basin of the Tay," prove conclusively that the site of "Mons Grampius," the historic battle between the Caledonians and Romans, was around Blairgowrie.

The Caledonians occupied the ridge of heights to the north of Blairgowrie, and extending from Mause to Forneth, a distance of about five miles. Their left flank was protected by the steep and lofty banks of the Ericht, their right by the deep ravine beyond Forneth and Loaning; Lochs Clunie, Marlee, Ardblair, and the Lunan Burn, strengthened by fortifications, which in parts can yet be traced, protected the front, a position which military judges have said was admirably chosen. The Romans were encamped along the banks of the Tay from Inchtuthil at Delvine eastwards as far as Meikleour, where their entrenchments can yet be traced. Tacitus, the Roman historian, who was present at the battle, thus describes it:—

"Galgacus (Galdus), the Commander of the Caledonians, harangued his host in one of the noblest speeches any General ever addressed to his soldiers. He concluded with these words:—'Your enemy is before you, and in his train heavy tributes, drudgery in the mines, and all the horrors of slavery. Are these calamities to be entailed upon us, or shall this day relieve us by a brave revenge? There is the field of battle, and let that determine. Let us seek the enemy, and, as we rush upon him, remember the glory delivered down to us by our ancestors, and let each man think that upon his sword depends the hope of all posterity.' This speech was received, according to the custom of the Barbarians, with war songs, savage howlings, and a wild uproar of military applause. Their battalions began to form the line of battle, the brave and warlike rushed forward to the front, and the field glittered with a blaze of arms.

"Agricola, the Roman General, also harangued his troops in most impassioned and eloquent strains, and concluded thus:—'Here you may end your labours and close a scene of fifty years by one great, one glorious day. Let your country see, and let the Commonwealth bear witness, if the conquest of Britain has been a lingering work, if the seeds of rebellion have not been crushed, that we, at least, have done our duty.' As soon as the General ended, the field rung with the shouts of applause, and, impatient for the offset, the soldiers grasped their arms. Agricola restrained their ardour till he formed his order of battle. The auxiliary infantry, in number 8000, occupied the centre; the wings consisted of 3000 horse. The legions were stationed in the rear at the head of their entrenchments to support the ranks if necessary, but otherwise to remain inactive, so that a victory obtained without the effusion of Roman blood might be of higher value. The Caledonians kept possession of the rising ground, extending their ranks as wide as possible to present a formidable show of battle. Their first line was ranged on the plain, the rest on a gradual ascent on the acclivity of the hill. The intermediate space between both armies was filled with the charioteers and cavalry of the Britons rushing to and fro in wild career and traversing the plain with noise and tumult. The enemy being greatly superior in number, there was reason to apprehend that the Romans might be attacked both in front and flank at the same time. To prevent that mischief, Agricola ordered his ranks to form wider range. Some of the officers saw that the lines were weakened into length, and therefore advised that the legions should be brought forward into the scene of action, but the General was not of a temper to be easily disuaded from his purpose. Flushed with hope, and firm in the hour of danger, he immediately dismounted, and, dismissing his horse, took his stand at the head of the colours. The battle began and at first was maintained at a distance. With their long swords and targets of small dimensions, the Caledons had the address to elude the massive weapons of the Romans and at the same time to discharge a thick volley of their own. To bring the conflict to a speedy decision, Agricola ordered three battalions of Bavarians and two Hungarian cohorts to charge the enemy sword in hand. To this mode of attack these troops had been long accustomed, but to the Britons it was in every way disadvantageous. Their small targets offered no protection, and their unwieldy swords, not sharpened to a point, could do but little execution in a close engagement. The Bavarians rushed to the attack with impetuous fury, they redoubled their blows, and with the bosses of their shields bruised the enemy on the face, and, having overpowered all resistance on the plain, began to force their way up the ascent of the hill in the order of battle. Incited by their example, the other cohorts advanced with a spirit of emulation, and cut their way with terrible slaughter. Eager in pursuit of victory, they pressed forward with determined fury, leaving behind them numbers wounded, but not slain, and others not so much hurt.

"The Roman cavalry in the meantime was forced to give ground; the Caledonians in their armed chariots rushed at full speed into the thick of battle where the infantry were engaged. Their first impression struck a general terror, but their career was soon checked by the inequalities of the ground and the close embodied ranks of the Romans.

"Nothing could less resemble an engagement of the cavalry. Pent up in narrow places the Barbarians crowded on each other, and were dragged or driven along with their horses. A scene of confusion followed. Chariots without a guide, and horses without a rider broke from the ranks in wild disorder, and, flying every way as fear and consternation urged, overwhelmed their own files, and trampled down all who came in their way.

"Meanwhile the Britons, who had kept their position on the hills, looking down with contempt on the scant numbers of the Romans, began to quit their station. Descending slowly, they hoped, by wheeling round the field of battle, to attack the victors in the rear. To counteract their design, Agricola ordered four squadrons of horse, which he had kept as a body of reserve, to advance to the charge. The Britons poured down with impetuosity and retired with equal precipitation. At the same time, the cavalry, by direction of the General, wheeled round from the wings and fell with great slaughter on the rear of the enemy, who now perceived their own stratagem was turned against themselves. The field presented a dreadful spectacle of carnage and destruction. The Britons fled, the Romans pursued; they wounded, mangled, and gashed the runaways, seized their prisoners, and butchered them on the spot. Despair and horror appeared in various shapes. In one part of the field the Caledons, sword in hand, fled in crowds from a handful of Romans; in other places, without a weapon left, they faced every danger and rushed on certain death. The field was red with blood. The vanquished Britons had their moments of returning courage, and gave proofs of virtue and brave despair. They fled to the woods, and, rallying their scattered numbers, surrounded such of the Romans as pursued with too much eagerness. Agricola saw the danger, and ordered the light cohorts to invest the woods.

"The Britons, seeing the pursuit was conducted in compact and regular order, dispersed a second time in consternation, each seeking his own personal safety. Night coming on, the Romans, weary of pursuit, desisted from the slaughter. 10,000 Caledonians fell in the engagement and about 5000 Romans. The Roman army, elated with success and enriched with plunder, spent the night in exultation; the Britons, on the other hand, wandered about helpless and disconsolate.

"The following day displayed to view the nature and melancholy silence all around, the hills deserted, houses at a distance involved in smoke and fire, and not a mortal discovered by the scouts; the whole a vast and dreary solitude.

"Agricola was at length informed by those who were sent out to explore the country that no trace of the enemy was anywhere to be seen, and no attempt made in any quarter to muster their forces."

Tacitus the historian, and son-in-law to Agricola, the Roman General, in the narrative of the battle just described, naturally gives his powerful father-in-law the advantage of any disputed victory to gild his illustrious arms.

Tacitus, moreover, gives the speeches of the Roman and Caledonian Generals before leading their armies to battle. It may have been the custom with the Roman Generals to address their soldiers, but if Galgacus delivered a speech, it was when he could be neither seen nor heard by any save his own soldiers, for it is recorded by other historians that the Caledonians attacked the Romans in the night, nearly seized their camp, but were prevented by the advance of other legions. Further, if we consider the limited boundaries of the Caledons, and the internal dissension prevalent in the country at the time, it is difficult to accede to the number of the army, Instead of 30,000 men, it is more likely that 15,000 would be the utmost figure. We are also informed by the Roman historian that the Caledonians were defeated. If this was so, why did the Roman army not keep possession of the field, and how do other historians inform us of the Romans' sad experience of the Barbarians?—"The Barbarians drive us to the sea, and the sea drives us back to the Barbarians, leaving us only the choice of being put to the sword or be drowned; nor have we any defence against either."

The reports of the campaigns in Britain, sent and carried to Rome, must have been beyond measure false and designing on the Emperor and the people, insomuch as Josephus, another historian, says of Vespasian:—"This was he who finished the conquest of Britain, which before was neither perfectly subdued nor known."

An eminent historian visiting these fields, and surveying the numerous evidences of the severe struggle, says:— "Virtuous men will revere the memory of Galgacus and the Caledonians who here bravely drew their swords for religious liberty. In this field 10,000 fell resisting the reckless ambition of Rome, and while we surveyed the mouldering cairns raised above their graves, we felt we were treading amongst the ashes of heroes and of patriots in righteous battle slain."

Another historian, speaking of the place, remarks:—"For miles around every yard of ground marks a soldier's sepulchre, and every inch of turf has been dyed with the best blood of Scotland."

Boetius, another historian, says that "the Picts had a town called Tulina on the elevated tract of land at Delvine, which they deserted and burnt on the approach of the Romans."

In 138 A.D. the Romans again traversed the district, and once again, in 207 A.D., Severus, the Roman Emperor, and his legions encamped at Meikleour. It is generally supposed that the lower arch of the bridge at Lornty was built at this time, the work being ascribed to the Romans.

St Ninian, one of the earliest Christian Celtic missionaries, on his tour through Scotland, pitched his camp where the Wellmeadow now is, and quenched his thirst at an old well or spring which ever afterwards bore the name of "St Ninian's Well," until it was covered in and the water led into the town drains.

History is silent regarding the events of the district for many hundred years, until about the year 831 A.D., when Alpin became king of the Scots. As grandson to Hungus, king of the Picts, he (being the only male survivor of the family), laid claim to the kingdom of the Picts. After a number of reverses, the Picts chose as their king, Brude, who immediately took active measures against Alpin. He levied a large army, crossed the Tay at the Castle of Caledonia (Dunkeld), and marched with all speed he could eastwards to the country of Horestia (Angus), where he was met by King Alpin with 20,000 men. At the time the armies joined battle Alpin was viewing the scene from a vantage point, and, observing one of the wings of his army to give way, he went forth with great force till, giving a fresh charge on his enemies, he was unfortunately taken prisoner. The Scots no sooner saw their king taken than they betook themselves to the mountains, while the Picts, remaining victors of the field, beheaded Alpin, and affixed his head to a pole which they erected in the centre of their chief city. Before the accession of Kenneth (or Kenneth MacAlpin, son of Alpin, as he is properly termed), at Dunkeld, in 843 A.D., the country was terribly ravaged by the Danes or Norsemen. Kenneth, making peace with the Scots of the West, engaged them in a common defence against their mutual foes. Daily incursions were made against the Danes, who had taken possession of and fed upon the rich lands of Strathmore.

Regner Lodbrog then ruled over the nations on the shores of the Baltic—a man who made every throne in Europe tremble. Word having been brought home of the doings in Scotland, he resolved in person to punish Kenneth for his audacity in interfering with his countrymen. Lodbrog landed an army in the Tay in 847, and at once advanced and took possession of the old Roman encampment at Inchtuthil (on the Delvine estate). The Vikings—as these sea-kings were called—first fortified their position by forming a camp on the south side of the Tay, to guard a ford of the river near the present Bridge of Caputh, in order to provide against surprise from that quarter, and then at once proceeded against the outworks provided by Kenneth for the defence of his capital, the principal of which were on Stenton Craig, where very considerable works had been executed, part of the remains of which exist to this day. After much hard fighting these advanced positions fell, and Lodbrog found himself with his army looking into the steep gorge leading to Dunkeld, with MacAlpin and his men strongly posted on the top and sides of the mountain, ready to dispute the passage. A more uninviting outlook than the Vikings had before them could scarcely be presented. Nevertheless, Lodbrog led his men to the assault, when a dreadful carnage ensued. Kenneth and his men were wholly victorious, and drove the Northmen out of the pass, when hundreds of them were drowned in the river Tay attempting to escape from the swords of the Scots and the rocks that were rolled down upon them. A tradition exists that, after the battle, Kenneth caused a cross to be erected near the spot where the bulk of the Danes were buried, on the little haugh near the river side, and by which the road then led. History also well records that in the following year Kenneth and his men signally defeated the Danes, led by Lodbrog, who lost upwards of 4000 of his men, vainly trying to ferret Kenneth out of his stronghold by approaching past Butterstone and Cairnie, at which places the brunt of the fighting took place.

After this disaster the Danes fled to their encampment at Inchtuthil followed by Kenneth and his victorious army, who, after a time, compelled Lodbrog and his men to quit their camp and take refuge on the islands of the Tay, a little lower down than their former camp at Inchtuthil. Here the Scots sat down before them until the river had sufficiently fallen to enable them to attack with success, and they had not long to wait before the assault was made, when Lodbrog was driven out with immense slaughter. In the old maps of the country these islands are called "The Bloody Inches." From them the Danish King was carried to his ship wounded, and he has referred to this fatal day in an epicidum, or death-song, still extant, for, along with his fighting propensities, he was also a poet.

The valley of Strathmore was a very favourite hunting-ground of Malcolm Canmore, who is accredited with the building of Kinclaven Castle, about the year 1080, as a hunting seat. The building of the Castle of Ardblair in 1175 is also credited to Alexander de Blair, one of the favourite courtiers of William the Lion.

It is recorded in the papers of the Monastery of St Marie, at Coupar Angus, that "an agreement was entered into between the churches of Blair and Coupar Angus, at a Synod held at Perth, on 1st of May, 1201," and on the 1st of June, 1235, Alexander II. granted, at Traquair, "lands in Meikle and Little Blair to the Abbey of Scone, excepting a small portion in the fen of Meikle Blair, which he gave to the monks of Cupar (Coupar) in exchange for the common Muir of Blair, of which they had the use."

The Church of Blair was consecrated by David de Bernham, the Bishop of St Andrews, on the 13th September, 1243.

The Castle of Kinclaven was held as a Royal residence by Alexander II., and is mentioned in the year 1264, when payments were made for the carriage of wine to Kinclaven and for the repairing of a boat.

The Scottish patriot, William Wallace, in his early years received his education at Dundee, where he formed an attachment to John Blair (of the family of Ardblair), a Benedictine Monk, who afterwards became his chaplain, and compiled a history in Latin of the Scottish hero's deeds.

In June, 1297, King Edward I., in his progress northwards, visited Kinclaven, and stayed there one night. Shortly afterwards, with a handful of men, Wallace besieged and took the castle—"a castell wondyr wycht" —putting the entire garrison to the sword, including Sir James Butler, the Governor. Blind Harry, the Minstrel, describes an engagement between the English garrison and Wallace, some little distance from the castle, the defeat and flight of the former, pursued by the Scots, toward their stronghold, where

> "Few men of fenss was left that place to kepe,
> Wemen and preistis upon the wall can wepe,
> For weill thai wend the fleais was their lord,
> To tuk them in thai maid thaim redy ford,
> Leit donn the bryg, kest up the yettis wide,
> The freyit folk entrit, and durst nocht byde."

Here Wallace and his followers stayed seven days, spoiled and wrecked the place, and, under cloud of night, betook themselves to the neighbouring woods, and

> "The contre folk, quhen it was lycht of day,
> Gret reik saw ryss, and to Kinclewyn thai socht:
> Bot wallis and stane, mar gud thai fund thai nocht."
>
> * * * * * *
>
> "In till Kinclewyn thar duelt nane agayne
> Thar was left nocht bot brokyn wallis in playne."

In 1309, at Dundee, King Robert I. confirmed a charter to the Abbey of Coupar, bestowing the lands of Muir of Blair upon it. There can be little doubt that the Blairs, Herons, and Drummonds, the three powerful families in the district at the time, with their retainers, such as were able to bear arms, assisted thé Bruce, and rendered him yeoman service in the grand engagement at Bannockburn in 1314.

In the chartulary of the Abbey of Scone is a letter, dated Clackmannan, 26th of March, 1326, from King Robert the Bruce to the Sheriff of Perth, commanding him to take charge of the Loch of Blair (Stormont Loch) in view of the King's arrival in the neighbourhood. In the chartulary is a second letter on other matters, dated Clunie, 4th August, 1326, and a third and fourth are dated Alyth, 5th and 6th August the same year. It is reasonable to suppose that in August, 1326, King Robert fulfilled his intention and fished the Stormont.

From another document in the Scone Chartulary, dated February, 1356, it appears that in the reign of David II. the ownership of the church lands of Blair was in dispute. The Bishop of St Andrews laid some claim to it; the Abbey of Cambuskenneth stretched out a ghostly hand; and the Abbey of Scone retained its hold. In the document referred to the question is settled. All the lawful rights to the lands and pertinents of the Church of Blair are finally and elaborately made over, by William the Bishop of St Andrews, to the Abbey of Scone. It is ordained that a payment of money shall be made or continued to the Abbey of Cambuskenneth, and as for the Bishop himself, the church of Carrington (in the Lothians) with the rights and pertinents, presently the property of Scone, shall be transferred to him. The Church of Blair, then, with it revenues, was given over to the Abbey of Scone in 1356, and confirmed to the Abbey in a Bull by Pope Gregory XI. of the year 1373. The Bull narrates "that Carrington, though it 'abounded in revenues,' was distant from Scone, and the way was difficult; whereas, Blair was close at hand, although its revenues were but small." A Bull of Benedict XIII., a duplicate Pope, dated 1390, in the reign of Robert III., narrates that "the Abbey of Scone had been put to great expense, and had suffered serious loss, by many different meetings of the nobility and magnates concerning the affairs of the kingdom." The Bull, therefore, confirms to the impoverished Abbot and Convent several churches, including that of Blair.

In 1384 an Act was passed for the suppression of masterful plunderers, who get in the statute their Highland name of cateran:—"*Qui transierint ut Katherani, comedendo patriam et consumendo bona comitatum et capiendo per vim et violenciam bona et victualia.*" By this statute all men might seize caterans and bring them to the Sheriff, and, should they refuse to come, might kill them without having to answer for the act. This is the first of a long succession of penal and denunciatory laws against the Highlanders, on whom, no doubt, there was ample provocation to retaliate.

King Robert the Third's brother, Alexander, named the Wolf of Badenoch, had an illegitimate son, also named Alexander, who made, during his life, a considerable figure both in Scotland and France as Earl of Mar. Whether or not he obtained any of the Highland property, he succeeded to his father's propensities and his influence over the Highlanders. With a large following he descended from the Braes of Angus on a grand plundering expedition against the agriculturists of the lowland districts of Forfar and Perth. The landed gentry of this district gathered for its defence, and met the invaders near Glasclune. They fought, of course, and the affair, though a small one, was sharpened by the hatred to each other of two races whose antipathy was all the more bitter that they were near neighbours and nominally under the same government.

It is the earliest recorded example of the method of Highland warfare such as it continued down to the latest of our civil wars. The method was a simple rush or bound upon the enemy, and a reliance upon the impetuosity of the blow breaking his defences. If it failed to do so, the assailants instantly turned; if strong enough they might make another rush, but if not they would disperse their several ways, and the war was at an end for a time.

In this instance, at Glasclune, 1392, the rush was successful: the Lowlanders, mounted men and footmen, were swept before the torrent. Sir David Lyndsay,

"that worthie was and wycht,"

in command of the Lowland force, trying to make head against the torrent, as a mounted man, had trodden several of the Highlanders down, and had one of them pinned to the earth with his long lance. Thereupon, in the words of Old Wyntoun, the chronicler—

>"That man held fast his own sword
>Into his neive, and up thrawing
>He pressed him, not again standing
>That he was pressed to the earth;
>And with a swake there of his sword,
>Through the stirrup-leather and the boot
>Three-ply or four, above the foot,
>He struck the Lyndsay to the bone.
>That man no stroke gave bot that one,
>For there he died."

Sir Walter Scott could not but see the value of such an incident in heroic narrative, and accordingly, in the poem "Lord of the Isles," he brings it in at the death of Colonsay's fierce lord:—

>"'Now then,' he said, and couched his spear,
>'My course is run, the goal is near;
>One effort more, one brave career
>Must close this race of mine.'
>Then in his stirrups rising high
>He shouted loud his battlecry,

'Saint James for Argentine!'
And of the bold pursuers, four
The gallant knight from saddle bore;
But not unharmed—a lance's point
Has found the breastplate's loosened joint,
An axe has raised his crest;
Yet still on Colonsay's fierce lord,
Who pressed the chase with gory sword,
He rode with spear in rest,
And through his bloody tartan's bored
And through his gallant breast,
Nailed to the earth: the mountaineer
Yet writhed him up against the spear
And swung his broadsword round!
Stirrup, steelboot, and cuish gave way
Beneath that blow's tremendous sway,
The blood gushed from the wound;
And the grim lord of Colonsay
Hath turned him on the ground;
And laughed in death pang, that his blade
The mortal thrust so well repaid."

In 1430 one of the Blairs of Ardblair was Abbot of Coupar Abbey. In 1500 Bishop Brown of Dunkeld erected Clunie Castle, and in it (in 1560), was born James Crichton, afterwards so well known as the Admirable Crichton, the greatest Scotsman of any age.

About this time, throughout Scotland, family feuds were very prevalent, and one very remarkable example of one of these deeds of violence, connected with the locality, is recorded in "Pitcairn's Criminal Trials" under the year 1554. On the third day of June of that year, the Lairds of Gormack, Ardblair, Drumlochy, Clayquhat, and Knockmahar—all places in the vicinity of the town —and their retainers, to the number of eighty, waylaid and attacked George Drummond and his son, William (of Newton Castle), "in ye hie mercate gate, behynde ye Kirke of Blair," and barbarously murdered them both. The trial is fully reported in "Pitcairn," and will be found well worth perusal, not only on account of the peculiar circumstances attending the murder, but also in connection with it, the Laird of Drumlochy, one of the delinquents, entered into one of those extraordinary obligations called "Bonds of Manrent," which bound the granter to serve the grantee, and fight on his side in any quarrel, just or unjust, in which he might be engaged with any of his neighbours, or, as the document expresses it, " agaiuis all aud sindrie persouis, our Soveraine Ladye and ye auctoritie of this realm allenarlie excepit." This extraordinary conspiracy and deliberate murder afford a most illustrative picture of the lawless condition of the country at the period, and the inveteracy and ferocity with which each petty laird took the law into his own hands, and, either with his retainers or the assistance of his friends and neighbours, fought out his particular feuds or quarrels. It was also too frequently the case that, in place of meeting the enemy in a fair field, every advantage was taken to surprise him unawares and unprepared; and that those outrages were but too common, little regarded, and very leniently dealt with, is proved by the fact that, for this shameful and deliberate murder, an attempt to compound it "by pilgromaigis, doing suffrage for the soule of the deid," and a certain money payment, although, as it happened in this case, "the wyf an' bairnis" of George Drummond could nowise be content with the offer, and so, at least, two of the guilty persons suffered the penalty of their crime by decapitation.

George Drummond, who apparently purchased the lands of Newton of Blair, about 1550, is the first whom we understand to have been styled George Drummond of Blair. He married Janet Halliburton of Buttergask, who bore to him two sons, George, who succeeded, and William.

The following is the summons for apprehending and bringing the Laird of Gormack and his accomplices before the Queen and Privy Council:—

"Marie, by the Grace of God, Quiene of Scottis to our own Shireff of Perth and his deputis and to our deputis and lovittis, Archibald Campbell, Thomas Drummond, messengeris our scheriffs, speciale constitute, grating and forasmeikl as it is humlie menit and complenit to us be ou lovittis the wiffe, bairnis, kin and friendis of umqle George Drummond of Leidcrief and William Drummond his sone, upon William Chalmer of Drumlochie, William Rory, George Tullyduff, etc. : George M'Neskar, fidlar, his householdmen, Robert Smith (and cottars) tenantis to ye laird of Drumlochie, John Blaire of Ardblaire, Andro Blair, Thomas Blair his sones, David M'Raithy his householdman, Patour Blair (and two others) tenentis to the said Laird of Ardblair, William Chalmer in Clayquhat, Alexander Buttir, half-brother to John Buttir of Gormack, William Blair, David Blair of Knockmahar, John Blair, Patrick Blair, his sones, William Young of Tornence, and Thomas Robertsone, tenentis to ye said Laird of Gormok, quhilk is with thair complices with convocation of our leigis to the nomer of 80 personis bodin in feir of weir with jakkis, coittis of mailye, steil bonnetis, lance staffis, bowis, lang culverings with lichtit luntis, and utheris wappinis, invasive recentlie upone Sounday, ye thirde day of June instant, before none, of ye counsalling, devysing, causing, sending, command assistance, fortefeing, and ratihabitioun of ye said John Buttir of Gormack, come to ye said umqle George Drummondis, Perroche Kirke of Blair, to haif slane him, the said William, his sone, and utheris being with him in company and, becaus they could nocht cum to thair perversit purpois, they passed to the Laird of Gormokis place of Gormok and thair dynit with him, and send furth spyis that he was cuming furth of his place, thai with thair complices with ye said Laird of Gormokis householdmen and servantis bodin in feir of weir of his causing, sending, devysing as said is with convocation of our leigis to ye nomer of 66 persouis, ye samin day at twa houris or thairby efter none ischit further of ye said Laird of Gormokis place foirsaid and imbeset ye gait to ye saidis umqle George and William his sone, where they were doublate alane at thair pastyme play and at ye rowbowlis in ye hie mercate gait behynde ye kirke of Blair in sober manner, traisting na truble nor harm to haif bein done to them, but to haif levit under Goddis peace and ouris, and thair crewellie slew them upon ald feid and forethocht felonie, set purpois, and provisioun in hie contemption," &c.

The murderers, finding themselves in an awkward predicament, and believing they were likely to obtain their deserts at the hands of the hangman, appeared to have endeavoured to compromise the matter with the family of the murdered men, and the following is the offer they made with that view :—

"The offeris offered be the laird of Gormok, etc., to young George Drummond of Blair for the slauchter of his father—Thir ar the offeris quhilk the Lordis of Gormok, Drumlochye, and Ardblair, and their collegis, offeris to my Lord Drummond and to ye sone of umquhile George Drummond, his wyf and bairnis, kyne and friendis—item :—

"In primis :—To going or cause to gang to the four heid pilgromaigis in Scotland.

"Secondlye :—To do suffrage for ye saull of ye deid at his Paroche Kirke or what uthir kirk they pleis for certaine yeiris to cum.

"Thirdlye :—To do honour to ye kyne and friendis as effeiris as use is.

"Ferdlye :—To assyth ye partye is content to gyf to ye kyne wyf and bairnis—Imp. 1000 merks.

"Fyfthlie :—Gif thir offeris be noch suffeycent thocht be ye partye and ye friendis of ye deid, we ar content to underlye and augment or pair as reasonabil friendis thinkis expedyent in so far as we may lefsumlie."

It appears that the foregoing "offeris" were not considered adequate by Lord Drummond and the other parties concerned. The first, second, and third offers were considered of no value, therefore "Chalmer of Drumlochye and otheris, his friendis," made an amended offer :—

"To offer to his Lordship and ye partye ane nakit sword be ye point, and siclike to do all uthir honour to my lord, his hous, and friendis that sall be thoucht reasonabil in siclike caisis—to give my lord and his airis his Bond of Manrent in competent and dew form sic as may stand in ye Actis of Parliament and lawis of this realme—because throu extrame persecutioun be ye lawis of this realme ye said William has nother landis, gudis, nor money, he thairfor offeris his sonis marriage to be mareit upon George Drummondis dochter frelie without onie tocher and siclike ye marriage of ye said Williame Chalmer his cousing to ye said George sister—to offer any uthir thing quhilk is possabil to him as pleis my lord and friendis to lay to his charge except his lyfe and heretage."

It does not appear whether or not the above modest proposal to marry the son and cousin of the "murderer" to the daughter and sister of the "murdered" man, "without ony tochir," was carried into effect; but the promised "Bond of Manrent" was duly executed, for which the said William Chalmer was freely pardoned by the said George Drummond, but although one of the principal murderers thus escaped the gallows, others of them met their due deserts.

"August 4, 1554.—John Buttir of Gormok, denounced rebel and put to the horn for not underlying the law for art and part of the cruel slauchter of George Drummond of Ledcrief and William, his son.

"John Crechton of Strathurd and James Hering of Glasclune, his cautioners, were accordingly amerciated."

"16th Nov., 1554.—George Gordon of Scheves, James Gordon of Lesmore and Gilbert Grey of Scheves found caution to underlye the law at the next aire in Aberdeen, for resetting, intercommuning, and supplying William Chalmer of Drumlochye and his accomplices, rebels, and at the horn fore the aforesaid slauchter and for affording them meat, drink, and otheris necessaries in the months of July and August last."

"12th Dec., 1554.—Patrick Blair, in Ardblair, and Robert Smyth, in Drumlochye, alias Henry, convicted of the slaughter of George Drummond and William, his son. Beheaded."

The following is a copy of the extraordinary document known as the "Bond of Manrent":—

"THE LAYRDE OF DRUMLOCHE.—BOND OF MANRENT."

"Be it kend til al men be thir present letteris me Williame Chalmir of Drumlochie that fforasmeikill as ane noble and michty lord David Lord Drummond and certaine utheris principalis of the four branchis and maist speciale and neirist of ye kin and friendis of umqle George Drummond of Leidcrief and Williame Drummonde his sone for thameselfis and remanant kin and friendis of ye said umqle George and Williame, bes remitet and foregevin to me thair slauchteris, and gevin and deliverit to me thair letteris of slanis thairupone: and that I am oblist be vertew of ane contract to gif ye said noble lord my Band of Manrent as ye said contract and letter of slanis deliverit to me fullie proportis — Thairfore to be boundin and oblist and be thir present letteris bindis and obligsis me and my airis in trew and awfald Band of Manrent to ye said noble and michty Lord as chief to ye saidis umqle George and Williame his sone, and ye saidis Lordis his airis, and sall take thair trew and awfald part in all and sundry thair actions and causis, and ride and gang with thame therein upon thair expenses when they require me or my airis thairto, againis all and sindry personis, our Soveraine Ladye and ye auctoritie of this realme allenarlie exceptit. And heirto I bind and obliss me and my airis to ye said noble and mychty lord and his airis in ye straightest form and sicker style of Band of Manrent that can be devisit na remied nor exceptioune to the contrary.

"In witness of ye quhilk theng to thir present letteris and Band of Manrent, subscrivit with my hand, my seil is hanging at Edinburgh yn fift day of December ye zier of God ane thousand five hundreth fiftie aucht zeiris befoir thir witnesses—Andro Rollock of Duncrub, James Rollock his sone, John Graham of Gormok, Maister John Spens of Condy and Lawrance Spens his bruthir with utheris divers.
     (Signed)
       "Willzam Chalmir of Drumloquhy."

From this time, 1558, for a period of nearly eighty years, we have no records, civil or political, regarding the district.

CHAPTER III.

King Charles I.—Charter of Burgh of Barony—Barony Court—Gallows Knowe—Montrose—Sacking of Newton Castle—Donald Cargill—John Erskine—The Ghost of Mause : Full Description—Prince Charlie and the Curlers' Dinner—Duke of Cumberland at Woodlands—Division of the Muir of Blair—Coble Pule—Boat Brae—Muckle Mill Erected—Purchase of Blairgowrie Estate—Military Service in Blairgowrie—Enrolment Returns, 1803—A Rifle Corps—A Distinguished Officer—Burgh Charters—Erection of Parish Church—Stage Coach—Introduction of Gas and Printing—Visits of the Queen—Auld Brig o' Blair—An Incident of the French Revolution—The First Newspaper—Introduction of Railway Service—A Good Story—Burns Centenary Celebration—Inauguration of Volunteer Movement, 1859.

DURING his first visit to Scotland, 1633-1634, King Charles I. granted a charter, dated 9th July, 1634, in favour of George Drummond of Blair, by which Blairgowrie was erected into a Burgh of Barony, whereby Barons or Lairds were empowered to hold Courts in their own districts for the trial of thieves and other characters disgraceful to society. A Barony Court was established at Blairgowrie, and held sittings for a considerable time. The Courthouse is supposed to have been on the "Hirchen Hill," where the offices of the Parish Church Manse are now erected, the place of execution being the "Gallows Knowe," immediately to the west of Newton Castle. Traces of the mound might have been observed till within a few years ago, when the ground was ploughed up. The fields still bear the name "Gallowbank."

King Charles, seeking to establish the Episcopacy of Scotland, as his father James I. vainly endeavoured to do, roused the people of the land to form together an Association for the Protection of Religious Liberty. A "Solemn League and Covenant" was entered into in 1638, and none was more enthusiastic in its support than James Graham, Marquis of Montrose, who ultimately became its bitterest enemy.

Montrose, for the gratification of his own passions, as

much as for the sake of the religious liberties of the people, conceived the idea of subduing the kingdom, and pursued for a number of years an excursive warfare against those who had so bound themselves against Episcopacy.

Descending suddenly where least expected, Montrose achieved many a victory, and took up residence for some time at Dunkeld. Here he was informed that the army under Generals Urrie and Baillie had crossed the Tay against him, but he thought it advisable to "hie" out of the way, and on his march to Dundee sacked Newton Castle, 1644. Urrie and Baillie, following up, encamped on the Blairgowrie estate, passing eastwards through Forfarshire to Dundee, where Montrose had posted himself, but the historian records that no engagement took place between the rival armies at this time.

Newton Castle must have been rebuilt again shortly after this, as it was once more burned down by Oliver Cromwell.

In the year 1653 the soldiers of Glencairn were ranging through the parish. In 1679 the famous Rattray Covenanter, Donald Cargill, while on a visit to his parents at the Hatton of Rattray, was pursued by dragoons, and only escaped by leaping the Keith above Blairgowrie.

In 1726 a Blairgowrie gentleman, John Erskine, was an unsuccessful candidate to represent Perthshire in Parliament.

The year 1730 was a memorable one for Blairgowrie, the whole parish being in a commotion regarding the extraordinary proceedings caused by Soutar, one of the tenants of Middle Mause, declaring he had been ordered by a supernatural being to seek for human bones in a certain place. The place was known as the "Isle," situated between two or three small streams on the estate of Rochalzie, near the south-east march adjacent to the old turnpike road from Blairgowrie to Cally which passes up by Woodhead.

Soutar declared that the apparition was in the form of a dog, but spoke with a human voice, declared itself to be a David Soutar who had left the country over a century ago, and that he (David) had killed a man at the "Isle" 35 years before, whose bones must now be disinterred and receive burial in a churchyard, assigning as a reason for his bestial form that he had used his dog as an instrument in the murder.

There is a tradition that the man was murdered for his money; that he was a Highland drover on his return from the south; that he had arrived late at night at the Mains of Mause and wished to get to Rochalzie; that he stayed at the Mains of Mause all night, and left it early next morning, when David Soutar, with his dog, accompanied him to show him the road, and that, with the assistance of his dog, he murdered the drover and took his money at the place mentioned; that there was a tailor at work in his father's house that morning when he returned after committing the murder, and that his mother, being surprised at his absence and appearance, asked him what he had been about, but he made no answer; that he did not remain long in the country afterwards; that he went to England and never returned; that the last time he was seen he went down the Brae of Cochrage; and that in answer to the question by William Soutar why the apparition troubled him, the apparition said, "Because, after I killed the man, yours was the first face I saw in your mother's arms."

An old woman who died near the end of last century used to say that "the siller of the drover paid for the wood with which the west loft in the old Kirk of Blair was made," but she gave no explanation of her meaning.

About midnight on Wednesday, 23rd December, 1730, being in bed, "I (William Soutar) heard a voice, but said nothing. The voice said, 'Come away.' Upon this I rose out of bed, cast on my coat, and went to the door, but did not open it, and said, 'In the name of God, what do you demand of me now?' It answered, 'Go, take up these bones.' I said, 'How shall I get these bones?' It answered again, 'At the side of a withered bush, and there are but seven or eight of them remaining.' I asked, 'Was there anyone in the action but you?' It answered, 'No.' I asked again, 'What is the reason that you trouble me more than the rest of us?' It answered, 'Because you are the youngest.' Then I said to it, 'Depart from me and give me a sign that I may know the particular place, and give me time.' The voice answered as if it had been at some distance from the door, 'You will find the bones at the side of a withered bush; there are but eight of them, and for a sign you will find the print of a cross impressed upon the ground.'"

On the 26th of December, William Soutar, his brother, and seven or eight men met at the "Isle," and on digging at a particular spot, as indicated by the apparition, several human bones were found, the unearthing being witnessed by the parish minister, the laird, and other persons to the number of forty.

The bush described by the apparition was found to be withered about half-way down, and the sign was about a foot from the bush. The sign was one exact cross, thus **X**, each of the two lines of which was about 18 inches long and 3 inches broad, and impressed into the ground, which was not cut, for an inch or two.

The following is the "Account by William Soutar, being extracts from the original MS. written by Bishop Rattray, taken down at the time from William Soutar's mouth ":—

"In the month of December, 1728, about the skysetting, I and my servant, with several others living in the same town, heard a shrieking, and, I following the horse with my servant a little way from the town, we both thought we saw what at the time we judged to be a fox, and hounded two dogs at it, but they would not pursue it.

"About a month after that, as I was coming from Blair alone about the same time of the night, a big dog appeared to me, of a dark grayish colour, betwixt the Hilltown and Knowhead of Mawes on a lie ridge a little below the road, and, in passing me, touched me sensibly on the thigh at my haunch bone, upon which I pulled my staff from under my arm and let a stroke at it, and I had a notion at the time that I hitt it, and my haunch was painful all that night; however, I had no great thought of its being anything extraordinary, but that it might have been a mad dog wandering.

"About a year after that (to the best of my memory), in December month, about the same time of the night and at the same place, when I was alone, it appeared to me again just as before, and passed by me at some distance, and then I began to have some suspicion that it might be something more than ordinary.

"In the month of June, 1730, as I was coming from Perth from the cloth market, a little before skysetting, being alone at the same place, it appeared to me again and passed by me as before. I had some suspicion of it then likewise, but I began to think that a neighbour of mine in the Hilltown having ane ox lately dead, it might be but a dog that had been at that carrion, by which I endeavour to put that suspicion out of my head.

"On the last Monday of November, 1730, as I was coming from Woodhead, a town in the ground of Drumlochy, it appeared to me again at the same place, and after it had passed by me, as it was near getting out of my sight, it spoke with a low voice, but so as I distinctly heard it, these words, "*Within eight or ten days, do or die*," and it having then disappeared no more passed at that time.

"On the morrow I went to my brother, who dwells in the Nether Aird of Drumlochy, and told him of this last and all the former appearances, which was the first time I ever spoke of it to anybody. He and I went that day to see a sister of ours in Glenballow, who was a-dying, but she was dead before we came. As we were returning home, I desired my brother (whose name is James Soutar) to go forward with me till I should be past that place where it used to appear to me, and just as we were come to it, at ten o'clock at night, it appeared to me again as formerly, and, as it was passing over some ice, I pointed to it with my finger and asked my brother if he saw it, but he said he did not nor did his servant who was with us. It spoke nothing at the time, but just disappeared as it crossed the ice.

"On the Saturday night thereafter (5th December, 1730), as I was at my sheep cotes putting in my sheep, it appeared to me again at daylight, betwixt day and skylight, and upon saying these words, '*Come to the spot of ground within half ane hour*,' it just disappeared, whereupon I came home to my own house and took up a staff and also a sword with me, off the head of the bed, and went straight to the place where it formerly used to appear, and after I had been there some minutes, and had drawn a circle about me with the staff, it appeared to me, and I spoke to it, saying, '*What are you that troubles me?*' and it answered me, '*I am David Soutar, George Soutar's brother; I killed a man more than five-and-thirty years ago, when you were but new born, at a bush be east the road as you go into the isle;*' and as I was going away I stood again and said, '*David Soutar was a man, and you appear like a dog*,' whereupon it spoke again and said, '*I killed him with a dog, and am made to speak out of the mouth of a dog and tell you, and you must go and burry these bones.*'

"When breaking up the ground at the bush we found the following bones, viz.:—the nether jaw with all the chaft teeth in it, one of the thigh bones, both arm bones, one of the shoulder blades, one of the collar bones, and two small bones of the fore arm."

The bones were carefully wrapt in linen and placed in a coffin made by a wright, who had been sent for from Clayquhat, and they were deposited in a grave in the Kirkyard of Blairgowrie the same evening.

It has generally been supposed that this William Soutar was labouring under a delusion, or that it was a trick played on him by one of his neighbours. As for the bones found, they have been supposed to be the remains of a calf which had been buried there some years before. The story is, even to this present time, believed as true by a few credulous and superstitious beings.

The winter of 1745 was hard, and the ice was keen, and the curlers of Blair, taking a day on the ice at the

"Lochy" (now a thing of the past), had a dinner of beef and greens preparing for them at Eppie Clarke's Inn, at the Hill o' Blair, when Prince Charlie and some of his Highlanders invaded the place, ate up everything, and departed, refreshing themselves again and washing the dinner down at a small well near Lornty Cottage, now known as "Charlie's well."

The army of the Duke of Cumberland, on the march to the north against the rebel forces, encamped on the Muir of Blair, the Duke, with his officers, occupying the old house of Woodlands, while his cavalry and outposts were garrisoned at Newton Castle.

THE BEECH HEDGE.

Early in the spring of 1746 the now famous Beech Hedge of Meikleour was planted.

About the year 1770 there were large muirs—some of

them many hundreds or thousands of acres in extent—attached to many parishes both in the Highlands and Lowlands of Scotland, and, with a general belief, with the object of promoting draining, cultivation, and the general improvement of the country, it was highly desirable that these muirs should be divided amongst all persons having any interest in them, in proportion to the extent of their respective interests.

The law of the time favoured this view of the question by empowering the Sheriffs or the Sheriffs'-Depute of the various counties of Scotland to make such partitions on submissions or applications being made to them by all persons having any interest whatever, either large or small, in any particular muir, and to apportion and divide it accordingly.

In terms of a submission to, and a decreet-arbitral by, John Swinton, Sheriff-Depute of Perthshire (proceedings with reference to which were commenced in 1770 and concluded in 1774), it appears that all persons having any interest in "The Common Muir of Blair" made application to have it divided among them in proportion to their legal interest therein.

It was accordingly so divided, in terms of the decreet-arbitral referred to, amongst the then proprietors of the estates of Meikleour, Rosemount, Ardblair, the two Welltowns, Parkhead, Carsie, and the then proprietor of Blairgowrie and his feuars. At this time the feuars numbered eleven in all, who (together with the minister of the parish, who got his share) represented the village of Blair congregated around the Parish Kirk.

The block allotted to and subdivided among them consisted of nearly fifty Scotch acres, divided into twelve lots of different sizes in proportion to their respective rights of each person concerned. On this block now stand the villas of Woodlands, Heathpark, Brownsville, Shawfield, and a number of smaller cottages. Leaving the glebe out of the reckoning there is not one of those eleven separate holdings now belonging to the descendants of the original feuars of Blair—from whom, or their assignees, the present owners have acquired their rights to purchase. The above described block was what the then feuars of Blair got for their interests, in terms of their charters, in exchange for their "servitude of pasturage, fewal, foull, divot, &c., in the 'Great Common Muir' of Blair recently divided."

In accordance with the terms of their Charters they had also similar servitudes on certain parts of the Blairgowrie Estate proper, and, for the convenience of themselves and the then proprietor, they jointly petitioned the Sheriff that these rights should also be valued, and that another block (or blocks) of land should be taken *out of the Blairgowrie Estate* and divided, in terms of law, amongst those having claim. Accordingly, on the 21st January, 1777, another submission was made and a decreet-arbitral was issued thereon by John Swinton, Sheriff-Depute of Perthshire.

It is described as being between Thomas Graham, Esq. of Balgowan (then the Superior), and William Raitt, feuar, Hill of Blair, and others, "the vassals of the town of Blairgowrie below the Hill."

To William Raitt and another were allotted eight acres on the Lornty Road, and to the vassals below the Hill "fourty acres" on the Perth Road, divided into different lots, as in the case of the feuar's share of the "Common Muir."

Before 1777 there was no bridge over the river at Blairgowrie, all vehicular traffic having to cross by a ford where the "weir" is now erected, access being had from Lower Mill Street, down by where Mr Fell's slaughter-house is, while foot-passengers were taken across in a small coble or boat, which ceased to ply when the bridge was built. The part of the river where the boat crossed was known as the "Coble Pule," and the ascent on the Rattray side as the "Boat Brae," which name it retains to this day.

The year 1778 saw the "Muckle Mill" erected, in which flax was first spun here by machinery.

On the 20th September, 1788, the estate of Blairgowrie was purchased by a predecessor of the present proprietor, Col. Allan MacPherson (17—-1817), from Thomas Graham, Esq. of Newton and Balgowan, the purchase, of course, including Graham's share of the "Common Muir" of Blair, in terms of the decreet-arbitral of 1774, situated immediately to the east of the feuars' share of the same.

At the time of the threatened invasion of Britain by Napoleon in 1804, service in the British Army was compulsory, and those drawn for it could only obtain exemption on paying either a penalty or finding a substitute. In the following list of the "Military Service in Blairgowrie, 1803," the first name in each couple is that of the principal, where a second name is given it is that of the substitute, whose age is stated:—

"SUBDIVISION OF THE BLAIRGOWRIE DISTRICT IN THE COUNTY OF PERTH.

"Return of Enrolment, dated the eleventh and twenty-eighth days of February, eighteen hundred and three years."

James Duffus, merchant, Blairgowrie.
William Blair, shoemaker, do. (39).

James Duncan, weaver, do.
Henry Henderson, weaver, do. (22).

John Fleeming, weaver, do.
James Downie, weaver, do. (24).

John Donaldson, weaver, East Banchory.
George Robertson, weaver, Dundee (24).

William Isles, weaver, Weltown.
David Yeaman, weaver, Rattray (18).

Robert Straiton, weaver, Blairgowrie.
Thomas Bog, weaver, do. (36).

John Playfair, saddler, Blairgowrie, was found unfit, and there was balloted in his room Duncan Keay, weaver, Blairgowrie, who paid the penalty of £10.

William Cowan, wright, Blairgowrie, paid penalty of £10.

Patrick M'Pherson, surgeon, Blairgowrie, did not appear.

In 1804, a corps of Volunteers was raised in the town to assist, if required, the regular army against invasion.

The corps comprised 8 officers, 65 privates, and 1 drummer.

One of the officers of this corps (2nd Lieut. James Dick) rather distinguished himself one morning by showing his readiness for action. It happened during a wet and stormy night that the meal mill took fire, and the flames rapidly spreading threatened to destroy the whole building.

In order to alarm the inhabitants and obtain assistance, the Volunteer drum was beaten through the streets. The rattle of the drum and the confused noise suddenly awoke the Lieutenant from his sleep, and, hastily getting out of bed, he seized his sword, rushed out into the street in his trousers and, shirt, and, flourishing his sword to the passers-by, exclaimed, " Where are they landed, boys! Where are they landed?" the gallant officer being under the delusion that the French had really crossed the Channel.

Early in the beginning of this century (18—) the Superior of the town, " by reason of the great increase of the town, judged it necessary to put the police and government thereof under proper regulations, and for this purpose selected and made choice, from among the most respectable inhabitants, of a Bailie and four Councillors, with a Treasurer, Clerk, and other officers of Court, by way of trial, for the management of the funds and common good of the Burgh, administration of justice, and maintenance of peace and good order."

This system was further extended in 1809, when Colonel MacPherson granted a charter conferring certain privileges on the burgesses holding feus or building-stances in the village under him as Superior, and empowering the Bailie, who should be elected in terms of that charter, to hold Baron Courts for the trial of offences not exceeding £2 in value, and petty criminal offences. This charter held good until further extensions were made in 1829, and again in 1873.

Under the Charter of 1809, James Scott was elected the first Bailie of the town in 1810.

In 1824 the present Parish Church on the Hill of Blair was erected on the site of the old " mercait gate," the foundation stone being laid with great ceremony by William MacPherson, Esq. of Blairgowrie.

For a number of years, beginning in 1831, a stage coach, named "Baron Clerk Rattray," ran twice a-week between Blairgowrie and Coupar Angus.

In 1833 the householders resident in the Burgh adopted part of the Police Act III. and IV., William IV., cap. 46, by which certain powers were vested in the Chief Magistrate and four Commissioners for the management and regulation of the Police Department of the town, and the jurisdiction of the Chief Magistrate in criminal matters was enlarged.

The town in 1834 was first lit up with gas, when the present gas works were erected, and 1838 marked another epoch when the first printing press was introduced.

The temperature, in common with all districts bordering on the Highlands, is subject to frequent and sudden variations. On the 23rd October, 1839, a most severe shock of earthquake was felt throughout the district about 10 p.m., and was accompanied by a noise resembling distant thunder, or the rapid passage of a heavily-loaded vehicle over a newly-metalled road. The motion at the commencement of the concussion was of a waving or undulating nature, and, terminating in a vibration or tremor, becoming gradually less distinct until it ceased altogether.

In 1842 Blairgowrie was first honoured by a visit from royalty in the person of Her Majesty Queen Victoria on her way to Balmoral. On her progress through the estate of Glenericht, then possessed by General Chalmers, a Peninsular hero, she conferred on him the honour of Knighthood (Sir William Chalmers of Glenericht).

During the great spate of October, 1847, one of the arches of the "Auld Brig o' Blair" gave way, but was speedily and substantially repaired.

About the time of the outbreaking of the French Revolution in 1848, the village of Blairgowrie, obscure and insignificant as it then was, shared in the general excitement of the nation. At the time that the Militia Act first came into operation the class of persons who were liable under its enactments, and the lower ranks in general throughout the country, were greatly discontented with the measure, and on the day when the Justices of the Peace for the district met in Blairgowrie for the purpose of balloting for those who should serve, this discontentment broke out into open violence. Great crowds from this and all other parishes collected in the district, made prisoners of Colonel MacPherson of Blairgowrie, Sir William Ramsay of Bamff, and other gentlemen assembled, and confined them in the Inn until they got hold of the only writer in the village, whom they compelled to draw out a bond, to be executed by the Justices, by which they should be bound to abstain in future from any measures for enforcing the obnoxious Act. This document was subscribed by the captives under the threats of the mob. Satisfied with this, in the belief that they had effectually extinguished the Militia Act, they allowed their prisoners to go free, and themselves dispersed peacefully to their respective homes. But a week had not passed over their heads when a body of the Sutherland Fencibles made their appearance and seized on the most active rioters. This vigorous proceeding quelled the disturbance, and the provisions of the Act were thenceforward carried into effect without further trouble.

On the 28th of April, 1855, the first number of a local newspaper was issued by Messrs Ross & Son from a very small office in the High Street. The paper bore the title: —"Ross's Compendium of the Week's News, to be issued occasionally," and consisted of a single sheet, 12½ inches long and 8½ inches wide, printed on both sides. Occasionally the week's news was so scant that one side was sufficient both for news and advertisements.

On the 28th July of the same year another epoch in the history of the town was the opening of the Blairgowrie branch of the Scottish Midland Junction Railway. Up to this time all cartage of goods had to be done from the neighbouring town of Coupar Angus or from Perth and Dundee. For passenger traffic the first train started at 8 a.m., consisting of two first class, one second class, and two third class cars. There was a rush to secure tickets long before the hour of starting, and the train was well filled.

There had been a pretty general impression that the line would be inaugurated by several excursion trains, gratis, but, as hope turned to disappointment, "no demonstration was made, no flags were waving, no shouts were heard, and no wish was expressed that the Blairgowrie branch railway would flourish."

A good story is told regarding the railway on its first introduction to the town. One day a party of clergy had been in town from Dundee attending a Presbytery meeting, dressed in black, with "white chokers." They arrived at the Station just before the 4.30 p.m. train should start, for the purpose of taking their places to return to Dundee. Suddenly, one of them recollected he had forgotten something, and the others promising to wait for him, he started to get the forgotten article. Train time was up, and the Station officials tried to get those who remained into the carriages, but they would not stir until their friend had returned. In vain they were told the train would start without them. They knew better; the train would not go off and leave a dozen well-dressed individuals standing on the platform. The guard's patience being exhausted the train did start. Just as it was leaving the platform, the individual appeared running down the bank at the foot of Rorry (Reform) Street, and, seeing the train on its way, took a slanting direction across the fields as if to intercept it. On seeing this, the whole party jumped upon the line and started in pursuit. The railway officials and the guard had some amusement watching them, but the pursuit of the "iron horse" was fruitless, the whole party losing the train.

Once again, on 29th August, 1857, did Her Majesty Queen Victoria and suite honour Blairgowrie by passing through it en route to Balmoral. The Royal train arrived at Blairgowrie Station at half-past twelve. A company of soldiers, partly of the 1st and partly of the 21st Royals, many of them decorated with medals, were in waiting at the terminus, and presented arms on Her Majesty's arrival.

On alighting from the carriage, Her Majesty was received by Captain Campbell and Lady of Achalader and a numerous party of the principal farmers. After receiving a beautiful bouquet from Captain Campbell's six-year-old son, Her Majesty retired to the waiting-room, which was beautifully fitted up under the direction of Mrs Campbell. After a stay of a little over five minutes, during which she partook of biscuits and fruit, the Queen entered her travelling carriage and drove off at an easy pace for her Highland Home. The road from the Station to New Rattray was lined with a crowd of spectators, who welcomed Her Majesty and Consort with enthusiastic cheers, which were gracefully acknowledged. Along the route, more especially at Glenericht, floral arches and banners were very abundant. The Royal party partook of lunch at Spittal of Glenshee, and reached Balmoral at six o'clock.

* * * * * *

The morning of Tuesday, 25th January, 1859—"a red-letter day" in the history of Scotland—dawned bright and beautiful in Blairgowrie. This day, long looked forward to by Scotsmen in all parts of the world, had come round, and Blairgowrie prepared to celebrate the centenary of the birth of Scotland's own Poet in its own way.

In celebration of the centenary of the birth of Burns, a party of 40 gentlemen, belonging to the town and district, met in the hall of MacLaren's (Royal) Hotel, about 4 p.m. The hall was decorated with evergreens, arranged upon the walls in various tasteful figures. The instrumental band, under Willie Scrimgeour, was in attendance for some time, and the music added greatly to the effect and enjoyment of the meeting. Mr Alexander Robertson, banker, presided, and, after a sumptuous supper, gave the toast of the evening, "The Memory of Robert Burns, Scotland's Immortal Bard," which was drunk to in solemn silence. A most enjoyable night was spent, enlivened with song and sentiment.

A demonstration was also held in the Malt Barns at "The Hill," which was perhaps the most successful meeting ever held in Blairgowrie up to this time. Between four and five hundred persons were present, from the youth of tender years to the sire of grey hairs, drawn from all ranks of society. Mr Allan Macpherson occupied the chair, and spirited addresses were given by the Chairman, Messrs Thomas Mitchell of Greenfield, William Davie of Millbank, John Bridie, and Thomas Steven, while a glee party and the Westfields Flute Band delighted the audience with music, the whole concluding with the singing of "There was a Lad was born in Kyle."

The year 1859 also saw the inauguation of the Volunteer movement; and the first meeting for the formation of a Rifle Corps in Blairgowrie was held 13th December, 1859. They were embodied under duly approved officers, 16th March, 1860. The corps was present in Edinburgh on the 7th August, 1860, at the review of the Scottish Volunteers by Her Majesty the Queen.

BLAIRGOWRIE 1860.

CHAPTER IV.

Founding of Public Hall—Earl Russell at Meikleour—Address from Inhabitants—Public Banquet—Address by Meikleour Tenantry—Earl Russell's Speech—Opinions of the Press—A French View—Introduction of Water Supply—Report and Analysis of Water—Drainage of Town—Erection of New Schools—Opening up of Commercial Street—Planting Trees in Wellmeadow—Franchise Demonstration—County Council—Boundary Commission—Public Park—A Generous Gift—Burgh Seal—Macpherson Memorial Fountain—New Sewage Works—Visit of Lord Wolseley—The Bailies of Blair—Magistrates—Provosts.

SINCE the year 1824, when the foundation-stone of the Parish Church was laid, no event excited so much general interest in the town and neighbourhood as the laying of the foundation-stone of the Public Hall, on the 20th October, 1860, by His Grace the Duke of Athole, Most Worshipful Grand Master Mason of Scotland. A grand banquet afterwards took place in the Queen's (Macdonald's) Hotel, upwards of 100 gentlemen being present. Alternately, during dinner, selections of music were given by the Duke of Athole's Flute Band and the Blairgowrie Brass Band.

The year 1863 was a memorable one for Blairgowrie. On the 10th of March it was *en fête*, the occasion being the marriage day of the Heir-Apparent to the Throne. Flags waved from the housetops; bells pealed forth merrily; processions were the order of the day, and illuminations of the night.

A banquet, attended by 80 gentlemen, was held in the Queen's Hotel, when Bailie Thomas Steven occupied the chair; another banquet, attended by 50 Volunteers, under Sergeant William Crockart as chairman, was also held in the Queen's; the shoemakers, to the number of 40, sat down to dinner in MacGregor's Temperance Hotel, Mr William Lauder in the chair; a public festival took place in the Free Church School, James Street; and the rejoicings were concluded by a grand ball in the Public

Hall in the evening. Everything passed off with great *éclat*, and a wish was expressed that such another pleasant reunion would be arranged ere many years would pass. This wished-for occasion came round very soon, and Blairgowrie once more assumed holiday appearance. On the 26th September, 1863, it did honour to itself by honouring one of Britain's noble men. Earl Russell, having chosen Meikleour House as a quiet retreat to enjoy a

MEIKLEOUR CROSS.

brief repose from his arduous Parliamentary duties and recruit his strength, a number of the Meikleour tenantry proposed to show their respect to his lordship by inviting him to a banquet, in the Public Hall, Blairgowrie, on the 26th September, 1863.

The authorities of the town entered heartily into the movement, and fraternised with the originators in order to make the demonstration worthy of the noble guest. At a meeting of the inhabitants of Blairgowrie, on the Tuesday evening previous, it was arranged that a public demonstration should be made, and that an address should be presented to the Earl.

At half-past one o'clock a procession started from the Wellmeadow, under the leadership of Capt. George B.

Anderson, of the Blairgowrie Rifles, to meet the Earl and bring him in honour to the town. The procession was led by the Volunteers and Brass Band, followed by the Masonic and Operative Bodies of the place, and a coach containing Bailie Steven and the Town Council. On arriving at the "Dark Falls" the procession stopped, and the Volunteers presented arms, the band playing, "Saw ye Johnnie coming?"

Earl Russell's carriage, which also contained Lady Russell and daughter, then took up position, and the procession returned to the Cross. On arriving in front of the Royal Hotel the Volunteers formed three sides of a square, and the carriages of Earl Russell and the Council drove into the open space, after which Bailie Steven presented the following address from the inhabitants of Blairgowrie:—

"Unto the Right Honourable John, Earl Russell, one of Her Majesty's principal Secretaries of State.

"May it please your Lordship—I have the honour, as representing the inhabitants of this burgh, to convey to your Lordship their sincere respect for your character, and their high appreciation of your long and distinguished services.

"We are grateful for this opportunity so courteously afforded us, of publicly acknowledging our high sense of your Lordship's character and ability as a statesman, and of your consistent unremitting efforts throughout all your public life in the cause of popular rights and privileges.

"It would ill become us, who enjoy the substantial fruits of your Lordship's labours, to refrain, at a time like this, from a hearty acknowledgment of the noble service it has been your fortune to render to your Sovereign and your country; for we feel assured that on the broad foundation of those Liberal principles so consistently advocated by your Lordship, the truest patriotism and the most intelligent loyalty are based. And, while it cannot but be gratifying to see that your labour has not been in vain, we trust it will be no less gratifying for you to know that it has not been forgotten or unappreciated by a grateful and intelligent people.

"We recognise the growing intelligence of the people,

their increasing interest in public questions, and their loyal attachment to the Constitution of their country, as the genuine fruits of that liberal and enlightened policy to which your Lordship, throughout your whole Parliamentary career, has so consistently adhered.

"While we are fully alive to the momentous interests involved in the right and able discharge of the duties of your high and responsible position, we feel assured that your Lordship's firm and consistent foreign policy will uphold the dignity of this great country throughout the world, and preserve the nation in peace and prosperity, whatever contingencies may arise.

"As a public servant, long tried and ever faithful to the great interests of civil and religious liberty, we desire to convey to your Lordship our high and grateful acknowledgment of the honourable and distinguished part you have acted throughout, and to express our utmost confidence that your Lordship, actuated by lofty principles and guided by the light of a long experience, will be found equal to any emergency, and will be enabled by your wise and judicious counsels to guide the country safely through every possible peril.

(Signed)   "THOMAS STEVEN, Chief Magistrate."

Earl Russell, in replying to the address, said :—

"Gentlemen, I beg to thank you for the very gratifying address which you have presented to me. It has been my good fortune, in co-operation with many others, to promote the civil and religious liberties of my countrymen. The enlightened state of public opinion and the progress of political knowledge have caused the success of measures which in former years had been obstructed by selfish interests or defeated by ignorance and apathy. Let us hope that, with the increased interest which is felt in public questions, loyalty to the Throne, attachment to the Constitution, and zeal for all useful reforms will pervade every class of the community."

In the evening a banquet was held in the Public Hall, attended by upwards of 160 gentlemen. The hall was beautifully decorated for the occasion by Mr John Bridie, painter. On the wall above the platform were displayed three heraldic coats of arms. In the niche in the centre was placed the arms of the County of Perth, and on each side the arms of Meikleour and Ramsay of Bamff. The Meikleour arms displayed two naked figures as supporters, and four stars on centre of shield—"*The Grit Pool*" and "*Crux Christi Nostra Corona.*" The Ramsay arms had two griffins rampant as supporters, and spread eagle in centre of shield—"*Spernit Pericula Virtus.*"

At the bottom of the hall, facing the Chairman, was an enormous "R," beautifully painted and having in several parts of it spaces in which the words "Reform," "Emancipation," "Free Trade," and "Neutrality" appeared. Slightly above and on the right and left of the letter were the arms of Earl Russell and the Earl of Airlie, with the Blairgowrie arms in the niche above. The Russell arms had a lion and an elk rampant as supporters, and a red lion rampant in centre of shield, three oyster shells, and Earl's crown above—"*Che sara sara.*" The Ogilvy arms displayed two bulls rampant as supporters, and red lion passant quadrant in centre of shield, a figure of Lady Ogilvy on top throwing down the Harrow—"*A Fin.*" The Right Hon. the Earl of Airlie took the chair, with Earl Russell, Lord Amberley, Provost Parker, Dundee, and Rev. Mr Marshall, Coupar Angus, on his right; on his left sat the Lord Provost of Perth, Dean of Guild Dewar, Perth, the Hon. Mr Elliot, &c.

At this banquet an address was presented by the Rev. Mr Marshall to Earl Russell from the tenantry on the Meikleour estate. Thereafter Earl Russell delivered a speech which echoed throughout the world, and Blairgowrie found itself to be famous above all places of the earth, and, what was thought of the banquet by the outside world, a few extracts from judicially competent authorities will show.

From *The Globe.*—"Earl Russell's speech at Blairgowrie will be read with deep interest in other lands besides our own. The organ of a powerful Government in all that relates to foreign affairs cannot well speak at length on great topics which move the passions and affect the interest of the nation, and demand the full judgment, without having a large circle of readers; still less one, who, for many years in the van of political life, has his name blended with the history of all great modern questions."

From *The Scotsman.*—" Blairgowrie has this year been blessed above all places in the three kingdoms with what is beyond doubt the speech of the recess. The addresses, indeed, in which his hosts complimented and congratulated him, were remarkably good, both in substance and expression, and supply several texts on which he might or might not have preached as he felt inclined. Waiving the past he entered quickly into the present, and spoke to his Blairgowrie audience words whose scope and might will be estimated with eager interest over all Europe and America."

From *The Witness.*—" The speech of Earl Russell at Blairgowrie is one worthy of a statesman, spoken as it is at an hour of more than ordinary interest in the history of the world. The topics of his speech are far from being commonplace; they have a wider range than even an Imperial speech; they belong to the world, and are such as fix at this moment the attention, and involve the interests of the leading nations of the earth. It is full of noble, generous, and just sentiment; its tone is manly and dignified; it is redolent of liberty, and there is about it a calm consciousness of strength, such as becomes the Minister of a great nation, which feels that it is strong and is determined not to abuse its strength by the perpetration of a wrong."

From the *Manchester Guardian.*—" Blairgowrie is not a place towards which the attention of mankind was strained in pursuit of political enlightenment, but that was because the honour designed for it was not generally known. This accidental circumstance is sufficient to elevate it from its natural condition to a centre of attraction for Englishmen and Frenchmen, Russians and Germans, Americans and Poles. It is evident that Earl Russell was not in a reticent mood; he was willing to regard the Meikleour tenantry as the representatives of a far wider circle of auditors, and came prepared to speak with authority of the affairs of state under his control."

" This morning " (says the *Dundee Advertiser*) " the spruce little village on the rocky banks of its romantic Ericht wakes up and finds itself famous, and feels that its name is to be carried to all ends of the earth. Such is fame.

Never before did this little manufacturing town do so ambitious a piece of business in the finer qualities of yarns."

The following is a French view of the banquet, from the *Revue des Deux Mondes*, by M. Eugene Fercade:—"Is it not a lucky occurrence for us that the farmers of Meikleour had the idea of entertaining Lord Russell in Blairgowrie? To the convivial humour of these honest men we are indebted for the first official disclosure of the impression produced on English policy by the last despatch of Prince Gortschakoff. Let us picture to ourselves these honest inhabitants of Blairgowrie, this pretty little town in Scotland, hastening to do honour to the illustrious veteran of British liberty. They walk forth in procession to meet the noble Lord, his Countess, and the family, a league from the town: a detachment of Volunteers serves as an escort, and gives to this half rustic fête a sort of military air, which is the fashion in our day. The Bailie presents an address to Lord Russell. At the dinner hour they enter the hall of the Town House, which is gaily decorated, where a table for a hundred-and-fifty guests is laid. The farmers of Meikleour entrust to their minister the reading of their address, and this composition gives a fair notion of the literature of the Scottish farmer. The classical allusion to the House of Russell is most happy—the blood of Russell moistened the plant of British liberty while it was yet young and weak: and the noble career of Lord Russell is traced in appropriate language. They sit down to dinner, and in that stands out the speech of the principal Secretary of State for Her Britannic Majesty—a speech simple, honest, spoken within the walls of a Scottish village, but is to England, Europe, and America."

For a long number of years the town was supplied with water from force pumps, erected in different parts of the district over sunk wells.

The water supply being generally of a bad quality and insufficient for the increasing population, the wells were gradually filled up on the introduction of a water system direct from Loch Ben-a-chally, about eight miles north-west from the town.

The plans in connection with this work were prepared

by Mr Leslie, C.E., Edinburgh, and a regular and complete inspection of the Lornty was made, the water from the burn being analysed by Professor Macadam, who pronounced it to be very pure, and above the average quality for domestic or other uses.

Several schemes were suggested as to the supply. At first the Lornty Burn was looked to as the probable source, and various small streams and tributaries of the Lornty were also believed to be sufficient, and the situation of the ground at Nether-Aird was considered likely to be turned into a natural basin or reservoir for the reception and distribution of the springs so to be collected.

The Glasclune burn was also speculated upon, but all these schemes were, after due consideration, set aside, and it was resolved to take the water supply direct from Loch Ben-a-chally, thereby getting rid of all vegetable and other impurities, and securing a permanent and thoroughly sufficient supply direct from the fountain head.

Loch Ben-a-chally lies a little over seven miles to the north-west of the town in a cavity at the eastern base of the hill Ben-a-chally, from which it takes its name. It lies 760 feet above the lower part of Blairgowrie; the reservoir at Burnhead, about half-a-mile north of the town, being 500 feet lower than the loch, and 260 feet higher than the lowest part of the town.

The gradient of the fire-clay in all the seven miles is not less than 1 in 200. In some parts it is as much as 1 in 35.

The extent of the loch, according to the Ordnance Survey, gives 131 acres of average area. In some parts it is over 30 feet in depth. By arrangement with the Duke of Athole, or his representatives, liberty was obtained to raise the loch five feet and lower it other five, thus giving ten feet additional storage. From the loch to the reservoir at Burnhead there are upwards of seven miles of fire-clay piping, and through the town and neighbourhood are over ten miles of cast-iron pipes as water mains for domestic and other supply.

The whole of the work, except furnishing of materials, was performed in a substantial manner by local contractors, at a cost of nearly £6,000, under the superintendence of

Mr Fenwick, a gentleman of skill and experience, acting as Inspector on behalf of Mr Leslie, C.E.; Mr David Tod acting as Engineer for the contractors.

The work was begun on the 14th March, and finished, after considerable delay in procuring iron pipes, on the 27th October; and the water was turned on with much ceremony on the 5th November, 1870.

Since 1870, the requirements of the district—which now includes a large portion of Rattray, &c.—have increased so rapidly, that a new reservoir, of four times the capacity of the old one, was built in 1893. In 1896 it was thought advisable to have a full report on the entire water system by an expert, and Mr George Baxter, C.E., Dundee, was engaged. After a most thorough survey from the reservoirs to Loch Ben-a-chally, Mr Baxter drew up and submitted a very elaborate report. On his recommendation new filter-beds and measuring boxes were laid down, with new screens at the loch. The whole system is now in first-class order, under the personal superintendence of a practical man.

The following is a copy of Professor MacAdam's report and analysis of the water:—

"ANALYTICAL LABORATORY, SURGEONS' HALL,
"EDINBURGH, 20th May. 1869.

"I have made a careful chemical analysis of a sample of water forwarded to me by the Local Board of Blairgowrie through James Leslie, C.E.

"The general characteristics of the water were excellent; as received for analysis, the water was clear and transparent, free from visible contamination, evolved no odour, and possessed an agreeable taste. On evaporation the water yielded the following results, calculated to one imperial gallon:—

Chloride of Sodium (common salt),	1·36 grains.
Sulphate of Lime (stucco),	0·83 ,,
Chloride of Magnesium,	0·21 ,,
Chloride of Potassium,	trace
Carbonate of Lime (chalk),	0·87 ,,
Carbonate of Magnesia,	0·43 ,,
Carbonate of Iron and Phosphates,	traces
Soluble Silica,	0·19 ,,
Organic matter of vegetable origin,	0·53 ,,
Total matter dissolved in one imperial gallon,	4·42 grains.

Hardness, 2 degrees.

"The foregoing results demonstrate that the water from Blairgowrie is of first-rate quality for domestic use. It is free from the presence of any impurity, and the saline and organic constituents dissolved therein are characteristic of all wholesome waters. The quality of the ingredients in solution is comparatively small, being decidedly below the amount found in domestic waters generally, and in this respect the water under examination ranks in the very highest scale. The degree of hardness is very small, and, indeed, the water is practically soft.

* * * * * *

"I consider that the inhabitants of Blairgowrie would be extremely fortunate in securing a water for domestic supply, which, alike as a beverage, for culinary purposes, and in washing operations, is eminently suitable, and ranks in the highest class.

(Signed) "S. THOMSON MACADAM, M.D."

* * * * * *

Under a Charter granted by the Superior of the Burgh, dated 10th September, 1873, the burgesses' privileges were extended, and they were empowered to elect twelve, instead of five, Councillors, with three Bailies instead of one; but the powers of local government possessed by the towns-people were still found to be unsatisfactory, and the General Police and Improvement (Scotland) Act, 1862, was adopted. The Burgh then had a Police Commission of twelve, including a Senior and two Junior Magistrates. Under this Act, Dr James Neilson was elected the first Chief Magistrate, and, during his term of office, a sewerage system was laid throughout the town, at a cost of £3000.

Some time after the introduction of School Boards for the management of school affairs and superintendence of education, the old denominational Church schools were closed, and new Public Schools were opened on the 19th of August, 1879, by Mr Allan Macpherson, Chairman of the School Board.

The Schools were built on the field immediately to the north of the parish manse garden, being part of the glebe belonging to the Established Church. The Schools, as originally built, cost £6000, but considerable alterations and additions have since then been made.

In 1882 a great improvement was made on the lower part of the town by the formation of Commercial Street. Prior to this, all foot and vehicular traffic to the Railway Station had to be done by Tannage Street. The new street was formed by subscription, and runs almost in line with Allan Street at north end of Wellmeadow, and down by the west side of Station Hotel, through what was formerly the hotel garden.

The square, still known by the old name of Wellmeadow, was also adorned with trees, after the fashion of the squares in our large towns.

During the autumn of the year 1884 the whole country was astir with demonstrations in protest against the Government urging that the franchise should be extended.

Blairgowrie, like its neighbours, contributed to the excitement. A processional demonstration, made up of over 1000 persons and 50 horses, was marshalled by Major D. Chalmers in a field at the east end of Old Rattray, and paraded through Old and New Rattray and Blairgowrie.

Towards the end of 1889 an Act was passed—the Local Government (Scotland) Act, 1889—which provides for the establishment of a County Council, to be entrusted with the management of the financial and administrative business of the county. Blairgowrie, by reason of population, was entitled to elect two representatives to this Council, wherefore the Burgh was divided into two wards or divisions.

The first ward includes all that is contained to the east of the boundaries, as follows:—" Up the east side of Wellmeadow crossing to Leslie Street, west north side of same to Croft Lane, up east side of same to High Street, along north side of same to John Street, and up east side of same to old Parochial School. The second ward embraces all contained to the west of said boundaries."

In January, 1890, Chief Magistrate Bridie and Mr James Ogilvy were nominated to contest the first ward; Mr James Stewart being nominated for the second ward; and for the landward part of the parish of Blairgowrie, Mr Allan Macpherson and Mr James Scott were nominated.

The election of the various representatives took place within the Public Schools, 4th February, 1890, when Mr James Ogilvy was elected representative of 1st ward by a majority of 6. Mr James Stewart was elected, unopposed, as representative of the 2nd ward; and Mr A. Macpherson was elected to represent the landward division by a majority of 36.

About the 25th of June, 1890, the Boundary Commissioners under the Local Government Act issued their proposals for the consolidation of parishes. The following were their proposals regarding the parish of Blairgowrie:—"Annex to this parish the detached part of Bendochy at Drimmie and the part of the parish of Kinloch known as Cochrage Farm, thus uniting the detached part of Blairgowrie, at Cochrage and Blackcraig, with the main part of the parish; detach from Blairgowrie and annex to Bendochy the detached part of Blairgowrie at the Welltown of Bamff and the part of the main parish of Blairgowrie lying to the east of Rosemount (Parkhead estate)."

In the beginning of August, 1890, the Boundary Commissioners issued orders relating to Blairgowrie:—"That a detached part of the parish of Bendochy, containing 904 acres, situated at Drimmie and adjoining the parishes of Rattray, Blairgowrie, and Alyth, shall form part of the parish of Blairgowrie; and that a detached part of the parish of Blairgowrie, containing 1742 acres, situated at Creuchies and adjoining the parishes of Rattray, Bendochy, and Alyth, shall form part of the parish of Bendochy. That so much of the parish of Kinloch as lies to the north of the march between the lands of Cochrage and Blackcraig on the north, and Millhole Farm, Middleton Farm and Muir, and Glasclune Farm on the south, shall form part of the parish of Blairgowrie."

Blairgowrie gave away, as foresaid, a detached part and a part of the main parish valued at £602 and £200 respectively, while it received a detached part of Bendochy renting at £656, and the farm of Cochrage from Kinloch. The total rental of the parish was therefore reduced from £28,009 to £27,888. (1890.)

On the 26th of March, 1892, a special meeting of a Committee elected in 1887 in connection with the proposal to have a Public Park for Blairgowrie, as a memento of the Queen Victoria Jubilee, was held in the office of the Secretary (Mr J. B. Miller). Mr Thomas Steven presided, and the following letter was read :—

"MILLBANK,
"BLAIRGOWRIE, 10th March, 1892.

"DEAR SIR,—At the first meeting of the Public Park Committee kindly intimate that, conjointly with my sister, Mrs Nicoll, we will have much pleasure in conveying by a deed of gift, in favour of the public body they may appoint, that field belonging to me at the Loonbrae as a public park for the inhabitants of Blairgowrie and Rattray, and hope that the Committee may now see their way to carry out successfully the very desirable object which they have been endeavouring to promote.—I am, yours faithfully, "WILLIAM DAVIE."

It was stated that it was Mr Davie's wish that the field should be conveyed to the Police Commissioners of Blairgowrie and Rattray, and be administered by a Committee consisting of three from each, with six elected by these bodies from the general public, preferably, in the first instance, from the Public Park Committee, the Chairmen to be alternately the Chief Magistrates of Blairgowrie and Rattray; and that part of the field be so utilised that the upkeep of the whole should necessitate no tax upon either of the two parishes.

The Chairman submitted the following resolution:— "That this Committee accept, on behalf of the communities of Blairgowrie and Rattray, of the offer of Mr William Davie and his sister, Mrs Nicoll, of a field for a public park; and tender them their united and cordial thanks for their most liberal gift, so freely and ungrudgingly given; and that a Committee be appointed to meet Mr Davie and his sister, and arrange the necessary preliminaries so that their intention may be carried into effect with as little delay as possible."

This was seconded by Mr James Isles, and a Committee, consisting of Messrs Thomas Steven, John Bridie, Thomas Doig, and the Secretary, was appointed.

In a second letter Mr Davie suggested the purchase of a field adjoining his, belonging to Mr James Thom, a letter from whom was read offering the same at £650. This field comprises about nine acres, Mr Davie's being eleven acres and costing £700.

A public meeting of the ratepayers of both burghs was held in Public Hall, Blairgowrie, on the 29th April, 1892, for the purpose of considering Mr Davie's generous gift. The chair was taken by Chief Magistrate Bridie, who, along with Mr James Isles, ex-Chief Magistrate Steven, Chief Magistrate Doig, and Junior Magistrate Stewart, spoke in the highest terms of the offer of Mr Davie in giving of his means to help the public of Blairgowrie and Rattray in their recreation and amusement. Upwards of thirty gentlemen were thereupon appointed a Provisional Committee to carry out the scheme and endeavour to raise funds to purchase the adjoining field.

The park was afterwards handed over by Mr Davie to Trustees who are empowered to let it until they accumulate funds sufficient to warrant them in opening it to the public.

On the 15th of May, 1893, the Burgh Police (Scotland) Act, 1892, came into operation, under which our Senior Magistrate was honoured with the title of "Provost"—(John Bridie being the first to have the honour). One section of this Act declares "that the Burgh shall have a Common Seal bearing a device to be fixed on by the Commissioners." After due consideration a design by Mr John A. R. Macdonald was approved of, the component parts being:—"A very ornate escutcheon entwined with the leaves of the strawberry—(that luscious fruit so abundant in the district). The escutcheon is

Burgh Seal.

divided into three divisions, each having a crest emblematic of different periods in the history of the town. The one on the left is a sheaf, the crest of the old family of Blair of Blair, now extinct; on the right a nest of young ravens, the crest of the Drummonds of Blair, one of whom, while proprietor of the estate and resident in Newton Castle, obtained a Charter, 9th July, 1634, from King Charles I., whereby the town was erected into a Burgh of Barony. The lower part has that well-known object of interest portrayed, the Brig o' Blair, with the motto underneath, 'Bhlair-gobhainn-righ,' the whole circumscribed with a buckled band bearing the inscription—'The Commissioners of the Burgh of Blairgowrie.'"

An artistic fountain, erected by Mrs Macpherson and family in memory of the late Mr Allan Macpherson, was gifted to the town on the 8th of May, 1893. The structure has been set up in a prominent position at the south-east corner of the Wellmeadow, opposite the Bridge, is of elegant design, and forms a pretty enhancement to the locality. The base and basin are of red Aberdeenshire granite, while the superstructure is of fine red freestone from Dumfries, the whole rising to a height of nearly 18 feet, richly ornamented with gablets, crockets, gargoyles, and other architectural devices with harmonious effect. The upper part, in the form of a spire, is surmounted by a cross, with lightning conductor attached.

The whole work was designed and carried out by Messrs Hicks & Charlewood, Newcastle-on-Tyne. All the different parts were fully prepared before being forwarded, all that was required where it was to be put up being preparation of the site, piecing the sections together, and fixing up the water arrangements.

On the east side of the fountain, from which the water flows over a shell design into the basin, the pedestal bears the following inscription :—

"In memory of Allan Macpherson of Blairgowrie, who entered into rest 6th November, 1891, aged 73."

On the three other sides are :—"Whatsoever thy hand findeth to do, do it with thy might." "Not with eye service as men pleasers, but in singleness of heart, fearing God." "For the righteous Lord loveth righteousness, His countenance doth behold the upright."

The ceremony of formally handing over the fountain to the town was of a simple nature. The Magistrates, Commissioners, Town Council, and others connected with the public bodies assembled, along with representatives from Blairgowrie House, &c.

Mr Alan Macpherson said :—"Mr Chief Magistrate and gentlemen, as some of you know, my eldest brother being in India, Mrs Macpherson has asked me to read to you a letter expressing her views and wishes as to this fountain."

MACPHERSON MEMORIAL FOUNTAIN.

"To the Police Commissioners of Blairgowrie, the Bailies and Town Council, and the Water Commissioners for the town and district of Blairgowrie.

"GENTLEMEN,—I have much pleasure in handing over to you, for the use of the people of Blairgowrie, the fountain just put up by me in Wellmeadow, in memory of my husband, the late Mr Macpherson of Blairgowrie. I may mention that I am anxious to be permitted to retain during my lifetime the privilege of doing anything that may be deemed necessary for the due preservation of the memorial, and I trust you will kindly accede to this request. I take this opportunity of thanking you for the site you have given for the fountain, and for the interest you have taken in its erection.—I am, gentlemen, yours faithfully, "E. MACPHERSON.

"BLAIRGOWRIE HOUSE, *May 8th, 1893.*"

Chief Magistrate Bridie, on behalf of the Police Commission, the Town Council, and the Water Commission, and other bodies in the public service, accepted of the gift, and expressed the hope that nothing would be done to mar the memorial in the least degree, and assured the family (Macpherson) that the town would take the greatest care of it, as it deserved.

Master Alan D. Macpherson, son of the Laird of Blairgowrie, then turned on the water, and the proceedings terminated.

When the burgh was thoroughly drained in 1876-77, up till 1893 the whole of the sewage had been allowed to flow into the Ericht, unfiltered, at two outlets—one near the Bridge, the other opposite the Railway Station.

Various complaints had been made against this treatment, and the Board of Supervision more than once pressed upon the Commissioners the advisability of remedying the state of affairs. In 1891 a crisis was reached, negotiations were entered into with Mr Macpherson of Blairgowrie, and plans were prepared for carrying the whole sewage down the river a distance of 1600 yards beyond the Railway Station. The sewage was to be filtered there, and the effluent allowed to flow into the river; but objections were raised, and various actions by different proprietors, who held that it would destroy the amenity of their land, &c., obliged the Commissioners to carry the sewage works further down the river. Ground to the extent of 1½ acres having been acquired from Dr Rattray's Welltown estate, the filter-house was erected at the lower end of the ground. Constructed (after a model supplied by Mr Mackay, County Sanitary Inspector), of brick, it measures 40 feet long by 21 feet broad.

The sewage enters at one end of the building, is carried along one side in a channel, returns back again nearly to where it entered, and is again finally carried to the opposite end. In the channel a number of "interceptors," formed of whin pavement stones, are placed with angle deflected stones, the bed of the channel having a slight rise towards the point of exit, so as to cause the sediment to settle within the channel as much as possible.

At the extremity of the channel a filtering well is formed about four feet deep, the cover of which lies at an angle of about 45 degrees, and is formed by a hinged frame, about seven inches deep, covered on both sides with galvanised steel wire-cloth, the space between the two sheets of wire-cloth being filled in with fine gravel, the sewage having to force its way through this filtering medium. The whole apparatus is fitted up in duplicate, so that while one set is in operation the other is being allowed to settle for a few days, and the sediment is then cleaned out. Adjoining the filtering screens are two sludge wells, about nine feet deep, into which the sludge is allowed to pass by means of valves; this can then be lifted out by means of pumps fitted up for that purpose. The filtered effluent goes into a channel beyond the filters, carried to the outside of the house, passes through pipes for about 30 yards, and for a further 450 yards, through rough pasture and uncultivated ground, in a channel formed through a bed of sand and fine gravel, to the river.

All the works were carried out at an estimated cost of £1500, including £200 to proprietors for compensation. The works were first put into operation under the direction of the "City Fathers"—Provost Stewart, Bailies Clark and Lamb, and other members of Commission, 16th November, 1893.

During the night of the 17th and morning of the 18th November of that year, a fearful hurricane of wind swept over the district, devastating whole forests, and changing the general aspect of the country entirely.

On the 7th and 8th December, 1896, Lord Wolseley, the Commander-in-Chief of the British Army, honoured the town by a visit (staying over night at Craighall, the seat of Lieut.-Gen. (now Sir) James Clerk Rattray), and, on the 8th December, unveiled a monument on the North Inch at Perth to commemorate the deeds of the gallant 90th (Perthshire) regiment, which was raised in 1796 by Thomas Graham of Newton, afterwards Lord Lynedoch.

Under the Charters of 1809, 1829, 1873, &c., the following gentlemen have been elected Bailies of Blairgowrie:—

PROVOSTS.

James Scott,	elected	1810.
James Dick,	,,	1811 and 1823.
Robert Dow,	,,	1813.
Thomas Johnstone,	,,	1815.
David Kidd,	,,	1817.
James M'Nab,	,,	1819.
George Constable,	,,	1821.
William Robertson,	,,	1825 and 1829.
Thomas Whitson,	,,	1827.
Robert Ayson,	,,	1831 and 1835.
Robert Robertson,	,,	1833.
James Leslie,	,,	1837.
John Brown,	,,	1839 and 1843 and 1847.
David Wilson,	,,	1841.
William J. Ayson,	,,	1845.
Thomas Mitchell,	,,	1847 (interim).
George Robertson,	,,	1849 and 1853.
James Young,	,,	1851 and 1857.
Robert Lunan,	,,	1855.
John Fleming,	,,	1859 and 1863.
Thomas Steven,	,,	1861 and 1865.
Alexander Buchan,	,,	1867.
James Chalmers,	,,	1869 and 1873.
John Bridie,	,,	1871.

Senior Bailies—		Junior Bailies—	
John Bridie,	1873.	1st Dr James Neilson,	1873.
James Chalmers,	1874.	2nd Thomas Steven,	1873.
David Chalmers,	1879.	William Craigie,	1879.
		James Chalmers,	1879.
John Bridie,	1884.	William Craigie,	1884.
		James Chalmers,	1884.
James Stewart,	1887.	George Brown,	1890.
		David Chalmers,	1890.
John Bridie,	1893.	George Brown,	1893.
		Thomas Low,	1893.
George Brown,	1894.	Thomas Low,	1894.
		John D. Fell,	1894.

Chief Magistrates—

Dr James Neilson, 1873-75 and 1876-78.
Thomas Steven, 1878-1887.
John Bridie, 1887-1893.

Provosts—

John Bridie, 1893.
James Stewart, 1893-1896.
James Chalmers, 1896-1897.
David Templeman, 1897.

CHAPTER V.

Original Inhabitants of Scotland—Druids and Druidical Remains—Standing Stones—Haer Cairns—Tumuli—Store Mount—Blairs—Buzzard Dykes—Bloody Inches—Steed Stalls—Roman Relics—Local Antiquarian Collections—Relics in Scottish Antiquarian Museum—French Bell—Hirchen Hill—Agreements and Charters—Interesting Map—Seals of Families—Pedigree of Drummonds of Blair—Copy of Two Letters by King James the Seventh—Notes from Rental Book of Coupar Abbey—Cally—Murtoun—Blair—Old Parish Tokens.

IT has since the beginning of this century up to the present time been a vexed question among archæologists—who were the first discoverers and occupiers of the kingdom? Evidences have been found from time to time which antiquarians believe to be the remains of several distinct races who inhabited those regions many thousand years ago. According to some, the Druids, a very learned and enlightened people from the borders of the Caspian Sea, traversed Europe nearly along the 45th parallel of north latitude, crossed the Channel, and were the first discoverers and occupiers of the country.

How long that nation peopled the land, or where their descendants migrated to, is mystery alike, but the monuments they have left behind attest their genius and power.

The unhewn stones found in Hindostan and the East are attributed by the natives there to a fabulous being named Pandoo and his sons; and, with a similarity of character attesting their common origin, they are also to be found in many parts of Europe, on the shores of, and in the interior of, Britain. About a mile south-west of the town, near the Darrach Wood, on the Essendy Road, are the remains of one of these Druidical monuments. It is in the form of a hexagon, and is supposed to be one of the earliest erected in this part of the country. Further examples are to be found at Glenballoch and Easter Rattray.

Many of these monoliths, as at Glenballoch, show cup markings and grooves, which, according to the traditions of the Celts, are in honour of departed heroes. When in stones singly they represent only one distinguished hero, but when in great numbers, many heroes fallen in battle. The stone at Glenballoch shows thirteen of these cups, while one unearthed in 1897 at Aikenhead shows a large number of various sizes. The last has, unfortunately, been ruthlessly destroyed.

The parish contains few remains of antiquity possessing much interest. Among those deserving of notice are the "Haer Cairns," marking the scene of mortal conflict and last resting-place of the slain.

Most of these cairns have now been wholly removed to allow of agricultural improvements, and in process of excavation, stone coffins, formed of four flat slabs, have been discovered, containing, in many instances, human bones, urns, &c. Two Roman cinerary urns, containing burnt bones, were found in a field at Cottershade, but they were, unfortunately, broken and thrown away as being of no value. At the same place a stone cist containing human bones was uncovered, but the bones crumbled to dust on exposure to the air.

In a moor a few miles west are 8 tumuli or cairns, termed the Westerly Cairns. There are also in the neighbourhood Kincairney, the head of the Cairns; Balcairn, the town of Cairns—(that is, the resting-place of the dead); Cairnmoor, the moor with the cairns; Pitcairn, the cairn of graves; and Cairnbutts, the ridge of cairns. There is a cairn at Morganstone in which stone cists were found, and a cairn to the north of Netheraird, where a bronze celt was found; there are also numerous cairns west of Middle Mause and on the Muir of Gormok. Urns have been found in tumulus near Milton of Drumlochy; two bronze swords were found near the Teuchat Knowe, west of Nether Aird, and urns were found at Meethillock, Gowanbrae, Blairgowrie. A Roman spear was found in the Moss of Cochrage, and another near the bed of the river. Coins of the Emperor Hadrian were found in a cairn near Greenbank, and also in a cairn near Dark Falls.

On an island in Stormont Loch (Loch Bog), there are traces of a building, to which, tradition states, the inhabitants of the surrounding district removed their effects for safety in times of dispeace—hence its name, Store Mount Loch.

There are also the "blairs"—Blairgowrie, Ardblair, Blairhill, Blairloch, Gormack (Gorblair); the "Buzzard Dykes" near Lornty Burn, and the "Cleaven Dykes" at Meikleour; the Roman camps at Meikleour and Delvine, and the Caledonian camp at Knockmahar; the "Bloody Inches" on the Tay, and the "Steed Stalls" at Gourdie —the tombs of the Roman cavalry; Craig Roman, a mile north-west of the town, where the Romans left off pursuing the Caledonian army.

In the moss of Cochrage the body of a Roman soldier, in full armour and in an upright position, was found, besides other Roman relics, human teeth and bones mixed with charcoal, doubtless the remains of Caledonians or Romans who were slain there.

From a mound near Greenbank, several years ago, a large quantity of human bones were found, together with several flint arrow heads and flint knives.

An old Roman pot was found about six feet below the surface in the peat moss at Blackloch, near Clunie. It is supposed to have been one of the camp pots of the Roman army, and is made of a compound metal something like our brass or bell-metal. It stands upon three feet, is about 17 inches high, 40 inches in circumference, and is capable of holding about six Scotch pints. It is in the possession of Mr James Isles, St Ninians, who has numerous antiques from this and other districts. Mr G. S. Duncan, Dunmore Villa, has also an interesting collection.

The Antiquarian Museum in Edinburgh contains many relics from this neighbourhood, including—"Flint Knife," $3\frac{1}{2}$ inches in length, presented 10th March, 1890; "Donation of a Medal of George Drummond of Blair, Lord Provost of Edinburgh, with bust," 8th May, 1882; "Old Brick from Clunie Castle," 14th April, 1884.

The proceedings of the Scottish Antiquarian Society, 13th May, 1878, page 624, vol. XII., contains the following :—

"Notice of a small urn of the so-called 'Incense Cup' type, found within a large urn at Blairgowrie in March last, and presented to the Museum by (the late) Rev. Wm. Fraser, M.A., minister of Blairgowrie.

"About a fortnight ago, that is, in the last week of March, there was found, on a detached field of my glebe in the Moor of Blairgowrie, and about a mile and a-half from the Parish Church, a circular goblet-shaped urn containing bones. It was about a foot in diameter and a foot deep. It lay on gravelly soil on a large stone, which seems to have been hollowed out, probably by the action of the water of the Ericht, which flows near by, and the bed of which contains many stones of similar size, on which the action of water is very marked. Over the urn (slanting) was a large flattish unhewn stone. The urn rested about two feet below the surface of the ground, and, unfortunately, it was much broken in being removed from its bed. The fragments have been almost all given away by the feuar in whose feu of the glebe it was found; but it has been my good fortune to secure for the Museum the small vessel which was found along with the larger urn.

"The interior of the large urn was black as if from the burning of some substance in it, or from the substance within it having, in long process of time, inparted some of its blackness to the urn. The small vessel is not darker on the inside than on the outside, although it bears on the inside at the bottom the prints of the thumb-nail of the person who made it."

A considerable number of stone weapons have been found in this neighbourhood.

About a hundred years ago a very ancient tumulus, locally known as "The Hirchen Hill," stood at the side of the Kirkwynd to the north of the Parish Manse. The outbuildings close to the roadway have been built near to what was originally its western base, and part of the site is now used as a bleaching green.

Tradition has it that the Earls of Gowrie held baronial courts there for administering justice to vassals and retainers, and a ridge less than half-a-mile west still bears the name of "Gallow (Gallows) Bank," where the unfortunate victims were strung. The ridge in its original state had a flat space on the top, which was surrounded with a rampart of earth, but the levelling and squaring of the fields have obliterated all traces of it.

There is a bell, preserved in the Mechanics' Institute, which is supposed to have belonged to a French man-of-war. It is about 12 inches high, 14 inches wide at the mouth, heavy, of good tone, and bears the inscription:— "Messire Georges Francois de Cheverne Vicomte de Mortain, 1724." A companion bell was in use many years ago at the Auction Mart when a sale was to begin, but it has unaccountably disappeared.

In the papers of the Monastery of St Marie, at Coupar Angus, dated 1st May, 1201, is an "Agreement between the Churches of Blair and Coupar." On the 1st June, 1235, Alexander II. granted at Traquair "lands in Meikle and Little Blair to the Abbey of Scone, excepting a small portion in the feu of Meikle Blair, which he gave to the monks of Cupar (Coupar) in exchange for the Common Muir of Blair, of which they had the use."

"Carta donationis regis Alexandri 2ndi monachis de Cupro de duabus carvatus (sic) terrae cum dimedio in feodo de Magna Blare in excambiun communis more de Blar quod visi fuerant, &c. Testibus:—Villielmo, Episcopo Glasquensi Cancellaris; Patricio, Comite de Dunbar; Waltero filio Alani Senescalli, Justiciario Scotiæ. Apud Tresquere, primo die Juini anno regni domini regis xxi. (1235)."

By a Charter granted at Forfar, William the Lion gave to the Abbey of St Marie, at Coupar Angus, the marsh of Blair:—"Carta regis Villielmi eisdem monachis facta de toto maresio meo in territorio de Blair, quod pertinebat ad dominium meum de Blar, die qua marescum illud iis dedi, et Comes Duncanus, et Hengo de Kaledone, et Rogerus de Mortuomari, et Mackbeth Judex de Goury, et Duncanus filius Douenaldi, et alii probi homines per preceptum meum eiis tradiderunt, &c. Testibus; Rogero, Episcopo St Andrex; Comite Dauide, fratre meo; Duncano Justiciario; Comite Gillebryd; Phillipe de Walloun, Camerario meo; Roberto de Quinci; Malcolmo filio Comitis Duncani; Villielmo de Cumyn; Johann Hasting, &c."

In 1309 King Robert I. confirmed a charter to the Abbey of Coupar, bestowing the lands of Muir of Blair upon it (at Dundee).

In the Chartulary of the Abbey of Scone is a letter, dated Clackmannan, 26th March, 1326, from King Robert

I. to the Sheriff of Perth, commanding him to take charge of the Loch of Blair in view of his arrival in the district. There are also other letters on like matters, dated Clunie, 4th August, and Alyth, 5th and 6th August of the same year. There is also a letter, dated February, 1356, referring to the dispute as to ownership of the church lands of Blair.

There is a Bull by Pope Gregory XI., of the year 1373, confirming church lands of Blair to Abbey of Scone, again confirmed in a Bull by Benedict XIII., dated 1390.

"At the fest of Whitsonday, the zere of God a thousand v. hundredth and viij. zeiris, the hale muir of Blair above the wood of Campy (Carsie) is set to Patrick Bell, in assedacioun for the term of v. zeris."

"Campy (Carsie) Blayr, Whitsonday, 1517, the quarter of the muir of Blare is set to David Pullar."

The family papers of Drummond Moray of Blair-Drummond contain a fac-simile copy of the "Bond of Maurent" (page 40) between Chalmers of Drumlochie and Drummond of Newton, dated 1558.

In the original Feu-charter, of date 7th September, 1568, the family of MacCombie are referred to. This charter was given at Abbotshall, and was witnessed, among others, by George Drummond of Blayr; the sasine was given by George Drummond of Blayr in presence of witnesses.

An "Instrument of Tollerance," in favour of John Makcomas, for pasturing on the lands of Torridone (Corrydon), bearing date 11th November, 1577, was witnessed by George Drummond of Blair, &c.; and an "Instrument of Renunciation," of date 9th August, 1583, for the same, was given at Finnegand, and witnessed by George Drummond of Blair.

In the Register House, Edinburgh, is preserved the original Charter, granted on 9th July, 1634, by King Charles I. to George Drummond of Blair, erecting Blairgowrie into a Burgh of Barony. It is a very interesting document, nearly ten feet long and ten inches wide, closely written throughout in Dog Latin character.

A map of the Mid Provinces of Scotland, published by Gordon of Straloch in 1654, and reprinted by Messrs Shearer of Stirling, 1894, is very interesting to antiquarians and others—with the original spelling, &c. There is no Blairgowrie shown—only Blairgowrie K. (meaning kirk). Several of the places marked are Newtoun, Gormack, Rowchaille, Kochredge, Ercochy, Pitcharmik, Stron Calie, Bamilie, Dryomie, Rattray K., Bandoch, Coupargrangl.

In the Acts of the Parliaments, 1701, there is a grant to James Ramsay of a yearly fair at the Newtoun of Blairgowrie, on the Tuesday preceding Michaelmas.

In the Court records of Perthshire is the decreet-arbitral, of date 21st January, 1777, as to the division of lands of Common Muir of Blair, by Sheriff-Substitute Swinton, between Thomas Graham of Newtoun and the Blair Feuars.

On the 5th December, 1809, Mr Allan Macpherson, Superior of the town, granted a Charter to put the police and government of the Burgh of Barony under proper regulations. Its principal provision was "the election of a Bailie and four Councillors, with Treasurer, Clerk, and other officers of Court, from among the burgesses of the town, with powers to manage the funds and common goods of the town and burgh; to suggest rules and statutes for the advantage of the burgh; orders and regulations for granting relief from the town's funds to burgesses or their families; to receive and admit all feuars, sub-feuars, long lessees, respectable householders, merchants, manufacturers, and tradesmen to be free burgesses upon payment of certain fees; . . . to erect a Town and Court House, and to erect a Market Cross, &c."

This Charter was further extended by another one, granted by Mr William Macpherson in 1829. A meeting of the burgesses, held 29th October, 1825, petitioned the Superior "to alter the mode of election as granted in 1809," which he accordingly did. "A new Bailie was to be elected every two years from among the four Councillors, one of whom was to retire and a new Councillor take his room," &c., all as set forth fully in said Charter.

This Charter was again extended by Mr Allan Macpherson, by a Charter dated October, 1873, at the request of the Bailie and Council, to enlarge and confirm their authority. It enacted that "the number of Councillors be increased to twelve; that a Senior and two Junior Bailies be elected from among the said Councillors; that one-third of the whole Council Board retire annually, but be eligible for re-election," &c.

In the family papers of Balthayock there are numerous charters bearing seals connected with the district:—

"S' Johannis de Drumunt, 1407. Seal of John Drummond. Couche—three bars wavy; crest on a helmet—an eagle's head and wings; supporters—two savages. This seal is very imperfect, which gives the shield the impression of being wavy, but there can be no doubt of the blazon.

"Lord Drummond of Cargill, bearing date, 1465. Eagle displayed, bearing on its breast a shield with four bars wavy. A label with three points—the inscription is imperfect.

"Seal of John Drummond, 'de Cargil.' Couche—three bars wavy; crest on a helmet—a goat's head, the background ornamented with foliage.

"S' Johannis Drummond 'de Cargil,' 1491."

"Seal, bearing date, 13th May, 1496, of William Chalmers of Drumlochie, appended to 'obligation by William Chaumer of Drumlochy to Thomas Blair of Balthyak'—three pheons." The seal, however, is very much damaged, and the inscription is illegible.

"Seal, bearing date, 1558, of William Chalmers of Drumlochie, appended to 'Bond of Manrent'—Chalmers of Drumlochy to Drummond of Newton—(Blair Drummond Charters). Per fess, in chief a demi-lion rampant; three pheons in base; at the top and sides of the shield, a scroll ornament. 'S' Vilelmi Chalmer.'"

"Seal (official) of Bishop Rattray of Dunkeld. An apostolic person seated with hands uplifted, on his left three crossed crosses, or crosses of Jerusalem, with the inscription —'Sigillium Thomæ Rattray Episcopi Brechinensis.'"

The following pedigree of the Drummonds of Blair appears in Fraser's "Drummond of Blair Drummond":—

I. SIR WALTER DRUMMOND, Lord of Stobhall and Cargill,

Who lived in the reigns of King James I. and King James II., and was killed by the latter. He succeeded 1428, died about 1445. Issue:—Sir Malcolm, Sir John, Walter.

II. WALTER DRUMMOND,

Who, in 1486, received from his grand-nephew John, first Lord Drummond, a Charter of the lands of Ledcrief, and was thereafter designed of Ledcrief. Living 1508. Issue:—John, James.

III. JOHN DRUMMOND, Second of Flaskhill and Ledcrief,

Who, with his brother James, was a bailie-depute to his uncle Sir Malcolm Drummond of Cargill, in 1447. Issue:—George.

IV. GEORGE DRUMMOND, Third of Flaskhill and Ledcrief.

He and his son William were killed by William Chalmer of Drumlochy and an armed party, near the Kirk of Blair, on Sunday, the 3rd June, 1554, as they were "playand at the rowbowlis in the hie marcate gait," near the said church. The marauders were afterwards compelled to make submission, and to give manrents, &c., to David, Lord Drummond. Issue :

V. GEORGE DRUMMOND of BLAIR, Fourth of Flaskhill and Ledcrief,

Sold Ledcrief and bought Newton of Blair in the Stormont (15—), from Patrick, Bishop of Moray and Commendator of Scone. He was a Sheriff-Depute of the County of Perth to John, Duke of Athole, in 1566, and a Curator to John, fifth Earl, in 1581. He died 4th January, 1594.

William Drummond slain with his father, 3rd June, 1554.

Janet Drummond married George Rattray of Craighall.

VI. GEORGE DRUMMOND, Second of Blair,

Who succeeded his father. He died 11th August, 1596. Issue :—4 sons, 4 daughters.

VII. JOHN DRUMMOND, Third of Blair,

Who succeeded. He married Agnes, daughter of Sir David Herring (Heron) of Lethnide and Glasclune. He died 2nd May, 1620.

George Drummond married Grizel, daughter of Daniel Cargill of Haltown (Hatton). Issue:—Daniel and Patrick.

VIII. George Drummond, Fourth of Blair.

He married, 17th August, 1633, Marjory, daughter of George Græme, Bishop of Orkney, Laird of Gorthy.

Jean Drummond married, about 1630, Henry Drummond, son of Andrew Drummond, minister of Panbride, fourth son of George Drummond, first laird of Blair.

IX. George Drummond, Fifth of Blair,

Born 29th November, 1638. He sold the lands of Blair 1682, and in 1684 purchased the lands of what was afterwards called the barony of Blair Drummond. He died 24th June, 1717.

The following is copy of "Precept by King James the Seventh to James, Earl of Perth. Chancellor, and the Lords of the Treasury in Scotland, to pay George Drummond of Blair the fifth part of the Royal duties uplifted by him on behalf of the King, and also the fifth part of all compositions," 10th November, 1687.

"James R.

"Right trusty," &c., "wee greet you well. Having by our Commission, dated the 16th day of April, 1686, granted power unto George Drummond of Blair to pursue for and uplift all wards and non-entries simple or taxt, with the reliefes thereof. which are fallen due to us or our dearest royall brother (of ever blessed memory) of all yeares and termes bygone since the first day of August, 1674, by the decease in that time of any of our vassals holding their lands off us or our dearest royall brother aforesaid, as Kings, Princes, or Stewards of Scotland, in simple or taxt ward, with the availles, marriages, simple or taxt, of all lands holden of us in simple or taxt ward, or few cum maritagiis, fallen due as aforesaid, and in time coming, during our royal pleasure; by which Commission wee did allow unto the said George Drummond a fifth part of what he should recover, and compt for by vertue thereof, for his paines in lifting the said casualities which fifth part wee did appoint to be allowed unto him in the first end thereof, together with his

necessary charges in recovering the same. And by our
new Commission to him, bearing date the 8th of this
instant, wee have not only ratified the former Commission, but also impowered him to receive the non-entries
of all lands holden of us in blench or few ferme, with
the non-entries of all annual rents fallen due to us since
the first day of August, 1674, and in time coming, during
our royall pleasure, which formerly he received as having
commission from our right trusty and right well beloved
cousin and councellor, James, Earl of Perth, our chancellor, to whom wee did assigne the same untill he shall
be paid of the summe of eight thousand pounds sterline,
granting hereby unto the said George Drummond the
same allowance for recovery thereof as is contained in the
first commission. And considering the good and faithful
service done to us by the said George Drummond in discovering and pursuing for the said casualities (whereof
formerly small benefite did arise to us) and which by
his industry is increased to more than wee could reasonably have expected, severalls, by his discovery and
dilligence, being obleidged to present gifts of the said
casualities, which otherwise would have lyen latent (as
they have been heretofore) to be componed by you, the
compositiones whereof he receives without any allowance
from the parties; wee, to take off all scruples that may
hereafter arise, as to our intention of allowing unto the
said George Drummond a fifth part of the said compositiones, have now thought fit to order and allow unto him
a just fifth part of the same, as well as of what shall
otherwise be received by him either from the vassals or
other intromitters with the said casualities.

"Requiring you in the accompts that are to be fitted
by the said George Drummond to allow unto him, in the
first end thereof, the fifth part of the said compositiones
received by him from time to time, as well as of what
otherwayes shall be received by him of the said casualities
together with his necessary charges aforesaid, the remainder being always allowed unto the said Earl of
Perth, our chancellor, until he shall be paid of the said
summe of eight thousand pounds sterline, free of all
expenses conforme to the gift thereof granted by us unto
him. For all which this shall be to you, and all others

respectively who may be therein any way concerned, a sufficient warrant. And so wee bid you heartily farewell.

"Given at our Court at Whitehall, the 10th day of November, 1687, and of our reigne the 3rd year. By his Majesties Command, "MELFORT."

The following is copy of "Precept by King James the Seventh to James, Earl of Perth, and the Lords of the Treasury in Scotland, for payment of an annual salary of £100 to . . . . and George Drummond of Blair, keepers of the Signet," 17th July, 1688.

"James R.—Right trusty," &c., "wee greet you well. Whereas a good while agoe wee have taken into our consideration the paines and charges that . . . . . . and George Drummond of Blair (keepers of our Signet there under our Secretaries of State) have been and still are at about their receiving the black box thrice every week, and as often sending the same; and wee being fully satisfied with their care and diligence in that matter, and being resolved to bestow a constant yearly allowance hereafter upon them for the same. It is now our will and pleasure, and wee doe hereby authorise and require you, out of the first and readiest of our rents, revenues, customes, and casualities whatsoever of that our ancient kingdome, to pay or cause to be paid yearly to the said . . . . . . and George Drummond the summe of one hundred pounds sterline money to be equally divided betwixt them, and to be paid at two termes every year, Whitsunday and Mertimes, by equal portions, whereof the first termes payment is to be at Mertimes next, ensuing the date of these presents, and so forth, to continue yearly and termely thereafter during our royall pleasure, which yearly allowance of one hundred pounds sterline wee doe hereby authorize and require you to adde to the list of fees formerly granted by us to our servants there, and to be constantly paid at the same times and in the same manners as our said servants are usually paid of the respective allowances granted by us as aforesaid unto them. And in regard it is long since wee were graciously pleased to settle the foresaid yearly allowance of £100 sterline upon the said . . . . . . and George Drummond. It is now our further will and pleasure, and wee doe also hereby authorize and require you presently to pay or cause to be paid unto them the summe of fifty pounds money foresaid, as an halfe year's allowance from us unto them preceding the terme of Whitsunday last past in this present year of God. For all which these presents (together with their respective receipts for what shall be paid unto them from time to time) shall be to you, and all others respectively, who may be therein any way concerned, particularly to the Lords Auditors of your accompts for allowing the same as sufficient warrant. And so wee bid you heartily farewell.

"Given at our Court at Whitehall, the 17th day of July, 1688, and of our reigne the 4th year. By his Majesties Command, "MELFORT."

The following are Notes from Rental Book of Coupar Abbey:—"Willelmum Blair de Bargillo" (a cadet of the house of Ardblair), was one of four bailies of the Monastery at Coupar.

Of the family of Chalmers, which lately owned the lands of Glenericht, the predecessors were husbandmen on the Abbey estate. To Thomas de Camera was let, about 1444, the town of Calady (Cally); he is, in 1463, described as Thomas Chamer. By the Abbot, in 1477, Robert Chawmyr obtained a life lease of the quarter of Murtoun, which was also to be enjoyed by his son William; and, on the 2nd October, 1510, John, "son of William Chawmer of Drumlochy," had a lease of the land of Mydilbait.

At Pentecost, 1457, Thomas Soutar obtained from the Abbey a lease of a portion of the lands of Murton in which he and his three sons were afterwards liferented.

"CALADY WITH TIEND SHEAVES.

"18. This town with tiend sheaves is let to Thomas de Camera."

"41. Is let to the same Thomas for 40 merks, six kids, his surety being Donald Robertson of Drwmy."

"FISHINGS OF DRWMY AND CALADY.

"42. Are let to the same Thomas for same period for yearly rent of fourscore salmon."

"CALADY AT PENTECOST (1464).

"110. A fourth part of Calady is let to Finlay Makeden, and a quarter to Donald Makeden, a fourth part to Nagel Makeden, an eighth part to John Rede, and another eighth part to Donald Randale, for five years, for usual payment of 10 merks and 10 kids, with usual service."

"CALLE.

"372. At Pentecost, 1488, a half of the town of Calle is let for five years to Henry Neylson for 8 merks yearly, with 3 dozen salmon, and 40s to the fabric of the monastery; and he shall keep the wood from all others as forester, under penalty."

"516. At Pentecost, 1508, Cally is let to the tenants dwelling therein, for five years."

"MWRTOUN.

"105, 119. At Pentecost, in 1457 and 1464, Mwrtoun is let to Thomas Page, Thomas Sowtar, and John Thomson for five years, for yearly payment of 10 merks, three dozen capons, and 12 hens, with carriage corresponding and usual service."

"262. Be it kend til al men be thir present letres ws Danid be the permissioun of God Abbot of the Abbey of Coupar, and our connont of that ilk . . . til haf grantyt, &c., the quartar of our landis of the Murtoun, with al pertynens, profitis, and eyementis, to Robert Chawmyr as he lachfally brukyt obefor for al the days of his lyfe; and to Wilzam his soun, eftyr his fadris disses, for al the days of his lyfe; tha payand tharof yerly to ws twa pundis xs of vsual mone at ij vsual termes of the zere, a bol of hors corn, &c. . . . In witness of the quhilkis to this present wryt we haf put our common sele at our forsad Abbay, the tend day of Septembre, the zere of our Lord, Jm iiije seuynti and seuyn."

BLAIR.

"549. At the fest of Witsonday, the zere of God a thousand v. hundreth and viij. zeris, the hale Blair aboue the wod of Campsy is set to Patrick Bell, in assedacioun for the terme of v. zeris, with the pastour of xxx. sowmys in the mour of Monkquhell, and he sal haf pastour to vj. ky and a hors in our forest of Campsy . . . and he sal superintend til our fischin of Campsy, and warne ws lawtefully quhen that he knawis any falt with the fissaris, with all odir dew seruice aucht and wont."

"574. Precept of sasine by William, Abbot of the Monastery of Cupar, addressed to Master Antonio Dwly . . . for infefting John Chawmer as heir to his father, William Chawmer of Drumlochy, in the Mydilbait and lands thereof, lying in the Sheriffdom of Perth, for payment of 20 shillings Scots in name of yearly rent of few ferme. (Dated 2nd October, 1510.)"

"Campy Blayre.

"648. Whitsunday, 1517, 'the quartar of the Blayre is set to Dauid Pullour.'"

"649. Whitsunday, 1513, 'the thyrd onder the wod and the quartar bown the wod of Campsy is set to John of Crago with the forstar land for . . . fif zeris . . . he payand thairfor xviij. bollis of meil and bere, ij. bollis of horse corn, xxij. cok and hen, and to hald wp the thyrd of the net of Campsy,'" &c.

"650. The quarter of Blare is set to Dauid Pullour."

Old Parish Tokens.

There are only four examples of the old Communion tokens now to be found, viz.:—those in use 1723-1768—Rev. James Lyon; 1769-1786—Rev. William Dow; 1787-1836—Rev. James Johnstone; and 1839-1852—Rev. A. O. Greig.

CHAPTER VI.

Ecclesiastical State—Parish Church and Ministers—Associate-Antiburgher Secession Church—Brown Street Chapel—St Mary's Church—First Free Church—Free South Church—St Catherine's Church—St Stephen's Church—Congregational Church—Extracts from Parochial Registers—Shearing on Sabbath—Selling Aile in Time of Sermon—Fasts Ordered—English Army in Scotland—Collection in Aid of Glasgow—No Session—Applicant for Schoolmastership—An Indigent Baronet—Act Anent Brydals—In the Jouggs—The Boatman of Blair—Administering the Lord's Supper—Irregularities—Sabbath Breach—Communion Cups—New Schoolhouse—Poor's Rates Established—Sunday Shooting Match for a Sow—Population—Schools and Schoolmasters—Parish School—James Street School—William Street School—New Public Schools—Episcopal School—Dames' Schools—Adventure Schools—St Stephen's R. C. School—Sextons of Parish of Blair.

Ecclesiastical State—Parish Church.

THE situation of the town determined that of the Parish Church, which is situated close to it, yet, in a parish of such extent as Blairgowrie, it follows that the church is inconveniently situated as regards some of the congregation, but as its site is nearly equi-distant from the northern or southern extremity of the parish, it is quite accessible to the majority of the inhabitants. The Parish Kirk was erected in 1824, the foundation-stone being laid by Mr William M'Pherson of Blairgowrie on the site of the old Church, which had become much too small for the accommodation of the rapidly-increasing population. It has within recent years been considerably improved by end porches, alteration of the seats, and general renovation. The church is calculated to hold about 800 people.

The parish manse was built 1771, but in 1838 the whole house and offices, with the exception of the wing containing the dining and drawing-rooms, were taken down, rebuilt, and several additional rooms added to the house.

The glebe, including 5 acres, which were given in lieu of a right of pasturage formerly enjoyed by the incumbent, extends to about $9\frac{1}{2}$ acres.

The stipend about the year 1840 was partly of money and partly "victual" in the following proportions:— Money stipend, £100 1s 7½d; meal, 71 bolls, 2 lippies, 2 pecks; barley, 62 bolls, 3 firlots, 1 lippy, and 3½ pecks, convertible into money at the highest fiars' prices of the year.

The Parish Kirk prior to the Reformation belonged to the Abbey of Scone.

The following are the ministers who have been placed there since the Reformation:—

16—. John Ross, A.M., graduated at the University of St Andrews in 1599; pres. to the Parsonage and Vicarage by James VI., 25th January, 1603. He went with a view to attend the Assembly at Aberdeen, 2nd July, 1603, but arrived three days after they had met, yet he approved of their proceedings; was summoned before the Privy Council, 3rd October, and confined to the Castle of Stirling; joined with 13 others in declining the authority of the Council, 24th October; was one of seven who were not again called, and liberated soon after. He continued 11th September, 1631.

16—. John Ramsay, A.M., was laureated at the University of St Andrews in 1634, admitted prior to, 19th April, 1649, and died in October, 1663, aged 49.

1664. Thomas Blaire, A.M., second son of James Blaire of Ardblair, took his degree at the University of St Andrews, 28th July, 1656, presented by Charles II., passed trials before the Presbytery, got a testimonial for ordination, 26th January, and was admitted 23rd March, 1664, and translated to Bendochy in 1668.

1688. Gilbert Blair, second son of John Blair of Balude, presented by James VII., 25th May, and admitted 12th August, deprived by the Privy Council, 10th October, 1689, for not reading the Proclamation of the Estates, not praying in terms thereof, nor observing the Fast. He still continued there, 17th April, 1701, and was alive 1731.

1702. William Stewart, A.M., studied at St Salvador's College, and had his degree from the University of St Andrews, 23rd July, 1697, licensed by the Presbytery of Perth, 21st November, 1700, called 5th August, 1701, and ordained, 3rd February, 1702, translated to Perth, 2nd charge, 9th April, 1721.

PARISH CHURCH AND MINISTERS.

1723. James Lyon, licensed by the Presbytery, 9th November, 1720, called 14th August, 1722, and ordained 4th September, 1723. He got a new church built in 1767, and died 22nd December, 1768, in the 46th year of his ministry.

1769. William Dow, A.M., obtained his degree at the University of St Andrews in 1755, called 5th January, and ordained, 20th April, 1769. Died on 13th May, 1786, in the 18th year of his ministry.

1787. James Johnstone, licensed by the Presbytery of Perth, 29th March, 1786, pres. by Thomas Graham of Balgowan, in October, 1786, and ordained, 26th April, 1787. He got a new church built in 1824. He wrote a Statistical Account of the Parish in 1796. A marble tablet to his memory is placed in the Parish Church. He died 12th October, 1836, aged 78, and 50th year of ministry.

1837. Robert Macdonald, licensed by the Presbytery of Perth, 8th June, 1836, pres. by Mrs Oliphant of Gask and Ardblair, in February, and ordained, 15th February, 1837. On joining in the Free Secession and signing the Deed of Demission, he was declared no longer a member of this Church, 19th June, 1843.

1843. Archibald Ochiltree Greig, from Brown Street Chapel, inducted 4th August, 1843, and died 1852.

1852. William Fraser, licensed by the Presbytery of Perth, educated at Paisley and University of Edinburgh, taking degree of M.A., 1845. Occupied chair of Moral Philosophy, 1845-46, at Aberdeen. Inducted 1852, and died 24th February, 1881.

1881. Robert Kemp, M.A., from Glasgow.

REV. WILLIAM FRASER.

Associate-Antiburgher Secession Church.

There are few records remaining regarding this church, except from the Statistical Account of 1796; it seemed to be a small body of 100 members.

It must, however, have flourished considerably during the early years of this century, from the fact that, about the year 1829, it was thought advisable to proceed with the erection of a new place of worship. In 1830 that stance of ground situated at corner of Brown Street and George Street was feued by John Brown, Writer, Edinburgh, to John Lawson and others as trustees of the Antiburgher congregation. A plain, substantial building of hewn stone was erected, with sitting accommodation for about 430 persons.

For a few years it continued to do well, but, owing to diminishing numbers, the body ultimately became extinct in October, 1837. Mr Smith, minister.

The church was therefore disposed of for £399 to the congregation of the Parish Church.

Brown Street Chapel.

In 1837 the Parish Church at Hill of Blair having been found to be too small for the accommodation of the parishoners, and the chapel of Antiburgher congregation being then for sale, subscriptions to the amount of over £400 were raised, and the chapel was purchased in November, 1837, for £399.

The titles were disponed and assigned by John Lawson and others, trustees of Antiburgher congregation, in favour of Sir James Ramsay of Bamff and others, as trustees of subscribers of new congregation, 14th March, 1838.

The chapel was first opened as a preaching station, in connection with Parish Church, in December, 1837, Mr Smith being asked to continue his services as minister, 3rd April, 1838, at an accepted salary of £20 to begin.

While the congregation of the Parish Church, at the Disruption, 1843, left the Establishment almost to a man —along with their minister, Robert Macdonald—the Brown Street congregation continued to adhere, and so prevented the entire disappearance of the Establishment.

Mr A. O. Greig being elected successor to Mr Macdonald of the Parish Church (deposed 1843), he and his hearers removed to the Parish Church, where he kept alive the almost extinguished sparks of Established fire in the parish.

In March, 1840, a request was made by the Sheriff-Substitute of Perthshire for the use of the chapel to hold Quarterly Small Debt Courts, but refused. It was, however, granted on 19th June, 1845.

In consequence of the Disruption, and the congregation removing to the Parish Church at the Hill, the chapel was for a number of years shut up. In course of time, however, it was reopened after thorough investigation, as a separate and distinct charge, the constitution being obtained from the General Assembly in May, 1870.

The records of the chapel from 1844 to 30th April, 1870, are awanting.

About the year 1882 the chapel was found to be rather small for the increasing congregation, and means were taken to have another church built and endowed. By the beneficence of friends of the church, &c., this object was ultimately attained. It was further found desirable that the parish of Blairgowrie should be subdivided into another distinct parish allocated to this Church.

This was also carried into effect by powers from the higher Church Courts, and on the 17th April, 1879, Brown Street Church gave place to the *quoad sacra* Parish and Church of St Mary.

St Mary's Church.

A splendid site for the new Church was obtained in Reform Street. Building operations were commenced early in 1884, and, towards the end of that year, the foundation-stone was laid with full Masonic honours by the Right Honourable the Earl of Breadalbane. The new church, of the early English style of architecture, is in the form of a cross, the head being towards the west. It is comfortably seated for about 800 persons. The windows in the alcove behind the minister's desk are filled in with beautiful figures symbolical of New Testament doctrine, executed in stained glass.

At the north-east angle is a massive tower, square, about 40 feet high, whence above this is an octagonal spire, executed in stone, about 50 feet high, small columns with pyramidal caps being at each square corner of the base. Altogether, both external and internal, it presents a fine appearance, and, besides being an ornament to, is one of the distinguishing landmarks of the town. In 1885, having no further use for their old chapel, the trustees, acting for the congregation, sold it, and it was converted by an enterprising tradesman into a dwelling-house and furniture saloon.

Mr Smith (of Antiburgher Secession Church), continued 3rd April, 1838; died July, 1839.

Mr Cowans (interim), 1839.

Archibald O. Greig, elected 23rd October, 1839, resigned 29th July, 1843, and appointed to Parish Church, August, 1843.

Alex. S. Willison, from Auchmithie, elected November, 1870, resigned September, 1876.

Robert D. Hutchison, from Glasgow, elected 23rd April, 1877, translated to Persie, June, 1878.

Robert Stewart, from Glasgow, elected 27th August, and inducted 29th October, 1878. First minister of new parish, *quoad sacra*.

First Free Church.

In 1843, during the struggle of the Church with the State for religious liberty, the Disruption took place, many hundred ministers leaving their manses and the Establishment, and many thousands of the people the Church of their forefathers. At this eventful time Robert Macdonald was minister of the parish, but he cast in his lot with the Free Church (so the new section was termed), as also did many of his congregation.

For some time they worshipped in a large tent, which was erected in the Glebe Park where the Public Schools are now situated. Early in June of 1843 the Church was commenced to be built, and it was opened for public worship in November of that year, although not quite in a finished state. It is a very plain structure, oblong on plan, with a square tower, and spire about 80 feet high, at the south end. Internally it is arranged similarly to all other old Disruption churches, the pulpit being to one side and the seats circling round with radiating passages. To the south of the church are the old Free Church Schools, now used as Sunday School, Prayer Hall, &c.

ST MARY'S PARISH CHURCH

The manse is a very large and commodious building, situated in Newton Terrace, behind the church, and commands an extensive view over the town and strath.

1843. Robert Macdonald, deposed from the Parish Church (which see), 19th June, 1843. Called after the Disruption by the Free Church Presbytery of Meigle, he was ordained minister of First Free Church, November, 1843. He was indefatigable in getting Schools erected in this community. He was admitted to the Free Church of North Leith, 12th March, 1857. Had D.D. from University of St Andrews, 12th February, 1870, retired 1886, and died 1893.

1858. John Baxter, M.A., licensed by the Established Church Presbytery of Meigle, 4th April, 1831, ordained to Persie Chapel, August, 1831, and translated to Hilltown Church, Dundee, 8th November, 1838. Cast in his lot with the Free Church, at the Disruption, 1843, followed by most of his congregation, to whom he ministered till 1858, when he accepted a call to the First Free Church, Blairgowrie, where he was inducted 1st September, 1858. He had the honour of D.D. from the University of St Andrews, 1881, and in 1887 was proposed for the Moderatorship of the Free General Assembly. He died in 1892, in his 84th year and the 61st of his ministry.

1894. William Muir, B.D., B.L., from Glasgow.

Free South Church.

The Free Church (South) is a chaste, although comparatively plain, Gothic structure, consisting of a principal nave about 85 feet in length by 44 in breadth, and from the floor to the ceiling about 50 feet. It has a tower at the left angle 16 feet square and 60 feet high, with clock gables on each square, and, rising 50 feet above all, is a tapering octagonal spire. The church as a whole, in its external aspect and its internal arrangements, is such as secures in a high degree the comfort of the congregation.

The church was opened, on 2nd December, 1858, by the Rev. Dr Guthrie, of Edinburgh.

1858. Robert Taylor, transferred to London (now Dr Robert Taylor, Regent's Square).

18—. Charles G. M'Crie, transferred to Ayr (now Dr C. G. M'Crie, Ayr).

1874. Malcolm White, M.A.

St Catherine's Episcopal Church.

According to the "Statistical Account" of 1796 there were 12 Episcopalians in the parish. There are, however, no further records until 1841, when a congregation in connection with the Scottish Episcopalian Church was formed. Its founder, James Marshall, chiefly at his own expense, erected St Catherine's Church, at the east end of George Street. It is a handsome Gothic edifice, built in the early English style, and was opened in 1842.

Being intended as a model of the style and form of ecclesiastical edifices previous to the Reformation, it consists of a nave and chancel, the latter containing a beautiful window of stained glass, ornamented with various devices relating to sacred subjects.

To the east end is a building once used as a school in connection with the church, latterly as a Drill Hall and Armoury of the Volunteers, and now as the rooms of the Photographic Association.

1841. John Marshall, from Forfar: published two discourses on "Christian Priesthood" at the particular request of Very Rev. Heneage Horsely, Dean of Brechin, Prebendary of St Asaph.

18—. J. Abbey, from Ireland. Got a chaplaincy abroad.

18—. John Burton, removed to Alyth and Meigle, and then appointed Provost of St Ninian's, Perth.

18—. Mr Minniken.

1869. Mr Richardson, from England, educated at Cumbrae College, translated to Rothesay and Bletchley.

1870. F. W. Davis, from Yorkshire.

St Stephen's Roman Catholic Church.

About 70 years ago the Roman Catholics in Blairgowrie numbered about a dozen. James M'Kay, then stationed at Perth, came once a month, and they met in the old Town Hall.

Mr M'Kay was the first priest known in Blairgowrie since the Reformation, and such was the prejudice against Papists in those days that he was mobbed on the streets.

About the year 1835, finding the numbers increasing, Mr M'Kay purchased the ground in Bank Street, where the church now stands. Two houses were built, and the upper flat of one was used as a church until the present church was built. Mr M'Kay officiated for a good few years, coming once a month from Perth and Murthly.

He was succeeded by John (now Dr) Carmont, who served the mission most successfully and efficiently for about 30 years. It was through his zeal and energy the new church and schools were built, and when he resigned his charge, in 1882, the congregation numbered over 600, the same as it is now.

Dr Carmont was succeeded by Thomas Crumley, who was afterwards translated to Doune and Dunblane. Mr Crumley had a very able assistant for two years—Michael M'Manus; but the congregation was too poor to keep two, and that arrangement was given up.

Services were given occasionally at Alyth, and at Woodhill, in Strathardle, in a private chapel, the property of Mr Charles Trotter.

The present incumbent is John Malcolm, a talented priest, who served a short time in Perth and Montrose. He studied first at Blair's College and finished at Douay, in France, being sent to Blairgowrie in 1889.

St Stephen's Church was built by Dr Carmont, and opened with great ceremony, in 1856, by Bishop Gillies, of Edinburgh, and Mr William Smith, afterwards Archbishop of Edinburgh, preached the opening sermon.

The interior of the church is Gothic, and consists of nave and two aisles; the High Altar is in the centre, and the Lady Altar in one of the aisles. In the other aisle a door leads into the vestry, and the choir is at the south end of the church.

Several years ago, at his death, Mr Charles Trotter of Woodhill bequeathed that magnificent estate of about 3000 acres, with mansion-house, policies, chapel, &c., to the Diocese of Dunkeld.

18—. James M'Kay came from Perth once a month and officiated till a resident priest was ordained.

1853. Dr John Carmont appointed resident clergyman. He built the Church of St Stephen's in 1856, and resigned about 1882.

1882. Thomas Crumley, translated in 1889 to Doune and Dunblane; was assisted for two years by Michael M'Manus

1889. John Malcolm, from Perth and Montrose, studied at Blair's College and finished at Douay, in France.

The Congregational Church.

About the commencement of this century many good men throughout Scotland were led to think that some special effort should be made to stimulate and advance vital godliness in the country. Among the others, a few in Blairgowrie banded themselves together for this purpose.

After various labours they formed themselves into a small Congregational Church, and at length called Mr Peter Grant, a student of Divinity in Edinburgh, to be their pastor. Mr Grant and his congregation speedily erected a chapel, which, though somewhat rustic, answered its purpose, and he laboured faithfully and zealously in the village and country round about.

1807. Peter Grant, from Edinburgh, died 1817.

1817. Mr Lyall, from Glasgow, resigned 18—.

1834. John Tait, studied at King's College, Aberdeen; ordained in December, 1834; translated to Newport-on-Tay, 1866; died 1896.

1867. Mr Dobson, resigned 1869.

1869. John Miller, from Inverurie, died 1878.

1878. E. M. Tennant, from Alexandria.

Extracts from Parochial Registers.

The earliest Parochial register now extant belonging to the parish commences in the year 1647, and continues on to August, 1658. There is no register from this date down to 1702, from which time to the present the books are complete and appear to have been very accurately kept.

The book or books in which the register betwixt 1658 and 1702 was kept have been lost. In the more ancient Session records there are several rather curious entries, illustrative of the strictness of discipline enforced in the Presbyterian Church, the internal discord and contentions which then distracted the kingdom, and the rude and ignorant condition of the population.

Shearing on Sabbath.

"15th Oct., 1648. The minister asking if there was any new scandal, the session declare that George Clyde, Andrew Keay, and Walter Butchart were shearing come the last Sabbath, and George Watson did thresh on the last Sabbath. The kirk officer ordained to summon them against ye next day."

"29th Oct., 1648. The above parties called, compearit, quho, after long denying, at last being convinced, confessed ye breach of ye Sabbath, as they alleged, after sunsetting. After ye minister had aggravated yair sinne by shewing yat ye whole Sabbath is religiouslie to be observit not only in ye kirke but in yair private families, the sessione ordain them to satisfie ye next Lord's day before ye pulpit in humbling themselves and acknowledging their breach of Sabbath before ye congregation."

Selling Aile in Time of Sermon.

"27th Nov., 1648. Sundrie people fined and ordained to satisfie before ye pulpit, and ye sessione, for ye suppressing of this sinne, upon the Lord's day, doe also hereby ordain that every tavern-keeper or seller of aile, who runs aile in tyme of sermon, or ye whole day, in ane excessive manner to any, sall pay hereafter as much as ye drinkers, toties quoties, it sall be found they are guilty therein."

"5th Aug., 1649. An ordinance of sessione was made that the elders should search the taverne houses during the afternoon service for contemners of the word."

"12th Aug., 1649. The elders being required to give account of yair diligence anent searching ye taverne houses for contemners of God's worship, reported that two of them had gone through the town and searched and had found sundrie in their awin houses, quho declared to them that they were presentlie going to ye church, before yair coming to them. The sessione, therefore, to this end that the wicked prevaricatione of these persons may be better detected, ordaine that hereafter they search not immediately at ye beginning of afternoon service, but betwixt ye closure of ye sermon and ye blessing, or betwixt ye last blessing and ye Psalm, that such persons as then sall be found may be clearly rendered inexcusable."

16th Jan., 1654. One George Ambrose having been called before ye sessione to answer a charge of being absent from church and "selling of aile" on the preceding Sabbath, appeared and gave the following curious account of the cause of his absence from church:—"The said George Ambrose denyed that he sold any aile that day in tyme of Divine service, and that the trow cause of his absence was that he had but ane playd betwixt him and his wife, and that she had the use thereof that day and was in church. Notwithstanding this naive excuse, however, the sessione reprove him of his sinne and ordaine him to keepe the kirke in tyme cummand under ye pain of censure."

The records also contain numerous entries of historical interest, such as intimations of fasts on account of national occurrences, &c., of which the following are a few of the most curious:—

Fasts Ordered.

"16th Dec., 1648. The Covenant and ane publick acknowledgment of the sinnes of the land were publickly read before the blessing, and a fast for this effect intimated to be keeped on Thursday first and the next Sabbath immediately following; and ye Covenant intimated to be renewed on ye said Lord's day according to ye ordinance of the Commission of ye General Assemblie."

"16th Aug., 1649. The same day there was intimat and read causes of a solemn fast appointed be ye General Assemblie to be kept throughout all the congregations of the kingdom upon the last Sabbath of thir instant."

The causes thereof were, inter alia, the following:—

"1. We are to mourne for the continuance and increase of sinne and profanity, especially of the abominable sinne of witchcraft, which abounds in ye land, as appears from ye frequent discoveries thairof in all corners and quarters of the countrie.

"2. We are to afflict our souls before ye Lord for the sad interruption of the Lord's work in England and Ireland, and for the sore oppressions of his people and such as ar steadfast in his cause in these kingdoms by a prevailing partie of sectaries in ye one and of malignants in the other.

"3. It is a matter of humiliatione to us that our king had not as yet granted the just and necessarie desires of this kirke and kingdom for serving of religioun, and that he hath made peace with Irish rebels who have shed so much blood of ye Lord's people and hath granted them the full liberty of Poperie," &c.

"14th Nov., 1649. Again another fast was intimated, one of the causes of which was stated to be 'ye pregnant scandall of witchcraft and charming within this part of the land.'"

"26th May, 1650. A solemn thanksgiving is intimated to be keepit upon the 2nd of June, the next Lord's day, for that wonderful victorie over James Grahame and his associates, in the north, of late."

ENGLISH ARMY IN SCOTLAND.

"28th July, 1650. Thar was read from ye pulpit a declaratione of the General Assemblie in answer to a declaratione of the army of England upon their march into Scotland, and intimatione of a fast given for the sinnes of ye land and for the great danger the cause and work of God are into by the invasione of sectaries."

COLLECTION IN AID OF GLASGOW.

"28th Oct., 1652. Intimation is given of a collection 'for the sadd condition of the towne of Glasgow, being half brunt.'"

NO SESSION.

"12th Dec., 1653. It is intimated that ther was 'na sessione, in respect the elders were withdrawin in attending some of Glencairn's soldiers who were ranging throw the paroch.'"

There are also several curious entries respecting parochial matters and discipline, and of a miscellaneous nature, a few of which are here noted:—

APPLICANT FOR SCHOOLMASTERSHIP.

24th Dec., 1648. A schoolmaster being required for the parish school, a person of the name of Fittie had presented himself to the sessione as a candidate for that office, and attended on them for several Sundays to obtain their decision on his application.

The following rather naive minute at last occurs under the above date, from which it may be inferred that the applicant had at length become rather importunate, and that the sessione stood somewhat in awe of the bold "troupier."

"Compear Mr Patrick Fittie desyring ane answer. The session (he being removed) declare yt he was presentlie a troupier before he presented himself, and yt he was cashiered as being upone ye unlawful engagement. The sessione resolve, calling him in again, to discharge him in a fair way, in respect ther was not a competent provision yet agreed on, and ordained to give him 'twenty-foure shillings Scots.'"

A Twenty-Fourth Appearance.

"12th Aug., 1649. Compeared James Ireland (adult) in ye public place of repentance (for the twenty-fourth time), and his minister aggravating his sinne and exhorting him to sorrow and grief of heart for the same, was continued to give further evidence of the truth of his repentance."

An Indigent Baronet.

"17th Feb., 1650. Given this day to Sir Robert Moubray, sometime laird of Barnbougal, now become througlr 'indigence' ane poor supplicant, twenty-foure shillings."

Act anent Brydals.

"24th Feb., 1650. The Presbytery Act anent brydals, ordaining thair suld not be above eight persons in ye side, that thair sauld be no debaucht pypars, nor fiddlers, nor promiscuous dancing, nor excessive drunkennesse, likewise intimate out of ye pulpit."

In the Jouggs.

"19th July, 1650. The minister inquiring if thir was anie new scandall, it was declared be some yat Andro Malchre had most dispytefullie and devilishlic railed against ye sessione, cursing minister and elders. The said Andro ordained to evidence his repentance in face of the congregation, but proving refractory and contumacious was put 'into the jouggs' till he agreed to obey the former ordinance."

The Boatman of Blair.

"11th Oct., 1713. Robert Bennet, boatman at Blair, received moneys from the collection bag for mending his boat, in regard he gets much trouble from the people of the paroch and others passing to the Church."

Administering the Lord's Supper.

"11th March, 1719. Session constituted according to appointment. And taking into consideration how to go about this work in administering the Sacrament of the Lord's Supper, and how to demean ymselves in this weighty affair, do hereby order yt up the Sabbath day that :—

"(1). Tho. Spankie and William Soutar take care of the elements and serve ym up to the table.

"(2). James Chalmers to take care of the Isle door.

"(3). Yt William Turnbull and Tho. Gilruth wait upon the High Church door.

"(4). Yt David Gellatly and Tho. Soutar attend the collection at the churchyard style.

"(5). Thom. Soutar is appointed to take care yt none come into the churchyard but at the ordinary entries.

"(6). Tho. Saunders and John Fferqusone are to wait upon the east door.

"(7). Pat. Mackie and James Reid to wait upon the collection at the tent, upon the Sabbath day, on the west side, and Andrew Chaplin on the east side.

"(8). Charles Robertsone to wait upon the collection att ye east end of the churchyard dyck.

"(9). James Skinner to take charge of the west door.

"(10). The collection is ordered to be gathered att the churchyard style and east of the churchyard, if sermon be in the church upon the rest of ye days, and if in the tent the elders are to take yr posts timeously.

"These to gather the collection on the Fast day are John Fferqusone, Tho. Saunders, Tho. Spankie, Wm. Turnbull.

"Upon Saturday—David Gellatly, Tho. Gilruth, Ja. Chalmers, Ja. Skinner.

"Upon Monday—Ja. Reid, Andrew Chaplin, Tho. Soutar, Pat. Mackie."

IRREGULARITIES.

"20th Dec., 1743. The session being informed that Isabel Cirkgill in Skermic had been guilty of some irregularities on the Lord's day, and, understanding that she was waiting on, desired their officer to call her, who, on being called, compeared and confessed herself guilty of some indecencies about one of her sheep that was worried on Sabbath morning, for which she was rebuked and exhorted to repentance and dismissed."

SABBATH BREACH.

"18th Nov., 1744. John Cochran, in ground of Gormak, compeared and confessed himself guilty of Sabbath breach by turning over peese which were rotting with the great rains they had got, whereupon the minister seriously exhorted him, rebuked, and dismissed, with certification.

"6th Oct., 1745. William Owlar and Margaret Lammer, in ground of Drumlochie, 'confessed themselves guilty of Sabbath breach by scolding and fighting with each other in the fields,' were 'sharply' and 'gravely' rebuked by the Moderator, and exhorted to repentance and better behaviour."

31st Aug., 1746. Reported that "on our late Fast Day before the Sacrament, Donald Scot, in Woodsyde, did, with his shearers, employ the whole day in cutting down his corn, which gave great offence to all around him."

14th Sept., 1746. Scot appeared, "confessed he had sinned and given offence, and resolves never to be guilty of any such practices for the future," was rebuked and dismissed.

COMMUNION CUPS.

16th Sept., 1771. Gift of two silver cups for the use of the Church at the Communion, with the following inscription on each :—"This cup was gifted to the Church of Blairgowrie by George Soutar, merchant in Blairgowrie, Sept. 6th, 1771."

NEW SCHOOLHOUSE.

11th Sept., 1772. The plan of new school and teacher's house was laid before the session, which the schoolmaster offered to build (except the plaster work) and finish for £45.

Poors' Rates Established.

1776. The heritors agreed that poors' rates be established, and that, after applying the interest of the poors' funds, the sum necessary should be levied, one half from the heritors and the other half from the tenants according to their circumstances. The levying of the tenants' portion was found extremely difficult and, in course of time, had to be abandoned.

Sabbath Shooting Match for a Sow.

24th Dec., 1780. Reported "James Duncan Mair, officer in Hill of Blairgowrie, proclaimed last Lord's Day, after the dismission of the congregation, that there was a sow to be shot for on same day of the week thereafter, and that James Rattray, at the Mills of Rattray, was the owner thereof, which thing the session considering as a breach of the Lord's Day, and that it gave general offence, they hereby appoint both persons to be summoned against next Lord's Day, that the matter be enquired into.

Next Lord's Day accordingly, both parties "compeared, confessed they had done wrong, were seriously exhorted, and promised not to be guilty of the said crime again," and were dismissed.

Population.

11th Aug., 1801. "On account of the great scarcity of provisions for the last two years, and its having been alleged by persons of high station that the proportion of land in the kingdom, under cultivation, was not able to support the increasing population *in communibus annis*, to ascertain this fact and for other important considerations, the Legislature passed an Act for taking an account of the population of the kingdom.

"An abstract of the population of the parish was given by me this day upon oath; a copy of which abstract is, by said Act, ordered to be kept by every schoolmaster and delivered to their successors in office, therefore I have stitched a copy of my abstract in this place that it may be preserved along with the book.

(Sgd.) "Peter Forbes, Session Clerk."

The abstract is endorsed by Thomas Whitson, Clerk of the Peace, and shows there were in the parish 396 houses, occupied by 447 families; and 28 unoccupied houses, only two of which were in the village; that the population of the parish consisted of 882 males;

1032 females—

Total, 1914

Of these, 322 were engaged chiefly in agriculture; 281 chiefly in trade, manufacture or handicraft; "all other persons," including all the women in the parish, numbering 1311.

Schools and Schoolmasters—The Parish School.

The earlier parish registers being lost, there are no authentic records about the school and its masters until the beginning of the 18th century. The schoolhouse for a long period of years was situated where the smithy in Upper Allan Street now stands, end to end with the teacher's house. In 1710 we have it recorded that the schoolhouse was repaired, and on 3rd July, 1714, there is a notice of "ane account ordered to be paid to David Reid of Blair, ten shillings, to subscribe a disposition of the school and schoolmrs house," which the session had bought from a Joseph Watsone for one hundred pounds Scots, out of the poor box. The schoolmaster had to undertake to keep the school and house in proper repair unless relieved by the session. In 1717 it was rethatched by order of kirk session, at a cost of nearly 20 pounds Scots, and again in October, 1721, it seems to have got a new roof, as the following account notes:—

To Thomas Saunders, Wright in Loch Blair, for the great and small timbers thereof,	04	00	00
To Alexr. Duncan there for putting on the thack,	01	04	00
To James Blair, Officer, for his carriages, the timber lying at Eastmiln, and his own pains about the same,	03	00	00
For two thwaws of thack,	01	04	00
To John Butter, in Bankhead, for four days work, meal, and wages,	01	12	00
To David Waker, in Blair, for two days work,	00	16	00
To the schoolmr for maintaining a boy for leading the earth, the old rotten timber,			
To Thomas Donaldsone, in Hill of Blair, for four days wages, meal, and drink, notwithstanding of his precorded engagement to assist at the work,	01	00	00
Summa.	11	16	00

(The error in the "Summa" is due to the Session Clerk.)

On the 11th September, 1772, a new school and schoolmaster's house was built, 32 feet long and 15 feet wide, within the walls, two stories high, the schoolmaster building the same, except the plaster work and lath, for forty-five pounds, getting the use of the materials from the old school and upholding the new buildings at his own expense during his incumbency.

On the 4th November, 1803, the schoolmaster's salary was fixed at 400 merks Scots, with £1 1s yearly for a garden, besides a small garden possessed by him, with schoolhouse and close belonging thereto.

The school continued to be held in Upper Allan Street until the year 1840, when the kirk session built and opened a new Parish School at top of John Street, which continued to be used as a parish school until it was closed in 1879, after the opening of the new schools. The Parish School was latterly sold to the congregation of St Stephen's Roman Catholic Church, who still conduct it as a school.

16——Thomas Blair, schoolmaster.

1st March, 1702—Mr Oliphant, schoolmaster.

24th March, 1706—John Anderson, schoolmaster.

25th September, 1709—Alexander Stoddart, schoolmaster, from Dumbarnie, removed to Dunkeld 19th September, 1714.

19th December, 1714—Patrick Rae, from Ely, removed to Edinburgh March, 1716.

11th March, 1716—William Gelloch, resigned 9th November, 1719.

22nd November, 1719—David Ogilvy, from Bendochy, dismissed 1742.

25th August, 1742—Alex. Badenach, from Kingoldrum, appointed minister of St Martins, 1750.

11th February, 1750 — David Kermock, resigned 1st December, 1752.

10th December, 1752—Andrew Haly, from Methven, resigned 17—.

4th December, 1760—William Dow, elected minister of the parish, 20th April, 1769.

21st June, 1769—Thomas MacGlashan, from Bendochy, resigned 17—.

9th July, 1798—Peter Forbes, from Murroes, resigned

16th November, 1804—Thomas Soutar appointed [went to College 1806], assisted by David Wilkie, Robert Johnston, A. Hislop, James Douglas.

1806—Interim teacher, Robert Robertson, student of Edinburgh University, started business as lawyer, appointed first Bank agent in the town, 17th August, 1832.

Parish School—John Street.

1841—Robert Johnston, deposed 1843 on joining the Free Church at the Disruption.

———A. Hislop.

———James Douglas, left to be a minister.

1846—Peter Sturrock, from Fife, continued till 1879, when Parish School closed, He retired with a yearly pension of £60, and died 1895.

James Street School—First Free. (First year at top of Jessie Street.)

1843—James Macdonald.

18——Mr Reid.

18——Mr Donald Sinclair.

1851—Mr John Inch, from west of Scotland, died 1867.

1867—Mr John Geddes (left to be a minister), a few months only.

1867—Mr John Malcolm, from Kilbirnie.

School closed in 1879; Mr Malcolm transferred to new schools as Headmaster, 1879.

William Street School—South Free.

Several gentlemen in Blairgowrie banded together and procured a teacher who taught for some time here, but, ultimately, during Rev. C. M'Crie's incumbency, it was opened in connection with the church.

1865—Mr Binnie; retired after 9 months; appointed Inspector of Schools.

August, 1866—John Barbour.

School closed in 1879; Mr Barbour transferred to new schools.

New Public School.

Some years after the introduction of School Boards for the management of school affairs and the superintendence of education, the schools originally in connection with the various churches—the Parish, First Free, and South Free—were shut up, and new School Buildings were erected, and opened on 19th August, 1879, at a cost of over £6000. Since that time considerable additions and improvements have been effected on the buildings, and they are now considered a well-equipped educational institution.

PUBLIC SCHOOL.

1879—John Malcolm, from James Street School.
1879—John Barbour, from William Street, School.
1884—John Malcolm, resigned.
1884—D. H. Lowson, M.A., removed to Perth, 1887.
1887—D. S. Calderwood, M.A.; appointed in 1896 Principal of Established Church Training College, Edinburgh.
W. Hamilton Bell, M.A., B.Sc., from Fort William, August, 1896.

EPISCOPAL SCHOOL.

Commenced by Mr Burton, followed by
Mr and Miss Lothan, from Northumberland.
Miss Thomson, from Edinburgh.
Miss Anderson, from Craighall.

DAMES' SCHOOLS.

1836—Miss Kennedy, Granada Cottage, Perth Street, now occupied by Mr E. Geddes, artist.

1838—Jeannie Mackie, Rorry Street.
18——Miss Murray, Meadow Bank Cottage, went to Australia and married there.
18——Miss Robertson, High Street.
18——Miss Amelia Brodie, above J. L. Ford's shop, High Street.
18——Miss Jeannie Brodie, in same place, and afterwards in James Street.
18——Misses Chalmers, at Erichtside, now the Station Hotel, removed to Greengait, Rattray.

Adventure Schools.

1833—James Macfarlane, school in Gas Brae, went to Canada 1835.
1838—Rev. Mr Buttar, school at Tannage.
1839—John Hunter, High Street. This building still remains, opposite 61 High Street, and till within a few years past the name Hunter was to be seen painted on the stone front.
1840—A. M'Donald, Gas Brae.
1842—James Johnstone was a grocer in shop in Allan Street (John Maclaren's property, now demolished); kept a school in Martin's Lane; delivered lectures on astronomy in old Parish School; for many years teacher of half-timers at the Haugh.
18—— Wyllie, in Jessie Street, built Wyllie's land, now Kinloch Place.
18—— Campbell, in Gas Brae, was previously rector of Grammar School, Dunkeld. He mysteriously disappeared.
1860—P. Grant, M.A., Brown Street.

St Stephen's R. C. School.

The schools beside the church, now used as a hall, were built by Dr Carmont in 1856. During Father Crumley's incumbency the congregation purchased from the School Board the Parish School at top of John Street, where education in all its branches is carried on under certificated teachers, the Government Inspector's report being always favourable.

SEXTONS OF PARISH OF BLAIR.

17——Walter Rodger.
28th June, 1713—James Blair, Murtown of Ardblair.
1714—James Blair.
17——John Blair, resigned 23rd November, 1774.
23rd November, 1774—William Curr, Muirton of Ardblair.
1780—James Duncan, Mair.
28th October, 1798—John MacLachlan.
1818—John MacLachlan (son of),
1849—John MacLachlan (son of).
1880—Robert Reid (in office at present date).

TOWN CRIERS—

28th October, 1798—John MacLachlan, died 1818.
1818—John MacLachlan (son of), died August, 1848.
August, 1848—Francis Law, died February, 1849.
January, 1849—Alex. Reid (Posty), for three weeks.
9th February, 1849—John MacLachlan (in office at present date.)

CHAPTER VII.

Statistical Account of Parish, 1796—Population and Statistical Table—Conditions and Professions—Births, &c.—Religious Persuasions—Stock, Rent, &c.—Population—Character—Origin—Extent, Surface, Situation, Soil, &c.—Cattle—Prices of Provisions and Labour—Bleachfield, Cloth, Stamp Office—Climates and Diseases—Rivers, Cascades, Fish, Birds, Scenery, &c.—Lakes, Islands, &c.—Minerals and Mineral Springs—Woods—Manufactures, Mills, &c.—Ecclesiastical State, Schools, &c.—Poor—Village and Markets—State of Property, Inclosures, &c.—Agriculture, Produce, &c.—Improvements, Farm Rents, &c.—Roads and Bridges—Gentlemen's Seats—Eminent Men—Antiquities—Disadvantages.

THIS chapter is devoted to the "Statistical Account of the Parish of Blairgowrie, by Rev. James Johnstone, 1796."

POPULATION AND STATISTICAL TABLE.

	FAMILIES		MALES	FEMALES	TOTAL
Resident in the country,	261	of	590	636	1226
Resident in the village,	133	,,	183	242	425
	394		773	878	1651

Majority of Females, 105
Population in 1755, = 1596
Increase, 55

CONDITIONS AND PROFESSIONS.

Proprietors,	...	22	Smiths,	...	...	7
Clergy,	...	1	Masons,	...	...	13
Shoemakers,	...	8	Carriers,	...	...	4
Weavers,	...	100	Bakers,	...	...	1
Tailors,	...	10	Cornmillers,	...	...	7
Joiners,	...	14	Shopkeepers,	...	...	18
Wheelwrights,		3	Flaxdressers,	...	...	8
Coopers,	...	1	Lintmillers,	...	...	7
Dyers,		1	Butchers,	...	...	8
Surgeons,	...	1	Ale and spirit sellers,			28

Births, &c.

Annual average of births for 7 years past, ... 36
Annual average of deaths for 7 years past, ... 27

Religious Persuasions.

Members of Established Church,	1507
Members of Presbytery of Relief,	30
Members of Antiburgher Seceders,	100
Members of Episcopalians,	12
Members of Roman Catholics,	2
	1651

Stock, Rent, &c.

Horses,	311	Sheep,	1220
Ploughs,	111	Pairs of cart wheels,	233

Black Cattle, 1269.
Valued rent in Scotch money, £5515 14s 0½d.

Population.

No dependence can be had on the parish registers for the number or proportion of births and burials. This may, in some measure, be accounted for from the large influx of emigrants from other parishes, especially from the Highlands, who settle here as servants, &c. By comparing the report made to Dr Webster, however, with the result of an accurate enumeration made in October, November, and December, 1793, we are enabled to state the exact increase, which is but small in proportion to the influx of strangers within these years.

Character.

The inhabitants of the parish are, in general, sober, industrious, attentive to their respective callings, and exemplarily regular in their attendance on divine ordinances. They are charitably disposed, and seem contented with their condition. They enjoy in a remarkable degree the benefits and comforts of society, and their houses, dress, and manners of living are considerably improved.

Origin.

The name of the parish of Blairgowrie, so called from the village near which the church stands; in old papers it is sometimes written Blair in Gowrie. Various etymologies and interpretations of it have been suggested. Like many other names in the parish, it is probably Gaelic. In that language "Blaar" is said to be descriptive of a place where muir and moss abound. Thus Ardblair is the "Height in the Muir or Moss." The Muir of Blair abounding with moss is in the near neighbourhood of the village. The Walton of Blair, the Lochend of Blair, Little Blair, and Ardblair are names of places on the borders of the muir.

Extent, Surface, Situation, Soil, &c.

The extent of it is considerable, being about 11 English miles long from S. to N., in some places not less than 8 (as may be seen from Mr Stobie's map of Perthshire). The figure is irregular, being frequently intersected by the parishes of Kinloch, Bendochy, and Rattray.

The connected part of it is only about 9 miles long and from 1 to 2 broad. The parish is divided into two districts by a branch of the Grampian Mountains which is the north boundary of this part of the beautiful valley of Strathmore.

The southern district, which lies in the strath, is about 4 miles long and 1 to 2 broad. In general it is flat. The northern district, which includes the detached ground, is high ground, very uneven in the surface. The arable land in it is, in general, sloping, and in many places very steep. The hills are mostly covered with heath. Some of them may be about 600 feet above sea level. The soil in both places as may be supposed is various. Alongside of the Isla it is a deep rich loam, free from stones. Immediately north of that is a stiff loam upon a till bottom, wet and spoutty. This last is a prevailing soil in the parish, and also a light dry earth full of stones on a gravel bottom; in many places there is a thin stratum of a light black earth, either upon gravel or cold till. There are considerable tracks of hill, muir, and moss, and more than 1000 acres are covered with wood. Not above a third part of the parish consists of arable land.

Cattle.

A good number of horses are reared in the parish.

They are of very different sizes and value. A considerable portion of them are very good draught horses, but a still greater proportion are small and ill kept. The former kind are worth from £15 to £25 each; the latter from £8 to £12.

Many black cattle are also reared in the parish. Those in the northern district are small, but they are considerably larger in the other. Great numbers are sold out of the parish when 3 or 4 years old, particularly the stots. The stock of sheep is much diminished. They are mostly of the white-faced kind, of a very small size, and are sold at from 6s to 9s each. Their wool sells about 14s per stone.

Prices of Provisions and Labour.

A boll of oatmeal, weighing 8 stones, sells on an average at from 14s 8d to 16s; a boll of wheat at 20s; a boll of barley at 15s; a boll of oats at 13s; a boll of peas at 13s 4d.

Beef, mutton, and pork are sold at from 3d to 4d a lb. Dutch weight. Little good veal is sold in the parish.

A hen sells at from 10d to 1s; a chicken at 4d; eggs, 3d a dozen; butter at 8d to 9d a lb.; cheese according to quality and age.

A day labourer receives, during 3 months of the year, 6d per day, and 8d during the other months, with his maintenance.

Masons and wrights, when they furnish their own provisions, receive 1s 8d.

A good ploughman receives £8 to £10; a maid-servant £3 with a crop of 2 lippies of lint seed sown in her master's ground or an equivalent for it if he be not a farmer.

Bleachfield, Cloth, Stamp Office.

There is a bleachfield in the parish of Rattray, about a mile from Blairgowrie. The cloth is whitened as it is sent from different quarters. About 50,000 may be the average number of yards annually wove in the parish; the cloth sells at about 8½d. Considerable quantities of household cloth and some Hessian stuffs are also wove in the district. There was formerly a stamp office in the village. This was discontinued for some years, but was again established in 1785. The following abstract was taken from the books containing the number of yards stamped for the last 8 years, and refers not only to the cloth wove in the parish of Blairgowrie, but also what comes from the neighbouring parishes, as well as what is whitened in the bleachfields:—

ANNO.	NUMBER OF YARDS.
1785,	17,197
1786,	50,380
1787,	128,559
1788,	130,602
1789,	165,364
1790,	190,682
1791,	220,371
1792,	252,485
Total,	1,155,640 yards

Or about 144,455 yearly.

CLIMATES AND DISEASES.

The climate varies in the different parts of the parish. It is often mild and temperate in the southern district, while it is sharp in the northern.

A remarkable difference is felt on leaving the former to go to the latter. In both, however, the air on the whole is very salubrious, and the inhabitants are not subject to any peculiar distempers. Formerly, indeed, the lower part of the parish was much distressed with the ague, but since some of the lakes have been drained that disease has totally disappeared. The rheumatism is the most common disorder, particularly among the poorer class of people when well advanced in life. Inoculation for the smallpox is now a good deal practised, and is almost always successful in preventing the fatal effects of that disease. There are no instances of extraordinary longevity in the parish at present, yet there are many persons living and vigorous who are above 70, and some above 80. There is only one person above 90.

It may be here mentioned that the lady of a considerable proprietor in the parish died not long ago, who saw, in her own house, 84 returns of Christmas. The mansion-house is close to several lakes.

The Isla, which washes the northern part of this parish, is the most considerable of our rivers. It has been frequently mentioned in former reports. As its banks are low in this parish, it often suddenly overflows them and occasions considerable loss and disappointment to husbandmen. This was remarkably the case in harvest, 1789.

The next in size is the Ericht, which, from its rapidity, has acquired the appellation of the "Ireful Ericht." It is formed by the junction of the Ardle and Blackwater. It runs along the east side of the parish for about 9 miles. Its channel in general is very rocky and uneven, and it often varies in its depth and breadth.

The banks in many places are so low that the river frequently overflows them and does considerable damage, especially in harvest. In other parts the banks rise to a great height, are very rugged, and often covered with wood. About 2 miles north of the village of Blairgowrie they rise at least 200 feet above the bed of the river, and on the west side are formed, for about 700 feet in length and 220 feet in height, of the perpendicular rock, as smooth as if formed by the tool of the workman.

The place where this phenomenon is to be seen is called Craighall, where the traveller may be furnished with one of the most romantic scenes in North Britain. Here hawks nestle, and their young ones have been frequently carried away by falconers from different parts of the kingdom. Here, also, the natural philosopher and botanist may find ample amusement.

Two miles further down this river is the Keith, a natural cascade, considerably improved by art. It is so constructed that the salmon, which repair there in great numbers, cannot get over it unless when the river is very much swelled. The manner of fishing here is probably peculiar to the place. The fishers during the day dig considerable quantities of clay and wheel it to the river immediately above the fall. About sunset the clay is turned into mortar and hurled into the water. The fishers then ply their nets at different stations below while the water continues muddy. This is repeated two or three times in the space of a few hours. It is a kind of pot net fastened to a long pole which is

The river is very narrow, confined by rocks composed of sand and small stones. The scenery, especially on the west side, is very romantic and beautiful. Many gentlemen from all quarters repair to this river for amusement.

From the Keith for about 2 miles down the river there is the best rod fishing to be found in Scotland, especially for salmon. The fishing continues from the beginning of April to the 26th of August. The fishing with the pot net is confined to a small part of the river near the Keith. When the water is very small, which is often the case in summer, the fish are caught in great numbers in the different pools with a common net. They are neither so large nor so rich as those of the Tay. The fishing on this side of the river was long let at 100 merks; it now gives £30 sterling. Plenty of trout are found in the river Ericht. The Ardle also washes this parish for a short way on the north. Sometimes salmon are caught in it, and it abounds with trout. Like the Ericht and the Isla, it frequently overflows its banks.

There are two burns or rivulets remarkable only for their excellent trout and for driving some corn and lint mills.

Lakes, Islands, &c.

The parish abounds with lakes of different sizes. Till lately there were more, but some have been drained and now supply the neighbourhood with peats and marl. In digging marl out of one of these the skeleton of a large animal was uncovered at least twelve feet below the surface. The horns resemble those of a deer, and are of a very large size.

In the lakes which still remain great quantities of perch and pike are caught, partly with the rod and partly with nets. They are much frequented by wildfowl of different kinds.

In the middle of one of them are the remains of an old building on a small island in it, in which tradition says treasures were concealed in perilous times. A district in this country is said to have acquired the appellation of Storemount from this circumstance. Curling is an exercise at which the inhabitants of this district excel.

Minerals and Mineral Springs.

There is no lime-stone in the parish, neither is it well supplied with freestone, though there are two quarries of this kind. Some whinstone quarries have been wrought, and muirstone is found in great plenty. There is one chalybeate spring in the Cloves of Mawes, which was formerly much resorted to by persons in the neighbourhood. It has been used, it is said, with success in scorbutic disorders. There are appearances of several more springs of the same kind in different parts of the parish.

Woods.

There are two oak woods in the parish, one along the western bank of the Ericht which is now cutting; this cutting sold at £320.' There is a smaller wood of the same kind on the property of Ardblair, and there are several birch woods in the head of the parish. There are only a few ash, elm, and plane trees. In 1774 the muir of Blair, then a common of 500 acres, was divided, and in 1775 most of it was planted with Scotch firs and the rest of it has been gradually planted since that time, partly with larch and partly with Scotch firs. There are at least 900 acres planted partly with larch and partly with firs. It is to be regretted that similar plantations have not been made on the moorish grounds in the northern districts.

There are vast tracts of muir which turn to little account in their present state. Shelter is much needed where they abound. The mosses, the greatest source of fuel, are nearly exhausted and every year become more difficult of access. Coal is at a considerable distance, and there is no water carriage.

Manufactures, Mills, &c.

The principal branches of manufacture carried on in the parish are spinning and weaving. The women spin it with their hands. Besides the flax raised in the parish, considerable quantities of foreign flax are spun, and the yarn is either wove in the parish or neighbourhood or sent to Dundee.

Considerable quantities of household cloth are wove here and about 50,000 yards of yard-wides, part of which is bleached in the neighbouring parish of Rattray, but a greater proportion is sold in the village of Blairgowrie and sent green to London. There are 7 meal mills, 2 lint mills, and 1 fulling mill in the parish. The rate of multure paid at the meal mills is, in general, about 1-12th part of what is ground.

Ecclesiastical State, Schools, &c.

The stipend, as fixed by a decreet of the Court of Tiends, in 1791, is five chalders of grain, two-thirds meal, and one-third bear, with £45 sterling, and £5 for communion elements.

The glebe contains $9\frac{1}{2}$ acres, of which $4\frac{1}{2}$ are good ground, the other five, lately obtained in place of grass ground, are of an inferior quality and a considerable distance from the manse.

The right of patronage is vested in Col. Allan Macpherson of Blairgowrie and Col. William Lindsay of Spynie in consequence of his marriage with one of the co-heiresses of Ardblair.

The church stands on high ground about 200 yards north from the village of Blairgowrie, having a deep glen planted with different kinds of trees immediately behind it. It was built in 1767, and is a plain substantial edifice, at present in good repair but cold in winter.

It would be much improved with being ceiled and having porches at the doors which are in the ends of it. The manse and a set of offices were built in 1771, but the offices were so ill executed that, after the present incumbent was settled, it was found more expedient to repair than rebuild the greater part of them, which was accordingly done.

Both manse and offices are now in good order, as also the school and schoolhouse.

There is one established school in the parish in which reading, writing, arithmetic, English, book-keeping, and some branches of mathematics are taught. From 30 to 50 pupils attend, according to the season of the year. The present teacher, who has long taught successfully, lately obtained a small augmentation of salary, but even with this addition it is only 200 merks.

The school fees are, per quarter, 1s for reading, English,

1s 6d for writing, arithmetic, and Latin. The whole emoluments exclusive of a free house do not exceed £22 a year, a reward by no means adequate to the abilities and application of so important an office.

There is one charity school occasionally taught in the head of the parish. In the winter season there are two or three private schools kept up by the tenants in remote corners from the parochial school.

Poor.

There are no begging poor belonging to the parish. For many years past the average number on the poor's roll has been 14. The heritors and Kirk Session meet twice a year to settle the roll; from 2s to 5s are given to each, monthly, according to their respective circumstances. They also receive occasional donations, especial in winter; occasional charities are likewise given to individuals and families not on the roll, which is attended with good effects and often prevents them coming on to it. The fund for the support of the poor arises from the interests of a small stock, from the collections at the church doors, from the dues of the mortcloth, and from the rents of the seats in the galleries of the church, amounting in all to about £35 sterling. The sum expended has not varied very much for these last 16 years, except in 1783 when it was much greater than in any other year of the period mentioned. The members of the Kirk Session are very careful in guarding, on the one hand, against imposition, and on the other that no necessitous person be neglected. In 1782 the harvest was late and the crop was much injured. In 1783 the meal was scarce and high priced. The Kirk Session employed the poor's stock in purchasing meal at a distance, which was sold at prime cost.

A small proportion of the barley meal voted by Parliament for the relief of the Highlands was sent to this parish. Many of the heritors provided good seed corn for their tenants where it was necessary. Though there are no begging poor belonging to the parish, yet the parishioners are much oppressed with beggars and vagrants from other districts, many of whom are very worthless.

Village and Markets.

The village of Blairgowrie is pleasantly situated on the north side of Strathmore, almost close upon the River Ericht. It was made a burgh of barony by a charter from Charles I. in 1634. The whole of it belongs, in property or superiority, to Col. A. Macpherson, who is proprietor of about ¼ of the parish.

The situation of the village is very healthy, and it is well supplied with water.

There are three fairs held in it annually and some attempts have been made to have a weekly market in it, but with little success.

The village is well supplied with butcher meat and other articles. As it is situated on a military road, any of the inhabitants may retail ale and spirits on payment of 1s annually.

There are no less than 19 dram shops in it, which must be attended with bad consequences to the morals of the people.

State of Property, Inclosures, &c.

There are 22 heritors and a great many feuars in the village of Blairgowrie; only one of the greater heritors resides in the parish. Many of them are possessed of considerable estates in other parishes. Most of the smaller proprietors reside upon and farm part of their own property.

The real rent cannot, therefore, be easily ascertained. Good ground in farms gives from 15s to 21s and some of it 30s per acre. The land around the village lets at from 30s to 43s. The number of acres in the parish is not known, as part of it has not been measured. Some progress has been made in enclosing within these six years, but still, at least, three-fourths of the parish lie open, and very few farms have been sub-divided.

The enclosures are either stone dykes or hedges with ditch; probably sufficient attention is not paid to this last kind of fence; the young thorns should be more cherished and better defended in order to secure good fences.

One property at the northern district is almost completely inclosed and sub-divided and lets, from year to year, considerably higher for pasture than it would do upon an ordinary lease for tillage. About four years ago above ¼th of the parish was sold at 36 years' purchase, and is likely to turn out a good bargain. The rent of land continues to rise in the parish.

Agriculture, Produce, &c.

The plows are of the Scotch make, considerably improved. Within these twelve years there has been a considerable alteration in the mode of plowing. In general the plow is now drawn by two horses and driven by the man who holds it. In breaking up old ley or in giving the first plowing to stiff land 3 horses are sometimes yoked, and in one or two corners the plough is driven by 4 horses yoked abreast and driven by a man who holds the horses by the halters and walks backwards. In general the farmers in the northern districts are very industrious, but they are only emerging out of the old method of culture. The distinction of outfield and infield takes place in some degree. Turnips and sown grass are only beginning to find their way into this district.

The want of inclosures and winter herding are great obstacles to their progress, particularly in those places where sheep are kept. The tenantry here labour under many disadvantages. Much of their time in summer is consumed in procuring fuel; they are far from manure, the ground lies open, is full of baulks and large stones, and in some places is very wet and spouty. This last circumstance, with the coldness of the climate, many plead as an apology for not having more of their farms in sour grass for summer feeding and hay. They allow that white clover and ryegrass succeed with them, but complain that the roots of the red clover are frequently thrown out in spring.

Inclosing, draining, and clearing of the ground of stones are much wanted in this district.

The crops raised in it are barley, oats, potatoes, a small proportion of pease, turnips, sown grass, and some flax. All the flax raised in the parish is spun in it and the rents of many of the smaller farms are mostly paid with the money got for the yarn spun in the winter months.

Improvements, Farm Rents, &c.

Greater progress in improvement has been made in the

southern district than in the other. Here the new method of husbandry is more generally practised, and excellent crops are raised of wheat, pease, barley, oats, potatoes, turnips, grass, and also some flax. But even here sufficient attention is not paid to a proper rotation of cropping. The following rotations are most universally observed. Where wheat is raised the rotation is thus:—After grass comes oats with grass seeds, then summer fallowing, then wheat, pease, barley. The dung is given to the wheat. In the division for pease, potatoes and turnips are raised along with the pease and get a little dung; sometimes the grass is kept two or three years, but more frequently only one year. On the farms where the wheat is not sown, the following rotation takes place:—After three crops of grass the ground is broken up for oats, of which one crop is taken. The oats are followed with turnips, potatoes, and pease in one division. Barley with grass seeds succeed the green crop; the dung is given to the green crop.

In the division for oats a proportion of flax is sown, and not infrequently a crop both of barley and oats is taken after the green crop, and the grass seeds in that case are sown with the oats.

The farms in both districts are of different sizes, from £10 to £130. Part of the parish is let in small possessions of a few acres to tradespeople, and this is one reason for the great number of ploughs and horses, as there are often a plough and 2 horses where the possession does not exceed 12 acres. Where the farmer does not carry on his work with the assistance of his children, it is generally done by servants who live in the family, except in harvest, for which additional assistance is secured some months before. Sometimes a house, kailyard, and an acre of land are given to tradespeople who pay their rent by assisting in harvest and at turnip-cleaning.

Oats are sown about the middle of March to the middle of April, then pease and lintseed, bear is sown in May, and turnips in June. The harvest generally begins in the end of August. It is somewhat later in the district to the north. The parish more than supplies itself with grain. Considerable quantities, particularly of barley, are sold out of it.

Roads and Bridges.

The great road from Coupar Angus to Fort George passes through this parish. It was made at the expense of Government, and is kept in good repair by the statute labour of the country, with the occasional assistance of military parties. It was regretted that a different direction was not given it after it reached Blairgowrie. Had it been made to cross the Ericht at Blairgowrie, run along the east side of that river, recross it near Craighall, and keep lower down in its course through Mause, the high ground over which it now passes would have been avoided, and the traveller would have been saved many a long and steep ascent. The great road from Dunkeld to Kirriemuir also passes through the parish, and cuts the military road at right angles. It is kept in tolerable repair; the cross roads are many. Till lately the statute labour was enacted in kind; it is now commuted at the rate of from 8s to 12s for every ploughgate, or 10s for every £100 Scotch of valued rent. There are no turnpikes. Besides many small arches over small streams there are four bridges, two on the military road, one over the Blackwater, and one over the Ericht. The last two were built by subscription.

Gentlemen's Seats.

Newton House, once the seat of the Proprietor of the Barony of Blairgowrie, and lately possessed by the present proprietor, is an old building something in the style of a castle.

It stands about the middle of the south slope of high ground which bounds Strathmore on the north, and has a most commanding view, not only of Strathmore, but also of parts of different counties. About half a mile further west lies the mansion of the old family of the Blairs of Ardblair. That family were long the proprietors of a most extensive property in the parish, and are still possessed of a fifth part of it. The mansion-house seems evidently to have been surrounded with water on three sides. The lake has been drained, and considerable treasures of moss and marl have been discovered.

The proprietor of Blairgowrie and Mause lately built a most substantial and commodious house, with offices, about

a fourth-of-a-mile south from the village
on a beautiful flat near the banks of the
the planting has got up it will be a
habitation.

EMINENT MEN.

George Drummond, Esq., who long distin
as a public-spirited magistrate in Edinb
five or six times elected Lord Provost of
and who had so active a hand in promot
of the Royal Infirmary, Royal Exchange,
in Newton House of this parish.

ANTIQUITIES.

There are the remains of several Druid
the parish. Immediately behind the mans
cular mound or mote hill, where it is sa
held his Regality Courts. It consists of s
and is surrounded on the top with a dy
materials. There are some large cairns.
there are many smaller tumuli running thi
in different directions from an encampmen
bouring parish of Kinloch.

DISADVANTAGES.

The time consumed in providing seed,
and in bringing coals from Perth and Du
bar to improvement. The distance from t
great disadvantage. This will in some mea
by the proposed bridge over the Isla n
with the Tay, and the road leading fron
Perth, which will shorten the distance f
to that town about four miles.

The tenants are beginning to bring lii
they will do it more easily when the ro
the bridge built.

Converting into money the services pe
tenants, enclosing and sub-dividing th
making plantations of larches and Sco
hilly and moorish grounds, would doubt
to the cultivation and improvement of th

CHAPTER VIII.

Castles and Mansions:—Ardblair—Clunie—Drumlochy—Glasclune—Gormack—Knock-ma-har—Kinclaven—Lady Lindsay's Castle—Tower of Lethendy—Loch Blair—Murthly—Newton—Castle of Rattray—Craighall—Parkhill—Blairgowrie House—Druidsmere—Meikleour—Delvine—Ballied—Logie—Falcon House—Altamont—Mount Ericht.—Legends, Ballads, &c. :—"Oh! wae's me, Cluny"—"Hey! an' How!"—Elegaic Poem on Bishop Rattray—The Green Ladye o' Newton—Ye Bailzies o' Blair—The Curlers' Dinner, 1745.

ARDBLAIR CASTLE,

AN old building, about a mile west from Blairgowrie. Up to 1895 (when structural alterations were made to modernise it) it still retained its courtyard form, with a good entrance gateway surmounted by a coat of arms, monogram, and date-panel marked 1668. In the monogram the letter " B " is distinctly visible, referring to the family of "Blair," who long were in possession.

The dwelling-house was on the right, with cellars and servants' accommodation on the left. The former was a simple oblong, with vaulted cellars on the ground floor, and a room on each of the upper floors. The staircase is contained in a wing, which juts out to the west as well as to the south, so as to command two sides of the main block with shot-holes. The old entrance door of the house is in the re-entering angle of the wing, and is of a very remarkable design: the ornament and sculptured band surrounding the recess for owner's crest, bearing a similarity to 17th century monuments.

The estate was in the possession of Thomas Blair, son of Blair of Balthayock, from the reign of David II., and was of great extent. The site of the Castle was then defended by a loch, long since diminished by drainage, so that it is now at some distance from the building. The Blairs of Ardblair were mixed up with all the local feuds, and had occasionally to pay the penalty. The entrance to the Castle is through a beautiful avenue of trees, at once the glory and pride of Ardblair, said to have been planted after the Battle of Culloden in token of the loyalty to Prince Charlie of the Oliphants of Gask, to whom the estate had passed, and to whose descendants it now belongs.

THE CASTLE OF CLUNIE

Is a simple and well-preserved structure, which stands on an island in the loch of Clunie, about 5 miles west of Blairgowrie. The locality was in early times dignified with the presence of a much more imposing castle, said to have been the summer palace or hunting-seat of Kenneth M'Alpin in the ninth century. As a stronghold of some note it was occupied in 1296 by Edward I.

CLUNIE LOCH AND CASTLE.

It stood on the "Castle Hill," a level platform on the west side of the loch. In 1377 John De Ross was appointed, by Robert II., keeper of the Castle of Clunie, and the lands afterwards passed into the possession of the See of Dunkeld.

The existing Castle on the island is stated to have been built by Bishop Brown (1485-1514) as a quiet retreat. The building has been restored and put in good order, probably about the end of last century. At the Reformation the Bishop was a Crichton, who disposed of the Castle to a relative of his own, Robert Crichton of Eliock, in Dumfriesshire. This gentleman took up residence in the Castle, and a son was born to him in 1660—James Crichton, afterwards known as the "Admirable Crichton." The estate eventually passed into the hands of the Earls of Airlie, and is now possessed by Mr Cox of Snaigow.

The Castle of Drumlochy

Stood opposite Glasclune on the east side of the ravine which separates the parishes of Blairgowrie and Kinloch. The Blairs of Glasclune and the Herons of Drumlochy were at constant feud, "which the proximity of their strongholds afforded them abundant opportunity of gratifying by a constant and harassing system of petty warfare, attended with considerable bloodshed on both sides, till at length the struggle was ended in the total discomfiture of the Laird of Drumlochy and the demolition of his fortress." A few fragments are all that remain.

The Castle of Glasclune

(The home of the Blairs of Glasclune), now in ruins, stands on the west side of the ravine formed by a tributary of the Lornty, about 2 miles N.W. of Blairgowrie.

The foundations of the main portions are visible, but the round tower at the north-east angle, with the north gable and the southern part of the block, are pretty well preserved.

The stonework of the central block was ruthlessly demolished in order to be used elsewhere on the estate. The remains are so imperfect that the internal arrangements cannot now be made out. The entrance doorway and staircase were in the round tower connected with the south wing, and the principal rooms were no doubt on the first floor.

Close by, in 1392, was fought the Battle of Glasclune, and from this Castle marched the murderers to the Drummond Massacre, 1554.

Herring (or Heron) is half suspected of the Drummond conspiracy, though not named. With the "Hays" of Gourdie also he had an unsettled quarrel, which, but for his pride, might have been settled by a matrimonial alliance with the young laird. Hay was in love with one of Heron's daughters, and on the occasion of paying her a nocturnal visit, was shot by her father, who, feeling his cup about full and vengeance everywhere in the rear, betook himself to the army in the "Mar" rebellion, which made his bitter cup to run over, as on the suppression of the rebellion, he dared to retreat to his private stronghold, when they ferreted him out. Finding the Castle surrounded, he jumped out at a window, escaped, and sailed for France, where in remorse and misery he lingered out a wretched existence.

The Castle of Gormack.

There are now no remains of the Castle of Gormack to be traced, but it is supposed to have stood near the site of the present farm-house of West Gormack.

It belonged to the family of Buttar, and was a place of considerable strength in 1550.

The Castle of Knock-ma-har

Has, like its neighbour of Gormack, entirely disappeared, and no trace can be got where it existed.

The Castle of Kinclaven

Is situated on the right bank of the Tay, about 5 miles south-west from Blairgowrie. It consists of a square enclosure measuring about 130 feet over the walls which are $7\frac{1}{2}$ feet in thickness, and in height vary from 15 to 25 feet. Circular towers were at each of the angles, entered from the courtyard by narrow doors. The principal entrance was near the south end of the west side, and is 9 feet 8 inches wide, and was provided with portcullis. There is a postern about 2 feet wide in the centre of the south front, defended by a square tower of which only part of one side now remains. The walls show neither shot nor loop holes—these probably being confined to the flanking towers of the interior buildings, not a vestige of which remains. The Castle was a royal residence in the time of Alexander III., and is mentioned in 1264, when payments are made for the carriage of wine to Kinclaven, and for the repairing of a boat. Early in

1207, Edward I., in his progress northwards, visited Kinclaven and stayed there one night; and, in the year 1299, Wallace with a handful of men attacked it and put the entire garrison to the sword. An iron plate fixed on the Castle walls commemorates this exploit—"Wallace took this fort in the year 1299. Placed A.D., 1869."

Although demolished by the Scots, the castle was evidently put in order again, and in 1335 was held by Edward III., then master of Scotland, but in the following year was recaptured by the Scots.

In its decay the spacious court has been turned into an orchard, and its walls give support to innumerable creepers, which give a touch of the picturesque to the extensive ruins.

Lady Lindsay's Castle

Stood on an impending ledge near Crag Liach—the Eagle's Crag—north-west from Craighall. The crag is a huge mass of conglomerate, a sheer grey precipice, and almost as smooth as though dressed by a mason's chisel. At the base is a cave which seems to have been cut out by the violent removal of some masses of rock. Viewed from the top of the crag, the spectator becomes impressed with awe; far below the ireful Ericht wheels round an abrupt angle and suddenly composes itself in a great pool, calm, deep, and black as night.

Near the brink of the ledge are some uncertain vestiges of what is said to have been a round tower, part of a castle in which a Lady Lindsay was immured, in her latter days, to expiate a heinous crime.

That lady was Janet Gordon, of the noble house of Huntly, and grand-daughter of James I., and whose first husband was Alexander, master of Crawford. He was an unprincipled desperado, renewed a family feud with the house of Glamis, took part against his father in his struggle for James III., and became the leader of a lawless band who ravaged the lands of friends and foes alike. In one of his forays he came in contact with his younger brother John, and, joining in single combat, the younger brother wounded the elder.

Alexander was removed to Inverqueich Castle (east from Alyth), where he is said to have died of his wounds. The popular belief, however, was that he was smothered in his bed, with the knowledge and connivance of his wife. The family records support this view, as an M.S., dated 1586, says—"He was smorit be his wife."

Tradition says that the murder of Lord Lindsay was not unavenged. Although Lady Lindsay had two other husbands, her spirit, when she died, haunted the hoary Castle of Inverqueich, where her nightly lamentations were heard for ages. The forms of herself and her husband were often seen on the narrow cliff between the Castle and the Isla, where, on bended knee and clad in snowy weeds, she craved the forgiveness of her husband.

Tired of her importunities at Inverqueich, he is said to have doomed her latterly to live out her penance to the end of time on Crag Liach, where the unfortunate lady was not allowed to remain idle. as her restless spirit had to abide in the eerie tower of her Castle until she should have spun an unbroken thread long enough to reach the heavens and form a ladder for her ascent to the realms of peace, to enjoy for ever the society of her injured lord.

The Tower of Lethendy.

The residence of Col. Gammell, is situated on the steep banks of a small stream, about 4 miles south-west from Blairgowrie. The original building is supposed to have been founded about 1570, by Sir David Herring (Heron) of the family of Herring of Drumlochy. The structure was three storeys in height, with walls of great thickness, and the lower and some of the upper apartments are vaulted in mason work.

The old entrance door was on one face of the block, with the staircase to both floors on the adjoining wing. In a panel above the door is a shield bearing the arms of the Herrings (Heron), the family to whom the fortress belonged, with the date 1678. Extensive additions were made to the old edifice in 1885, in the Scottish baronial style, and the old "tower" was converted into the kitchen and servants' apartments. The new additions were built with the warm-tinted old red sandstone from a quarry on the estate. There is a lofty tower, surmounted by a penthouse and corner corbelled turrets, forming a most picturesque feature in the landscape. The old tower seems to have been surrounded by a moat, and there is a stately hedge-row on the west side.

THE CASTLE OF LOCH BLAIR

Was built on a slightly rising eminence about a mile south of Blairgowrie; it is supposed to have been a small structure built in a rude, rough style, early in the fifteenth century. It belonged to a family named Coupar, the only one of whom we have record being Andrew, who was brutally murdered near Meigle in 1706. He is said to have been a stubborn, morose, young gentleman, caring little for anything save what he got in the "aile stoup" or the saddle.

There are no vestiges to be found of this castle, and it is supposed to have been demolished and swept away by the ruthless destructors of property during the rebellion of '45. The site of it is said to be near where Rosemount mansion is now built, a few magnificent fir trees marking the spot.

THE CASTLE OF MURTHLY

Is a fine old building, situated on the Tay, about $7\frac{1}{2}$ miles west from Blairgowrie. The original Castle seems to have been a small keep at the south-west corner of the courtyard, with an apartment on each floor about 14 feet square, and a staircase in a slightly projecting turret at the south-east corner. The structure has at different times been very largely added to, and extended into three sides of a courtyard. The greatest extensions were probably erected after the estate came into the possession of the Stewarts Barons of Grandtully, in 1615. The central portion of the building is evidently the latest addition, containing the entrance door, hall, &c. These are on the first floor, and the entrance door is at the top of a double flight of exterior stairs. The whole series of erections form a striking and picturesque pile. In the beginning of this century the sixth baronet commenced a new mansion in the Elizabethan style, which still stands unfinished, not far from the old castle. In 1891, on the death of the last of the Stewarts, the estates passed into the possession of Mr Stewart Fothringham of Fothringham, Forfarshire.

The Old Castle of Newton

Is situated immediately to the north-west of the town, and is supposed to have been built in the early part of the 14th century.

To the south-east is an angle tower, square in form, which contains the staircase; the north-west tower is circular below, and brought out to the square form on the top storey with corbelling. It was sacked by the Marquis of Montrose in 1645, and again in 1650 by Cromwell. Several additions have been made to the structure at various times, 1735, 1839, and 1885, and it is now in good repair, quite modernised but retains many of its old features. Like many other old buildings it is said to be possessed of a ghost in the form of a lady dressed in green, "the green lady," who still haunts some apartments.

The Castle of Rattray,

All traces of which have now been lost, originally stood on the "Castle Hill," a large mound south-east of Rattray, and was built by Alanus de Rattray, a favourite of William the Lion, about 1170. An old MS. says "The Castle of Rattray hath a pleasant situation upon a little green mound about a quarter of a mile in length; the castell stood upon the east end thereof, with a chapel lower down. The arms of that family are—Shield—azure, three crosses of Jerusalem; supporters, two serpents, crest, above a mullet or heart proper. Motto—'Super siderae votum'—('My desires are above the stars.')"

There is traditionary evidence that the Rattrays took part in the Crusades, which would account for the crosses, the special symbol of the Crusaders.

About the time of the Reformation the family seem to have vacated the Castle of Rattray and erected a new fortress at Craighall, as in all records after 1650 the family are designated as of Craighall. The estates have, however, been in possession of the Rattray family and their descendants for about 800 years.

Craighall.

The present house of Craighall is generally supposed to have been built about 1650, as in all family records after that time the Rattrays are designated "of Craig-

CRAIGHALL

hall." The house is about three miles from Blairgowrie, and the scenery is of the most picturesque description. Pennant, the traveller, describes its position—"The situation of it is romantic beyond description; it is placed in the midst of a deep glen, surrounded on all sides with wide extended dreary heaths, where are still to be seen the rude monuments of thousands of our ancestors who fought and fell;" while Sir W. Hooker describes the mansion of Craighall as "clinging like a swallow's nest to the craggiest summit of the eastern bank, and harmonising perfectly with the adjoining rocks."

> "We stand upon the dizzy height
> And feel a thrill of strange delight;
> Far down below dark Ericht glides,
> The tall pines towering o'er its sides,
> On bank and brae wave birken bowers,
> And spreading beech guard mountain flowers.
>
> "Uprising from its rocky bed
> Thy noble mansion rears its head;
> For ages it hath firmly stood
> Unscathed by storm or angry flood,
> And long may Heaven protect and spare
> Craighall so wild and yet so fair!"

The view from the balcony overlooking the river is very striking. The restless and turbulent stream—"the ireful Ericht"—dashes through the deep ravine with resistless force, and its impetuous course can be traced from this point for a considerable distance. The foliage which clothes the naked rocks with verdure is abundant, but despite its appearance the spectator, placed on this giddy height, can never forget that he is standing on the verge of a dangerous precipice, whilst he sees the river boiling in fury far below him. From other parts of the mansion wide stretches of sylvan scenery are visible, though an irresistible fascination carries him always back to this balcony as the most wildly romantic standpoint of all.

Near Craighall the road is lined with venerable beeches, and their bright green foliage is a welcome shade in summer from the scorching heat of the sun. The house itself bursts quite unexpectedly upon the visitor, affording a most agreeable surprise. There are numerous walks among the policies around, those having the best views being up the ravine. A short way up the higher walk is placed a rustic seat, from which a most effective view is obtained, and no one has an idea of the extent of Craighall House, or the romantic beauty with which it blends itself, until he has seen it from this point. Almost opposite is Crag Liach, a rock rising from the river's side to the perpendicular height of over 200 feet, and so smooth that it looks as if Nature had used a plumb in its construction. A little further up and upon the verge of a precipice is the remains of a tower—Lady Lindsay's Castle. About a mile from the entrance is a foghouse, from which a fine view is seen down the ravine. Further up, at Land's End, where the walk ends, there is a beautiful cascade, formed by the waters of a burn falling from a height of 20 feet into a natural basin, which again discharges its waters over the rock into the Ericht.

The ravine, the bottom of which is reached by numerous zig-zag walks, along the face of, and far up the sides of the rocks, is lined with hazel and alder, so dense that the river in some places in scarcely discernible; nearer the top the birch and the rowan trees bloom in beauty, while in summer the air is redolent with incense—the breath of many noble specimens of pinnaceæ which adorn the grounds.

Craighall and neighbourhood have been invested with a new and powerful interest since the publication of the Life of Scott by his son-in-law, Mr J. Gibson Lockhart. During the greater part of the summer of 1793, Sir Walter Scott enjoyed an excursion which much extended his knowledge of Highland scenery and character, and, in particular, furnished him with the richest stores, which he afterwards turned to account in many of his poems and romances. After mentioning several of the places he visited, the narrative proceeds:—"Another resting-place was Craighall, in Perthshire, the seat of the Rattrays, a family relative to Mr Clerk who accompanied him. From the position of this striking place, as Mr Clerk at once perceived and as the author at once confessed to him, that of the Tullyveolan of Waverley was very faithfully copied."

The kindness of the Craighall family, in affording the

public free access to the grounds, is worthy of the highest commendation, and ought to inspire with gratitude all who have the privilege of visiting them. The boon, however, like too many other public privileges, has not been appreciated as it ought to have been—indeed, it has been frequently abused, and may lead to the grounds being made exclusively private. Tuesdays and Fridays are free days; on other days a small charge is made on visitors, the proceeds of which go to the Perth Infirmary.

Parkhill,

Occupying one of the best sites in Perthshire, and commanding a most extensive view of the Howe of Strathmore, was built in 1887 by Capt. Charles Hill-Whitson, whose ancestors first came to Parkhill about the year 1600.

This is the fourth mansion which succeeding lairds have built, but this present one exceeds former buildings in extent, choice of sight, substantiality, furnishing, and finishing.

Blairgowrie House,

The residence of the Superior of the Burgh, was built in 1792 by Col. Allan Macpherson. It is a plain building outwardly, but the internal arrangements are on a magnificent scale of elegance combined with comfort. Extensive additions were made in 1890. The house is beautifully situated within well laid-out policies.

Druidsmere,

The residence of Mr I. Henry-Anderson, S.S.C., and situated a mile south of Blairgowrie, forms a very dominant feature, reminding one of the old French chateaux, so frequently met with in the south of France, with their lofty corner turrets and high-pitched roofs.

Meikleour,

The property of the Marquis of Lansdowne, is an extensive pile, beautifully situated on the banks of the Tay, near its junction with the Isla. The house consists of a centre of three storeys, with parallel wings of two storeys, and a range in right angle behind the south wing.

Before the house, and bounded on the south by the

Tay, is a beautiful lawn, on which there are some noble specimens of the elm, beech, larch, plane, and oak. A little to the north-east of the house, on the margin of the lawn, is a bronze dial, on which is engraved the Meikleour Arms. About a fourth-of-a-mile east is the great Beech Hedge, recognised to be one of the arboreal wonders of the world.

Delvine House

Is situated on a square of 160 acres, steep on all sides, and elevated 60 feet above the surrounding plain.

There are traces of a Roman station about 500 yards square—part of a redoubt near the eastern point of the area on the top of the bank—a long line from east to west—and on the western part of the hill a strong semi-circular fort fenced on the east side by five ramparts of earth and as many ditches. This is recognised as one of the stations which Agricola established before his engagement with Galgacus, A.D. 84. Delvine is the residence of Sir Alexander Muir Mackenzie.

Ballied House,

The residence of Major Campbell of Achalader, on a commanding site, beautifully embosomed among the trees, is about 3 miles west from Blairgowrie.

Logie House,

3 miles west, is the residence of Mr David M'Ritchie, F.S.A., Scot.

Falcon House,

At the west end of the town, is the residence of Lieut.-Col. Surgeon G. G. MacLaren.

Altamont House

Is finely situated on the rising ground to the west of Blairgowrie House, and belongs to Dr George Ballingall.

Mount Ericht,

The property of Mr James Ogilvy, is a substantial residence on the rising ground up from the Bridge of Blairgowrie.

LEGENDS, BALLADS, &c.

"Oh, wae's me, Cluny!"

There is a legend connected with the district that the laird of Clunie shot the laird of Lochblair dead, in the Churchyard of Caputh, in consequence of the former marrying the sweetheart of the latter. A ballad, of which the following are a few lines, says:—

> Oh, wae's me, Cluny!
>   Wi' your ha's an' your towers,
> You've wedded my Jeanie
>   Wi' your orchards and flowers.
>
> . . . . .
>
> There's gold in my coffers
> But there's nane in Lochblair.
>
> . . . . .
>
> Bonnie Andro Coupar,
> His sword out he drew,
> And he swore that thro' Cluny
> He wad mak' it gae thro'.

"Hey! an' How!"

Part of a refrain of another and older ballad relates also to the neighbourhood, and to two rival families:—

> Hey! the Birds o' Benothy! and
> How! the Bissats o' Ferold!

Tradition says that a beautiful daughter of the former was sent daily by her parents to the kirkyard of Bendochy to walk there, to keep her in mind of her mortal change.

Elegaic Poem on Bishop Rattray.

There is preserved a Latin elegaic poem on Bishop Rattray's death in Hexameter and Pentameter verse, by the Rev. Mr Skinner, author of "Tullochgorum,":—

> "Dum numerat doctum renitens ecclesia prolem
> Totque videt sanctos undique læta patres.
> Dum depressa jacet, nec concutit hæresis arma,
> Opprimet, heu! subitus gaudia tanta dolor!
> Cessit Rattraius fato, Rattraius et ille,
> Quem timuere hostes, quem coluere boni." .

Which may be translated in the same measure:—

Now that our church again shining beholds a numerous offspring,
Now that, all around, fathers so holy abound,
Now that heresy vanquish'd lies, nor raises a weapon,
On a sudden, lo! joys are extinguished in woe.
By the Divine decree Rattray has gone, even he whom
Enemies all did fear, good men all did revere.

THE GREEN LADYE O' NEWTON.

The ladye Jean sits in her bower,
  Her cheeks are like the snaw;
She winna work, she canna play,
  Sin' Ronald's gaed awa'.

" Gae bring tae me the crimson silk,
  Gae bring tae me the blue;
Gae bring my siller-buckled shoon,
  My satyne boddice new.

" An' busk me in my cramasie,
  But an' the velvet black,
My perlin's fine, an' gowden kame,
  To wile my fause love back."

Up an' spak a grey auld wife,
  Was fourscore years an' mae:—
" Licht, licht's the luve that can be coft
  Wi' gowd an' buskins gay.

" But an' ye be young Ronald's bryde,
  A sair darg ye maun dree;
For the witchin' claith ye canna buy
  Wi' the red an' white monie.

" Gae cut a bout o' the kirkyard grass,
  An' a branch frae the rowan tree
That stands by itsel' on the Gallows Knowe,
  Whar they hanged the murderers three.

" Gae twist an ell-lang rashy wyth,
  An' tak' them doon alane
Tae the Coble Pule, 'tween the licht an' the dark,
  An' sit on the Corbie Stane."

She has ta'en her a bout o' the kirkyard grass,
  An' a branch frae the rowan tree,
That stands by itsel' on the Gallows Knowe,
  Whar they hang'd the murderers three.

She has twisted an ell-lang rashy wyth,
  An' sits in her bower alane,
Wi' her heart in a lowe, at the thocht o' her luve,
  An' she waits till the day is gane.

THE GREEN LADYE O' NEWTON.

An' at nicht she gaed tae the Coble Pule,
   The licht an' the dark atween,
An' a' that nicht, frae dark tae licht,
   She sat wi' steekit een.

She hadna sat an oor ava,
   Never an oor but ane,
Whan she heard the win' sough thro' the trees
   Wi' an eerie, eerie grane.

An' next she heard the howlets' cry
   Within the saughen wud,
An' next the water kelpies' rout
   Aboon the Ericht's flood.

An' then she heard, jist at her lug,
   A gruesome, eldritch lauch;
An' then a voice cam' up the stream
   Frae oot the Mill o' Haugh:—

"Warlock wabsters, ane an' a',
   Weave the witchin' claith;
Warp o' grass an' weft o' rash—
   Weave the web o' death."

But aye she sat, an' aye she sat,
   Nor spak' the lang nicht thro',
She was deadly cauld, an' her heart was glad
   Whan the early gor-cock crew.

An' at the dawin' o' the day,
   Whan she oped her steekit een,
She wis dinket out frae head tae heel
   In the witchin' claith o' green.

     . . . . . .

There's mirth an' daffin' in Newton Ha'—
   The lady Jean's a bryde;
She's cled in a gown o' the witchin' claith,
   An' she stands at Ronald's side.

"Wae's me for you, my ain true love,
   That ever this should be;
But a mortal cauld is at my heart,
   I fear that I maun dee.

"An' I hear a soon' that I heard afore,
   Whan a' my leafu' lane,
Thro' the mirk midnicht tae the mornin' licht
   I sat on the Corbie Stane."

They hae ta'en her up tae a chamber hie,
   An' sune she steekit her een;
They hae streekit her corpse on the brydal bed,
   In her brydal bed o' green.

YE BAILZIES O' BLAIR.

They hae streekit her oot i' the cauld munelicht,
   An' tae Knockie Hill they hae gane,
They hae howkit her grave, an' happit her doon,
   An' set at her head a stane.

An' every year at Hallowe'en,
   That stane, whan it hears the soon'
O' the midnicht bell frae the Paroch Kirk,
   Turns three times roun' an' roun'.

An' the ladye Jean comes oot frae the mools,
   An' doon tae the Newton Ha'.

. . . . .

Frae sic a sicht, on that ghaistly nicht,
   The gude Lord keep us a'.

YE BAILZIES O' BLAIR.

(By John Bridie, Bailie in 1871.)

Oh, mony a sang has been made aboot men
That never existed, or fowk dinna ken;
But for my sang an' subjec' ye're a' boun' tae care;
An' why should ye no? it's ye Bailzie o' Blair.

Some names dinna fully express what they mean,
An' your technical phrases are hard to be seen;
But this simple teetle should plainly declare
It's inherent importance—ye Bailzie o' Blair!

Does ony ane question the greatness an' worth
O' this awful official that reigns i' the north?
Jist let him get fou' an' disorderly there,
An' he'll sune ken what's meant by ye Bailzie o' Blair.

The frolicsome fellows that caper an' spree,
Excursionists starring frae Perth an' Dundee,
An' tinklers an' poachers ken hoo tae beware
O' the dread definition o' ye Bailzie o' Blair.

The laddies that pilfer the gardens o' fruit,
The carter or cadger that trachles his brute,
The bullies that fecht, an' the brawlers that swear,
A' try tae keep clear o' ye Bailzie o' Blair!

But, while evil-doers their terrors may tell,
There is praise an' protection for them that do well;
Though he punishes roguery, a' that is fair
Has aye the support o' ye Bailzie o' Blair.

I sing nae o' ane o' the lot, but them a'—
Some—peace to their memory—dead an' awa';
For through saxty simmers twa dizzen or mair
Hae rejoiced i' the name o' ye Bailzie o' Blair.

YE BAILZIES O' BLAIR.

Even far i' the past, whan the office was new,
Whan the toon was but sma', an' the fowk wir but few,
Great honour was shown tae the poo'ers that were,
An' a special respec' to ye Bailzie o' Blair.

The urchins wad look wi' the tail o' their e'e,
An' wonder a real live Justice tae see;
Oh! a demi-diveenity, passin' compare,
Wis that wonderfu' body, ye Bailzie o' Blair.

But time, that tries a'thing, has altered the scene—
Hoo changed is the village frae what it has been!
Hoo grand are the buildings, the Brig, an' the Square!
Hoo wide the domains o' ye Bailzie o' Blair!

Hoo changed are the fowk, too! they lang since began
To discover a Bailzie was only a man;
An', if it wis possible, sune they micht dare
Tae doot the guid sense o' ye Bailzie o' Blair.

Even now some vile bodies tak' counsel thegither
Tae rail at their chief quasi-clerk o' the weather,
An' if it be stormy, ower weet, or ower fair,
It's laid at the door o' ye Bailzie o' Blair.

If dust blaws about by the wind on the street;
If mud fyles the soles o' the burgesses' feet;
If your drains are deficient, or dirty your stair,
Wha else gets the blame, but ye Bailzie o' Blair.

Yet it's only a few that prefer sic a chairge,
An' find their amusement in swearin' at lairge;
The common guid feelin' aye saves frae despair
The sensitive heart o' ye Bailzie o' Blair.

What a comfort tae fowk in positions o' trust
To believe the great soul o' the world tae be just,
While dischargin' their duty but favour or fear
Frae the Queen on the throne to ye Bailzie o' Blair.

But what compensation for trouble sae fit
As tae bring up your biter to let him be bit?
Ah! the impudent sinner is sure o' his share
When he comes to the bench wi' ye Bailzie o' Blair.

Alas! for oor new-fangled notions, for now
We can never get up a municipal row;
Where noo are the cliques an' Committees? where
The fun an' the feastin' wi' ye Bailzie o' Blair?

Hoo mony a battle again and again
Did the burgesses fecht for their favourite men;
Aye, an' some o' the candidates, glamoured wi' glare,
Paid weel for the office o' Bailzie o' Blair.

But hoo pleasant tae think that the siller gaed doon
Wi' a singular e'e "to the guid o' the toon,"
An' tae see the recruited raw levies repair
Tae vote for ye generous Bailzie o' Blair.

Noo a' this amusement will soon be forgotten,
The ballot will alter the mode o' the votin',
An' fowk should be able tae tell tae a hair
The popular choice o' ye Bailzie o' Blair.

But mony mair changes are coming apace
Tae strengthen municipal rule i' the place;
We'll soon hae officials enough an' to spare—
For ane, we are getting three Bailzies tae Blair.

Whatever may happen may all of us "rest
An' be thankfu" to Providence, hopin' the best;
May we aye gie oor hearty guid wishes in prayer
For the toon, an' the fowk, an' ye Bailzies o' Blair.

THE CURLERS' DINNER, 1745.

There is a tradition which would lead us to believe that as far back as 1745 the Curlers of Blair were playing a keen match on the Lochy, when some of Prince Charlie's Highlanders invaded Eppie Clark's Inn at Hill of Blair, where the Curlers' dinner was set ready, and consumed all the beef and greens. Both sides on that occasion lost the prize, and the landlord more than likely lost the reckoning. In an "ode" written by the late Mr Bridie, and recited at the centenary celebration of the Club in 1883, we have this incident detailed:—

Tradition tells a story of the village,
 About "the forty-five" or still more early,
Of rude invasion, foraging, and pillage,
 By some bold soldiers following Prince Charlie,
  Who on a winter evening came to Blair
  And greedily ate up the Curlers' fare.

Ah! who can faithfully depict the scenes,
 How these marauders rallied in a body,
And made a mess of all the beef and greens,
 And swallowed rather than discussed the toddy,
  And put the innkeeper in consternation
  Awed by the military occupation!

What could he do? Though in himself a "host"
 He was confronted by an armed band
Of hungry fighting men, each to his post,
 Obeying his superior in command;
  What wonder if he got a little nervous
  So cavalierly pressed into "the service"?

Then who can realise the blank despair
 Of all the Curlers, tired and hungry, too?
Winners and losers of the game were there,
 Prepared to dine as Curlers always do,
  And round the festive board to meet and sink
  Their petty quarrels in a friendly drink.

CHAPTER IX.

Institutions, Societies. &c.—Banks—Barty Mortification—Blairgowrie and District Photographic Association—Choral Society—Constitutional Club—Dramatic Society—Dundee Blairgowrie and District Association—Edinburgh Blairgowrie Club—Evening Classes—Free Masonry—Horticultural Society—Literary Societies—Mechanics' Institute—Post Office—Press—Shepherds—Volunteer Rifle Brigade.

BANKS.

THE WESTERN BANK OF SCOTLAND

WAS the first to open a branch in Blairgowrie, on 17th August, 1832. A branch was also opened in Coupar Angus about the same time, but as it did not pay it was closed. Messengers in those days had to come and return by mail coach from Glasgow. The Bank first carried on business at the Cross, over shop now occupied by D. Adamson, ironmonger; then it removed to Leslie Street, shop now occupied by Miss Campbell, tobacconist; and thence to the present building in High Street. The Western Bank was incorporated with the BANK OF SCOTLAND in the autumn of 1838. Robert Robertson, some time parish schoolmaster at the Hill, was the first agent. He was succeeded by his son, Alexander Robertson, who also was succeeded by his son—the present agent—Robert Robertson.

THE COMMERCIAL BANK

Opened a branch in the town early in September, 1832. It carried on business in that house in Brown Street long afterwards occupied by Peter Sturrock, parochial schoolmaster; from thence it was transferred to Commercial Bank House at top of Brown Street; and ultimately down to Wellmeadow. The first agent was James Anderson, Solicitor, who was succeeded by his son, I. Henry-Anderson, S.S.C., and latterly by A. W. Bennett, transferred from Pitlochry.

Blairgowrie Deposit Company.

A meeting of the townspeople was held on the 5th August, 1836, to consider the formation of a Monthly Deposit Company. This was ultimately carried into effect under the name of the Blairgowrie Deposit Company, the following gentlemen being the first office-bearers:—Bailie Robert Ayson, Pres.; Geo. Gellatly, brewer, Vice-Pres.; Geo. Macdonald, shoemaker, Treasurer; and Wm. Johnstone, writer, Secretary.

The shares, limited to 150, were taken up by 116 subscribers, who had to make monthly payments as required, the monies being lent out on obligations, bills, bonds, and properties.

The Company seem to have got into difficulties, and efforts were made to wind up their affairs. The last minute recorded bears date 3rd March, 1840, when the properties held by the Company in Rattray and the Muir of Blair were exposed for sale.

The Perth Banking Company

Opened a branch of their Bank in Blairgowrie under the charge of Wm. S. Soutar, Solicitor, on the 11th November, 1851. This Bank existed here until it was bought up by the Union Bank of Scotland, in 1857. On the retirement of W. S. Soutar, Jas. D. Sharp, transferred from Rosehearty, was appointed agent.

The Royal Bank of Scotland

Opened a branch in Millbank House in 1857, and erected the present banking offices in Allan Street in 1872. John Panton, Solicitor, was agent from the opening till his death in 1898, when David Mitchell was appointed.

The North of Scotland Bank

Opened a branch in 1882, in Bleaton House, Leslie Street, John B. Miller, Solicitor, being appointed agent.

National Security Savings Bank of Perth.

A meeting of gentlemen interested in the establishment of a branch of the National Security Savings Bank in Blairgowrie, in connection with the Perth Savings Bank, was held on the 12th October, 1839—Robt. Geekie, Esq. of Rosemount, Chairman.

By intimation from the Parish Church pulpit on the 13th, a further meeting was held on the 14th October, when a branch was established, by the voluntary association of the leading inhabitants of the town and district as its trustees and managers, in terms of the Acts of Parliament, and agreeably to the printed regulations of the Perth Bank.

Shortly before the County and City of Perth Savings Bank had been established, and the District Trustees adopted as their Constitution the "Rules" formed on the basis of those which had been duly certified for the Perth Institution under the existing Savings Bank Statute.

The first rule noted that "this institution, formed for the safe custody and increase of small earnings belonging to the industrious classes of the Town of Blairgowrie and its vicinity, shall be named The Blairgowrie and Rattray Branch of the National Security Savings Bank of Perth."

W. S. Soutar, Writer, was appointed Cashier.

The minute-book finishes up very abruptly at 30th October, 1840, and further minutes are not available till the 3rd January, 1889, when Thomas Soutar was appointed Joint-Cashier along with his father.

For many years before this, great discrepancies had appeared in the ledgers, which led to a thorough investigation of the Bank's affairs, and Messrs W. S. & T. Soutar were relieved of their duties on 29th January, 1889. Mr John Panton, Solicitor, was appointed Cashier, and the business thereafter removed to his offices in Royal Bank Buildings.

Since the opening of the Branch the business has flourished. From 28th October, 1839 to 1st February, 1840, the sum lodged amounted to £509 8s; at 31st October, 1855, it amounted to £11,087, 15s 7½d; at 31st October, 1888, it amounted to £50,410 2s 7d. During this year it reached its greatest sum, but nearly £10,000 were withdrawn by depositors, owing to certain well-known circumstances. On 31st October, 1892, it had, however, regained its footing, the amount in the books being £47,219 19s 4d. On the death of John Panton the agency was transferred to R. Robertson Black, Solicitor, Bank of Scotland, November, 1898.

The Cheque Bank

Is represented by William Stewart, m⟨ ⟩ Street.

Barty Mortification.

Mr George Barty, a tobacconist in Perth of this parish, by his settlement bequeathe the free residue of his estate to the Dean Guild Council of Perth, in trust, for the pu it out on heritable security and paying the of annually to the Parish Schoolmaster of E his successors in office, to defray the expe ting "all the orphans, fatherless, and ⟨ ⟩ belonging to the parishes of Blairgowrie, dochy, and Kinloch, in the Parish School ⟨ ⟩ the children to be recommended by the Kirk-Sessions of these parishes, and thos name of Barty or Soutar to be preferred.

in June, 1838, and his bequest came into Martinmas, 1841. The fund mortified amoı and there were at one time upwards of ⟨ ⟩ joying the benefit of the bequest.

They were taught the same branches and advantages in all respects with the othe tending the schools.

When free education was instituted t country, the trustees of this Mortificati found yearly bursaries of £4 and upwards interest of the capital as far as it would a for competition among scholars attending and the other neighbouring parishes afor encourage them in the pursuit of knowlec tion.

Blairgowrie and District Photog Association.

This Club was formed on the initiative amateurs, who, finding the need for such advertised a meeting to be held in the Ten on 13th February, 1894, and there, under ship of the late Provost Bridie, the A formed, with Mr Alex. Geekie, of Coupar President. The necessity of the Associa local "habitation and a name," was at ⟨ ⟩

on the 17th April, 1894, club-rooms were opened—the old Masonic Hall, Brown Street. The first excursion of the Association was to Kettins, on the 11th June, and the first competition, on 10th July, for the best illustration of the word "Caught." In December, 1895, the Association had the first Photographic Exhibition ever held in the town. The result was a great success, artistically and financially. It was truly "International" in character — exhibits being forward from Scotland, England, Ireland, Spain, United States, Canada, and Australia. Since then the Association has been the pioneer of photographic advancement in the district. On the 25th November, 1896, they gave an exhibition of the "Rontgen rays," and the following night a public exhibition, in the Public Hall, of the Cinematograph or "Animated Photography." In January, 1898, they held their second International Exhibition, which was also a decided success.

In 1896 a Field Club Section was instituted in connection with the Photographic Association, with the object of studying Natural Science and Archæology by the exhibition and preservation of specimens, the reading of communications, the holding of lectures and excursions, and the formation of a natural history library and museum. In 1898 the Photographic Association opened new rooms in the old Volunteer Drill Hall, George Street.

The Choral Society.

Started in 1867, the Choral Society was, from the first, very well supported by the music-lovers of the district, some of them tried veterans with good voices and considerable musical cultivation, who encouraged and inspired those in the callow stage to do their best towards acquiring a mastery over that wonderful instrument, the voice.

The first concert was given on 29th January, 1868. The Society were fortunate in having Mr John Smith, teacher, Kinloch, for its first Conductor, who continued in the office for two years, till he left the district. In 1870 Mr Hirst became Conductor, and so hard did the chorus study that three concerts were given in 1873, including "Judas" and 'Israel." In 1879 Mr Neale was chosen Conductor, which position he held for many years. With the view of putting the Society on a more satisfactory financial basis, a bazaar was organised in 1881, which realised, after all expenses were paid, about £270. In 1804 Mr Howells was named Conductor, and continued till the Society became defunct in 1894. It was, however, resuscitated under the batons of Mr Fisher and Mr Parker, and again flourishes.

The Constitutional Club

Was opened 16th November, 1891, by Lord Stormont. Having acquired the upper flat of the Blairgowrie Hotel, a splendid suite of rooms, comprising billiard room, amusement room, reading room, library, &c., with rooms for keeper, was fitted up. In the reading room all the leading papers are to be had, while the library contains a grand collection of all the newest and best books published.

Meetings for the discussion of politics and the strengthening of the Constitution, smoking concerts, &c., are held occasionally.

Dramatic Society.

On the 6th October, 1875, a Dramatic Club was formed with the object of "studying the legitimate drama and the provision of harmless and innocent amusement during the winter months." For a number of years the Society was fairly successful, but members leaving the town and getting tired of the play, with little encouragement from the public, it became defunct. It, however, acquired a new lease of life about 1894 under the title of the "Garrick Club," which has also been fairly successful.

Dundee Blairgowrie and District Association.

A meeting of the natives of Blairgowrie and district resident in Dundee was called by advertisement to be held in Lamb's Hotel, on Thursday, 22nd December, 1870, at 8 p.m., for the purpose of forming an Association, when 25 gentlemen came forward. Mr Alex. Weddell was called to the Chair, after which the meeting proceeded with the business of the evening. A draft of the rules, previously drawn up, was submitted, approved of, and adopted.

Office-bearers and members of Committee being appointed, the Treasurer proceeded to enrol members, when 23 joined, forming the Association, to be called, as stated in the rules, "The Dundee Blairgowrie and District Association," its aim and objects being "to maintain and promote a friendly feeling amongst the natives of Blairgowrie and district resident in Dundee, and to advance their interests in every way which to the Association may seem desirable;" "the membership to consist of natives of Blairgowrie and district, and of others who, from an interest in Blairgowrie and its welfare, may wish to join the Association"—"the Association to meet on the first Monday of every month in order to consider and carry out measures for attaining its objects."

At the first Committee meeting, on 27th December, arrangements were gone through for the first annual festival of the Association, The festival, which was a grand success, was held in Lamb's Hotel, on Tuesday, 17th January, 1871—Provost Yeaman presiding, supported by Grimond, Tait, Weddell, &c.

Permanent meeting-rooms for the Association were secured below St James' Church, Euclid Crescent, at a rent of 12s a-year, with two lights but no fire, and on the 7th February, 1871, the first literary meeting was held, when Thomas M'Laggan read a very interesting and instructive paper. At the other monthly meetings during the year, debates on various subjects took place, papers were read, songs and humorous stories given, with extempore speeches and readings. On Saturday, 1st August, 1872, a pic-nic excursion of the members and friends to Glamis Castle was held, starting from the High School in machines. From this time up to 1875 there was a gradual falling away of members, till the membership was reduced to seven, who resolved to dispense with the monthly meetings, but act as Committee for the arranging of the annual festival.

On the 11th January, 1875, the Association was re-formed, with an attendance of 15, but, except for arrangements of the festivals, the meetings proved very uninteresting, and were held at irregular times and places, so that from the 12th February, 1876, to 28th February, 1881, the Secretary's books record no minute of any meeting being held.

The Association was once more resuscitated on 28th February, 1881, and continued for a few years, the meetings being held in Mathers' Hotel, Crichton Street, until the 19th July, 1884, when it again succumbed, only to be renewed with greater life on 3rd December, 1889, the chief object then being the annual re-union and festival, which came off successfully on 7th March, 1890, within the Thistle Hall, Union Street. Chief-Magistrate Bridie presided, and speeches were given by D. H. Saunders, John Malcolm, Rev. A. S. Inch, and others, enlivened with songs, recitations, &c., by Esplin, Fleming, Douglas, &c. A grand assembly followed, upwards of 50 couples taking part. The Association is now defunct.

EDINBURGH BLAIRGOWRIE CLUB.

This Club, popularly known as the E. B. C., was formed in 1859 by a number of students at Edinburgh University who had received their education in Blairgowrie or its neighbourhood. Most of them were natives of Blairgowrie and Rattray. The first President was D. K. Miller, afterwards U. P. Minister in Eyemouth, and the first Secretary was J. W. Pringle, afterward U. P. minister in Jedburgh. The original had all, with one exception, been for longer or shorter time pupils of John Inch in the Free Church School of Blairgowrie, and the first intention of the Club, in addition to that of promoting a kindly feeling among the members themselves, was to encourage scholarships in their old school by giving prizes to the best pupils in certain subjects in that school. Shortly after, however, the area of encouragement was widened to all the schools in Blairgowrie and Rattray that would accept of it. The meetings of the Club were held on Saturday evening (the first of each session of College being on the third Saturday of November), the others following every fourth Saturday thereafter till March or April. They were held by rotation in the lodgings of the various members, and at each meeting an essay was read and criticised. The session was generally wound up with a supper, at which the President read his retiring address.

Occasionally meetings were held in summer if sufficient members were available to form a meeting. After a few years the meetings began to take a more social turn, for, in addition to the literary character of the entertainment, which was carefully kept up, the members were invited to tea by the one in whose lodgings it was the turn of the Club to meet. This was kept up for a long time very successfully until some ungracious landladies began to find fault, and this difficulty resulted in the Club meeting in Adam's Temperance Hotel in High Street, each one paying for his own entertainment. The new atmosphere did not seem to be so congenial as the old, and the Club began from this time to decline in spirit till it sank into an instrument for convening an annual meeting for social purposes of a larger kind than had been formerly held. In this capacity it did not last long, but seems to have been merged into a wider organisation for convening the natives of Blairgowrie and District to a soiree and assembly once every year. Thus the Club has now ceased to exist. Not more than half-a-dozen of the original members, if even that number, now survive; some of the most brilliant of them died not many years after its formation. Among these were Thomas G. Stewart, Mathematical Master in the Edinburgh Institution, who met his death when experimenting with nitric acid preparatory to the illuminations for the Prince of Wales' marriage on the 10th March, 1863. Stewart was a brilliant mathematician, and bade fair to take a foremost place as a man of science. William Cowan, one of the most cultured Greek scholars that Edinburgh University has produced, died in December, 1865, of typhoid fever. Dr James Neilson, who for many years practised medicine in Blairgowrie, died more recently. The details of the various sessions are accurately and, in some cases, graphically recorded in the minute-book.

EVENING CLASSES.

Evening classes for the study of Science and Art subjects were first instituted about the year 1878, the pupils being taught privately and journeying to Dundee for examination. In 1881 they were first opened in the town under the auspices, and conform to rules, of Science and Art Department, and managed by a local Committee. The late George Dickson was the first teacher (Mathematics) under the Department, and the writer was the first student registered (No. 1). Since that time the Classes have been put upon a broader basis, and there is now scarcely a night during the session but several subjects are being taught, embracing all subjects in Science, Art, and Technology.

In 1885 the syllabus of the City and Guilds of London Institute was brought out, and classes started by local teachers. They were most successful for several years, the students, particularly in the textile branches, carrying off the highest prizes (medals and money) offered under competition to Great Britain.

For several years, from 1887, the classes were under the tuition of resident teachers; but latterly they have been allowed, through lack of energy on the part of the management, to gradually lose heartening. Local teachers are, however, doing their utmost to encourage and educate the pupils.

Under the School Board, in 1896, classes for Cookery and Laundry Work were started in a special building erected for that purpose in connection with the Public Schools. These, however, have not been a success.

FREEMASONRY.

About the year 1774 a Free Masons' Lodge was first instituted in the town, and for a considerable time it was in a flourishing condition, but, as in other places at that time, it gradually diminished and seemed as if it would perish altogether.

In 1859 Freemasonry took a fresh impetus in America and this country; consequently Blairgowrie was not wanting, and on the 12th October, 1859, the Lodge of St. John, 137, was revived. For some weeks before, a considerable number of the inhabitants were initiated into the mysteries of Masonry. On this evening (12th October) the brethren assembled in the Town Hall, at 6 o'clock, when the Lodge was opened by David Dickson, R.W.M., and the office-bearers of Lodge Ancient, Dundee, No. 49. The Charter of Confirmation having been read and the various jewels laid before the presiding brother, office-bearers were installed. Thereafter the brethren to the number of sixty were marshalled in procession, and marched through the town in full regalia, headed by the Coupar Angus Instrumental Band playing the Masonic Anthem, the Blairgowrie Band bringing up the rear. The first ceremony of any importance in which the Lodge took a part, after its resuscitation, was the laying of the foundation-stone of the new Public Hall of Blairgowrie on the 20th October,

1860, performed by the Right Hon. the Earl of Breadalbane, Right Worshipful Grand Master of Lodge of Scotland.

Since that time it has taken a part with Lodges in the surrounding cities and towns in matters pertaining to the Masonic craft. The Lodge has been in a highly-flourishing condition since 1859, and it is worthy of note that a separate Lodge was formed a number of years afterwards to suit the convenience of members—" Royal Arch Chapter, No. 168."

The members of Lodge St John, No. 137, meet for the business of the craft within the Town Hall, Blairgowrie.

HORTICULTURAL SOCIETY.

This Society was first instituted in 1857, and for a number of years was in a flourishing condition. Then it was the custom to have an exhibition of flowers, fruit, and vegetables twice a-year, but the want of public interest in its proceedings caused its failure.

In 1876, however, it was revived, and it now holds an annual display of flowers, fruit, vegetables, and works of industry, each year becoming more interesting and popular.

LITERARY SOCIETIES.

THE BLAIRGOWRIE PARISH CHURCH LITERARY ASSOCIATION

("The Lit.") was inaugurated in January, 1885. The Rev. Robert Kemp, having suggested its formation, convened a meeting, which not only adopted the suggestion, but made it assume a practical form on the spot. It has been very successful in its works, and for a number of years did good service to the town by introducing popular lectures and concerts by eminent lecturers and artistes. Under the Association's auspices Dr Moxey (Leo Ross), Professor Blackie, Paul Blouet (Max O'Rell), C. C. Maxwell, Rev. David Macrae, Andrew Osler, Miss Imandt, Madame Annie Grey, Dickson Moffat, and others, have given entertainments. In 1890 an annual Burns Concert on behalf of the Royal Infirmary, Edinburgh (founded in 1738 by George Drummond of Blair), was started, and with the help of local talent the Committee of the B.P.C.L.A. have since then forwarded over £120 to that noble institution. In October, 1890, the Association extended its usefulness by issuing a monthly magazine, while in session, continuing the same till March, 1892, when it ceased. At Xmas, in 1892, however, it was re-issued in the form of an "Annual," which has continued since, and is much appreciated at home and abroad, and speaks volumes for the energy and ability of the B.P.C.L.A. The session begins in November and ends in March, the members meeting every Monday evening at 8.30 in the Photographic Rooms.

THE YOUNG WOMEN'S LITERARY ASSOCIATION

Was started on the 18th February, 1892, and is in a flourishing condition. The members meet in the Session-House of the Parish Church on Monday evenings at 8.15.

ST STEPHEN'S CATHOLIC UNION

Was formed in 1890. Meetings are held fortnightly on Wednesdays in St Stephen's Hall; concerts and amateur dramatic entertainments are occasionally given. A reading room and lending library are also in connection with the Union for members' use.

THE FIRST FREE CHURCH LITERARY ASSOCIATION

Was formed on the 12th September, 1892, and has been very successful. The Association issued the first number of an admirably got up magazine, "The James Street Magazine," at the New Year, 1893.

MECHANICS' INSTITUTE AND WORKING MEN'S CLUB.

The Working Men's Library was first formed in 1853, in a small room in Leslie Street, and afterwards there were several changes of locality, till the present handsome buildings in the High Street were erected in 1870, at a cost of over £850. The block comprises two shops, reading room, library, &c. In the library there are upwards of 3,000 volumes, and in the reading room all the chief daily papers and periodicals are to be found.

In the autumn of 1890 it was proposed to adopt the Free Libraries' Act, and to form the Mechanics' Institute into a Public Library, if Blairgowrie and Rattray, two

THE PRESS. 159

, could legally co-operate. It was found
not be done, and the idea was abandoned.
of that year (1890) Andrew Carnegie,
merica, made the gift of £100 towards the
ks. On the 2nd November, 1896, a billiard
duced into the amusement room, and has
nse success.

POST OFFICE.

ost Office was first established in Blair-
een unable to find out, but about the end
business was carried on in a small shop
d) on the site of which Keay's buildings
are now erected. When business necessi-
accommodation, several changes were made
n Street, and latterly to 23 High Street,
ueen's Hotel.
master of which there is any record was
orn 1766, died 1860.)
taff consisted of a postmistress, 1 assistant,
for the town, and 2 rural postmen. There
deliveries of letters each day, while a
was introduced in 1869. In 1870 and
troduction of halfpenny postage and post-
arcel post increased the work and required
taff, as also in 1872, when telegrams were
 the Railway Company.
enience of the public, receiving boxes are
ot of Leslie Street, foot of Newton Street,
keld Road.
aff consisted of 1 Postmistress, 4 assistants,
arriers, 4 rural postmen, and 3 telegraph
 there are only two deliveries a-day of
delivery of parcels.

THE PRESS.

press was first introduced into Blairgowrie
was not until the year 1855 that a news-
uced.
ue was on Saturday, 21st April, 1855,
High Street, by Ross & Son, under the

title—"Ross's Compendium of Week's News"—to be issued occasionally, and consisted of a single sheet, 12½ inches long and 8½ inches wide, printed on both sides. It was thought at the time to be a foolish venture, the town not being large enough to warrant such a proceeding, yet steadily the paper flourished under various titles, increased in demand and size, till it now consists of four leaves, 21 inches by 16 inches, or eight pages of 6 columns each, with a weekly circulation of about 3,000 copies. It is now issued every Saturday morning, from the office in Reform Street, under the title of "The Blairgowrie Advertiser." Early in the 80's a mid-week paper, commenced during a Parliamentary election, was issued from the same office, but was, after a time, discontinued.

In 1876 a rival paper to the "Advertiser"—"The Blairgowrie News"—was started, but it survived only about three years. It was issued by Larg & Keir from an office in Leslie Street.

The year 1894 witnessed another epoch in the annals of the press in the town, by the birth on 29th September of the "Free Press and General Advertiser," from the office of D. C. & W. Gibson in Leslie Street. It is an eight page paper; size, 10 inches by 7½ inches, of 2 columns each; published every Saturday morning, and delivered gratuitously to every householder.

SHEPHERDS (ANCIENT ORDER OF.)

The Loyal Order of Ancient Shepherds (Lodge Tullyveolan), was instituted in Blairgowrie on 10th May, 1884, under the Dundee District, John Smith, painter, being elected first Chairman.

It has a large and influential membership, and is in a highly-flourishing condition. In 1887 the Society revived the Highland Games, which had been allowed to lapse, in the district, and through their energy these sports are now considered one of the events of the season among athletes.

In 1804, when this country was at war with France and Britain was threatened with invasion by Napoleon, the people of the land were roused to embody themselves into Companies for drill for protection of life and liberty. In Blairgowrie a small company of 8 officers, 65 privates, and 1 drummer was raised as the "Blairgowrie Volunteers." History does not record how long this corps existed; but, probably, after the defeat of the French at Trafalgar, it was disbanded.

On the institution of the Volunteer movement in the kingdom in 1859-60, the gentlemen of Blairgowrie resolved to form a corps, and a meeting was held in Brown Street Chapel, on 13th December, 1859, to make arrangements. John L. Campbell of Achalader presided, and expressed the hope that the movement would be successful; that, by having trained riflemen in the country, a stop would be put to the periodical panics so mischievous in their effects upon commerce; and that, if Volunteers came forward, the Government would be saved the necessity of increasing the standing army.

Subscription lists were at once opened, and soon upwards of £200 was raised.

James Young, brewer, offered the use of his extensive premises at Hill of Blair, in one flat of which he thought the corps might shoulder their rifles without interfering with the roof. James Crockart, gunmaker, was requested to undertake the duties of armourer, which he said he would willingly do, and a room for an armoury was taken, at a yearly rent of £5, from Wm. Robertson, baker, High Street. On Monday, 23rd January, 1860, J. L. Campbell received a communication from the Lord-Lieutenant of the County that Her Majesty had been graciously pleased to accept the services of the corps. On the 6th February officers were sent by Government to inspect ground for a range, and they chose the ground immediately behind Woodhead, near the Heughs of Mause. Ground at the Dark Fa's was first taken for a practice ground. For a considerable time the range was at Woodhead, when it was removed to the Welltown, from which it was removed to the Darroch, near Fengus Loch, and again to its present position at Castlehill, Rattray.

It was resolved to adopt the pattern of the Dundee Rifle dress, and the materials of the same colour and texture as those of Perth. The expense of the uniform was about £3 12s 6d, including belts.

On 15th February the following gentlemen were elected as sergeants:—James Young, David Chalmers, J. L. Robertson, Alex. Murdoch, Thomas M'Lachlan.

On the 25th March the oath of allegiance to Her Majesty was taken, John Fleming, Chief-Magistrate, and John Rattray of Coral Bank attending as Justices of the Peace; James Anderson, solicitor, acting as Clerk to the Justices.

The Company was drawn up, forming two sides of a square, in front of the Justices, and the oath was administered amid profound silence. The following is an extract from the "London Gazette" of 23rd March:—

"Commissions signed by Lord-Lieutenants, March 16th, 1860. 5th Perthshire Rifle Volunteers—John Livington Campbell, Esq., to be Captain; William Shaw Soutar, Esq., to be Lieutenant; Richard Penketh, Esq., to be Ensign; Rev. Wm. Herdman, to be Hon.-Chaplain; Robert A. Balfour, Esq., to be Hon.-Assistant Surgeon." Sergeant Seaton, Instructor.

In April the Government supply of rifles and ammunition arrived, consisting of 80 rifles and 25,000 rounds of ammunition, with caps, &c., to match. 16,000 of these cartridges were ball, whilst the remaining 9000 were blank, and the Lochy House was turned into a magazine for their storage.

On the 15th May, John Saunders of Bramblebank, George Sidey, Alex. Munro, and John Cowan, Rattray, were elected Corporals.

An Instrumental Brass Band was formed in connection with the corps, the drum being, by permission of Allan Macpherson, embellished with his crest and motto—"Touch not a cat but a glove."

On the 7th August, 1860, the corps was present in Edinburgh at the review of Scottish Volunteers by the Queen.

J. L. Campbell, Captain, retired after two years. R. Penketh succeeded in command, and when he left the district G. B. Anderson was appointed. On the death of that esteemed officer, 1868, D. Chalmers, who had meantime graduated from the ranks, was promoted to the Captaincy, and latterly to the rank of Major, retiring in 1890.

In 1860, on the retirement of Instructor Seaton, Sergeant-Major Wilson, late 71st Highland Light Infantry, was appointed Drill Instructor, which position he retained till 1892, when he retired, and was succeeded by Colour-Sergeant White, late of 93rd Highlanders.

In 1880 the old uniforms were cast aside and the Highland dress adopted, with the same tunic as formerly, the tartan being Athole tartan, which afterwards gave place to the tartan of the 42nd Highlanders ("Black Watch"), of which famous regiment, it, with other corps in the district, forms the 5th Battalion.

In 1881 the corps was again present at the second review of Scottish Volunteers by Her Majesty in the Queen's Park, Edinburgh.

During the annual holidays in July the Volunters have the benefit and enjoyment of a week in camp, where they go through their drill, &c., as though in camp with the regulars. The year 1890 saw the institution of this movement here, when the camp was at Delvine; it has since been at Birnam, Aberfeldy, &c.

In June, 1895, several members of the corps were presented with long-service volunteer medals by the Government. Those members were:—

Capt. John Baxter, Ashbank, ... 34 years' service.
Hon.-Major D. Chalmers, ... 30   ,,
Band-Sergt. William Hebenton (29 years' service), joined the corps at Brechin in 1861, and retired from the Blairgowrie corps in 1890.
Sergt. D. Paterson, ... 26 years' service.
Corpl. Gellatly, Oakbank, ... 25   ,,
Colour-Sergt. Adam Hill, ... 25   ,,
Colour-Sergt. Simpson, ... 24   ,,
Band-Sergt. Ambrose, ... 24   ,,
Colour-Sergt. D. Lamont, ... 22   ,,

Sergt. Wm. Davidson, ... 20 years' service.
Sergt.-Major Jas. Wilson,... ...long-service army medal.
Sergt.-Instructor White (18 years), ,, ,,
In 1898—Pvt. G. Low, ... 23 years' service.
         Corpl. B. Paterson, ... 22 ,,
In 1899—Pvt. H. Grant, ... 20 ,,

Several years ago the Instrumental Brass Band was dispensed with, and a Pipe Band took its place.

For nearly 30 years the corps had the use of the Episcopal School as an armoury and drill room; but it was considered advisable to erect a drill hall to suit the corps, which was done in 1897-98. The hall, opened in Feb., 1898, by the Earl of Breadalbane, is one well adapted for its purpose, and provides all necessary accommodation for drill and for armoury, &c.

CHAPTER X.

Manufactures—Lornty Mill—Brooklinn—Oakbank—The Meikle Mill—Ericht Linen Works—Greenbank Engineering Works—Millwright Works—Brewing—Ancient Trade—Recollections of the Past—A Merchant's Rhyme—The Whisky Roadie and its Associations—Duncan Watchie—Posty Reid—The Toon's Officers—The Guard-House—The Bell o' Blair—Lily Harris—Matthew Harris—Tammy Mann—Daft Harry—John Couper—Quoit Club—Candy Betty—Smith Lamont—Voluntary Constables—Abram Low and the Welltown Brownies—Isaac Low, the Ingenious Blacksmith.

MANUFACTURES.

BEFORE 1796 a considerable quantity of flax was grown in the parish, the produce of which was spun on the ordinary spinning-wheel by domestic servants and women who were not fit for any harder work, and it was quite a common thing for them to earn 2s 6d to 4s a-week in this way.

In days gone by the manufactures of Blairgowrie, as in most villages and towns in Scotland, were confined to the handloom. Over a century ago, spinning was first introduced, and Blairgowrie shortly after that period became the centre of a extensive handloom and hand-spinning industry.

It was common in the end of last century and earlier part of this century for a person to possess a little bit of land in the vicinity of the town, in which flax was cultivated, and afterwards, by the hand of the grower, manufactured, retted, and steeped in the neighbouring lochs. The flax harvest of those days was quite an event, and the strength of the domestic establishment of the flax cultivator was often employed in gathering the production of the earth. Now the cultivation has entirely ceased.

The founders in Blairgowrie of that important branch of commerce — the linen trade — were David Grimond, W. Fyfe, J. Milne, Baxter, Dick, Morrice, Cairncross,

M'Intosh, and G. Saunders—all men of great force of character, perseverance, and business energy.

Prior to 1840 the only branches of the manufacture carried on here were the spinning of flax and tow into yarn and the weaving of these yarns into cloth of various fabrics. There were five spinning-mills in the parish engaged in flax manufacture, all the machinery of which was driven by water. The following table shows the number of hands engaged at each of the mills:—

Blairgowrie Mill, ...	...	9 males,	32 females—	41 total.
Oakbank Mill,	...	35 ,,	36 ,,	71 ,,
Lornty Mill,	...	8 ,,	21 ,,	29 ,,
Ashbank Mill,	...	32 ,,	40 ,,	72 ,,
Carsie Mill, ...	...	1 ,,	5 ,,	6 ,,
		85	134	219

The flax used at these mills was imported into Dundee from the Baltic ports, and after being spun into yarn was either conveyed to Dundee for sale there or disposed of to the manufacturers in the neighbourhood and in Alyth and Coupar Angus. The value of flax weekly consumed in the three mills in operation in the immediate vicinity of the town in 1840 was from £400 to £500, or from £20,000 to £26,000 per annum, and the value of yarn spun at the same mills, from £650 to £700 per week, or about from £33,000 to £36,000 per annum.

The other branch of manufacture, the weaving of yarn into cloth, employed about 370 hands. The yarns were purchased by the master manufacturers of the place, who employed weavers to weave it into cloth, which was sent to Dundee and sold to the cloth-merchants there. Part of the cloth was shipped direct, at the risk of the manufacturers, to North and South America and France. The greater part of the cloth manufactured consisted of Osnaburgs and coarse sheetings, but there was also a considerable quantity of fine dowlas and drill manufactured. At an early period in the 18th century flax was grown to a moderate extent, and continued to be cultivated for a considerable time. During the winter months the whole of the quantity raised was spun in the parish, the rents of many of the smaller farmers being mostly paid for with the money got for the yarn. The husbandry was long of the rudest description, but in 1780 there was a decided improvement in it. More land was cultivated, and better crops were raised.

The flax was generally sown about the end of April, in a portion of the division for oats, and when the season was suitable a fair crop was produced. Considerable quantities of foreign flax, besides the home grown, were spun. About 1788 the two-handed wheel superseded the single one, and thus the spinning capabilities of the workers were doubled.

The weavers employed by the manufacturers were paid for their work by the piece, and their earnings averaged, for the men, 8s, and for the women, 5s per week, working 14 hours per day. The whole of the weaving was done by handlooms, no machinery being employed for that purpose.

Since the erection of the "Meikle Mill" in 1798, the banks of the beautiful and romantic Ericht have been studded with spinning mills, and the rush of its waters affords employment to a large population.

Throughout many parts of the country the flax spinning mills driven by water power have, from a variety of causes, been demolished or turned to other purposes; but this does not apply to the district of Blairgowrie. Here the water power is sufficient to drive moderate sized mills steadily and profitably, but it is not so large as to admit of great extensions, and many of the mills therefore remain as they were originally erected.

James Grimond, of Oakbank Mill, was the first spinner whom Watt induced to make a trial of jute. He cut it into lengths, heckled it, spun the line into 3-lb. yarn (16 lea), the quality of which was excellent. The jute first used by him was of remarkably fine fibre, soft and silky, with spinning properties superior to the bulk of what is now imported.

Jute has now the principal place in the staple trade, there being a number of small manufactories engaged entirely in the spinning of yarns.

The proprietors are a respectable body of spinners, most attentive to business, and well worthy of the wealth which they have acquired. They labour under the disadvantage of having to attend the markets in Dundee once or twice a-week for the purchase of the raw material and the sale of its produce, but this is a disadvantage shared by the spinners and manufacturers in other towns, and it is more than counterbalanced by the cheap motive power supplied by the Ericht. The extension of the railway system, in 1855, to Newtyle, Coupar Angus, and Blairgowrie, contributed greatly to the changing of the method of conducting business, and, in no less marked degree, on account of the facilities afforded by it for the rapid transmission of goods, to the increase of trade.

Lornty Mill.

Is situated on, and driven by, the Lornty Burn. It was built about the year 1814 by David Grimond, a progenitor of the present proprietor. Grimond, who was originally a millwright, observing that there was a fall which could be advantageously turned to account for driving flax-spinning machinery, arranged with Colonel Macpherson, the proprietor, for a site, and built a mill of modest dimensions, in which he had four frames, the clear profit on which was about £5 or £6 per week. This mill was subsequently extended, and, though it has a quiet, retired, and rather antiquated appearance compared with some of the other mills in the neighbourhood, a considerable amount of business is still done in it.

Brooklinn Mill.

Was built by David Grimond. It stands close on the banks of the Ericht, but the machinery is driven by the water of the Lornty Burn, which is collected in another dam after driving Lornty Mill. The water is retained in the dam by a strong wooded breastwork across the ravine, and is applied to the Brooklinn Mill by means of a wheel about five feet in diameter. It is on the lower end of a vertical shaft running up the gable of the mill. The water is conveyed in a pipe to the wheel, and the surface of the water in the dam being nearly 40 feet above the level of the wheel, there is a pressure of about 20 lbs. per square inch. The water is conducted to the lower side of the wheel, which it enters at the centre and leaves at tangential orifices at the circumference. The wheel takes 180 revolutions per minute, and gives nearly 25 horse power.

Ashbank Mill

Was built about 1836 by John Baxter, and was originally used for the spinning of flax and tow. New machinery was afterwards erected for spinning jute, of which about 5000 spindles per week were produced, in cops and weft, principally for the Dundee trade. Several years ago the entire mill was burned down; it was, however, re-erected, but has not been in operation. About 100 hands were wont to be employed in the mill. It is now possessed by John Grimond of Oakbank.

Oakbank Mill

Was commenced many years ago, and was successfully worked by James Grimond, brother of the originator of Lornty Mill.

On James Grimond's death, David Grimond (his nephew) succeeded. The mill was burned down in the spring of 1872, the fire arising from a gas jet igniting some of the tow.

The damage done was very great, and 170 people were temporarily thrown out of employment; but the proprietor soon had the mill erected and started again. It is entirely driven by water power.

The Meikle Mill

Has been familiar to the inhabitants of Blairgowrie for several generations, and it must have been regarded as a very important as well as extensive institution in its earlier days. About the beginning of the century it belonged to Peter M'Intosh, who first introduced the art of spinning by means of machinery into the district. Subsequent to M'Intosh's time Bailie Dick had the "Muckle Mill" but, unfortunately, he failed in business, and in consequence the mill stood idle for some time. It has since been in the hands of numerous owners, including John Adamson, formerly of Erichtside Works, and Drummond, who disposed of it to James Luke & Co., of Ericht Linen Works, which are situated on the other side of the road from it.

Luke & Co. had the mill fitted with new machinery adapted for their own business. Some of their machinery was also contained in a smaller building a little further down the river, and driven by a small turbine, where the old "Plash Mill" used to be.

Ericht Linen Works

Were erected in 1867 from designs by Thomson Bros., Dundee, and form a handsome and conveniently arranged block of buildings, which have the advantage of being situated within the town of Blairgowrie, and therefore near the homes of the operatives.

In 1894 Luke & Co., the proprietors of the "Muckle Mill" and Ericht Linen Works, suspended payment, and the works were closed. They were, however, put in operation again, with W. A. M'Intyre & Co. as managers, in the autumn of 1897.

Greenbank Engineering Works.

As makers of agricultural implements of all kinds, especially harvesting reapers—the Scotia, Speedwell, and Bisset Binder—the firm of J. Bisset & Sons has attained world-wide reputation.

It is now nearly half-a-century since the works were started at Marlee, on a comparatively small scale, by John Bisset. The demands of trade necessitated the extension of premises, and about 20 years ago Greenbank Works were erected.

Year by year additions have been made, and the works now cover a great extent of ground. A large staff of workmen are employed, and hundreds of reapers, binders, diggers, &c., are annually put out to all parts of the world.

In consequence of the death of Thos. S. Bisset, the managing partner, the proprietorship has been converted into a Limited Liability Company.

Millwright Works.

Since the beginning of the century a flourishing business of millwright work has been carried on by John Abercromby. The grandfather of the present proprietor erected the first thrashing-mill in the district at Blairgowrie House, about 100 years ago, which proved very successful, and his services were much sought after for many miles around.

Brewing.

The Scottish brewers have long been famed for the excellent quality of their beer and ales, and the liquor manufactured by James Ogilvy, in Allan Street, Blairgowrie, can bear comparison with any. It is well known and much appreciated in town and country. The bottling premises and brewery in Allan Street are of great extent, and capable of storing a large stock.

The manufacture of temperance beverages is carried on to a considerable extent by William Stewart in his premises at Croft Lane.

Ancient Trade—Recollections of the Past.

An old inhabitant, long since departed, used to relate that he recollected when "there were only 4 slated houses in Blairgowrie, and only 1 inhabitant for every 60 (of his latter days); then it had 1 minister and 1 dominie; it had a brewer and a few drinkers; a baker who lived a hungry life; a butcher, small of paunch, who seldom killed a beast; a miller not much troubled with dust;. a smith with too many irons in the fire; a cloth merchant who generally wore a very seedy coat, and came to serve his customers after dark by the light of a rozetty stick; a barber nick-named Skin-em-alive—the byeword ran thus:—

> 'You are like the barber o' Blair,
> Wha tak's the skin an' leaves the hair;'

a tailor who whipped the cat at twopence a-day; there were some laws, but no lawyers to teach them; broken bones and various diseases, but no doctor to scob and drug us; we had no banks and little money—the Bible was the only bank for paper notes and an 'old hugger' for coin; we had no brokers and nothing to pawn; the town's bellman used to perambulate the town with his bell and intimate to the inhabitants that 'good beef at fourpence a-pound is on sale at John Lowrie's— the Bailie's ta'en ae leg, an' the minister anither, but gif nae ither person tak's a third leg the ox will no be killed.'"

About the beginning of this (the 19th) century the whole mercantile space of the town was comprised between the foot of Brown Street and the Royal Bank.

An old shopkeeper used to remark that he could recollect every merchant and public man between these points upon the shady side of the street—which somehow was never so prosperous as the other—the names of whom were introduced into a rhyme taught the children then—

> "Jeems Doeg mak's shune;
> Jimmy Johnstone's saut's dune;
> Tinsmith Brisbane works the file;
> Peter tak's folk tae the jile;
> John Pennycook sells beef;
> Doctor Edward gi'es relief;
> Daniel Maclaren sells dear;
> Tammas Johnstone, auctioneer;
> Saddler Sim has little sale;
> John Tyrie brews ale."

He had no distinct recollection of the shopkeepers on the other side of the street, as they had no rhyme.

One of those buildings, long occupied as a public-house, and tenanted by a person named John M'Gregor about the year 1830, was demolished in 1890 to allow of improvements. (The property of Wm. Crockart, gunsmith, now occupies the site, in Allan Street.)

The house was built with the gable-end to the street, but about ten feet back from the line, and to increase the accommodation a peculiarly-shaped addition, known as "the coffin," was built. The sign over the house was very interesting, painted on a ground of plaster:—"John M'Gregor, Flesher; Ales and Whisky," with emblems of conviviality, viz., punch-bowl, mutchkin-stoup, a large dram-glass, a small glass, and water-jug. Though the rooms were small many a rowdy meeting made them resound with uproarious mirth.

Passing the front of the house, and through the garden to Croft Lane, was another lane, known as "The Whisky Roadie," which allowed drouthy neighbours to get unobserved to "The Coffin" at all hours.

The old Newton Burn, at the beginning of the century, ran open down through the fields to and east the High Street, descended to Allan Street by the back of M'Gregor's public-house, then down to the top of the Wellmeadow, and from thence past Lower Mill Street to the Ericht.

One of the old merchants, Duncan Robertson, familiarly

known as "Duncan Watchie," from his being a watchmaker, occupied a shop on the east side of the Cross. Another, William Todd, carried on a drapery business at the corner of Brown Street. About 1820 Todd erected a small gas work behind his house, which proved very successful, and his brilliantly-lighted premises contrasted strongly with the "rozetty sticks" and "cruizie" lamps of his neighbours. Where the Public Hall now stands, upwards of seventy years ago, Sandy Waddell carried on a business of blacksmith and farrier. Johnnie Tamson made barrels and tubs and plied his coopering adjoining John Tyrie's brewery, where Dr Charles S. Lunan's surgery now stands. John Bruce also carried on business as a brewer and distiller at the west side of the "Whisky Roadie." Honest Jamie Irvine was the town's bellman and public messenger. John M'Lachlan was the "kirke officer" and parish sexton. In order to keep the peace during the Fair, or on high occasions, a body of Special Constables were enrolled, and householders were thus saved the expense of keeping night watchmen. The chief of the "force" was Sandy Reid, more familiarly known as "Post" Reid. (He had been a post-carrier in his younger days.) He was, during his sojourn in Blairgowrie, the town officer, and was uniformed in a blue surtout with red collar and metal buttons, and an old tile hat for a head-piece. Archie Irons, for many years salmon fisher on the Ericht, was a constable as well as sheriff-officer, and Willie Mustard acted as his assistant. David Peters was a vintner and messenger-at-arms. (These all carried the small baton of authority in their pockets.) Willie Johnstone, the writer, was Town Clerk, with guid honest men for bailies.

In addition to his civic appointments, Post Reid had to fill up spare time with scavenger work. The town could not then boast of a Cleansing Department, so he had to keep the streets clean in all weathers. After a rainy season he scraped the mud with a large clatt, and formed what the children called "Post" heaps at the sides of the streets, where they were allowed to settle for months before being carted away.

The business of the town was usually conducted either in John Bruce's or John Tyrie's public-house, and, a generation later, in Gardiner's back shop. "Bookie" Robertson (another old worthy) used to remark—"If we do the town's business, we do it at the town's expense;" and, "pu'in' the hare's fit," he would call in another round.

The old "Guard-House" of Blair, demolished about 1830, occupied a site near where the shop of James Miller, watchmaker, now stands, in Allan Street. It stood back from the street, leaving an open space in front. It had two compartments—the guard-room and the inner ward where the prisoners were kept. The window sills were level with the ground, and the opening was strongly stanchioned with iron bars, and at the windows the unfortunate inmates were consoled, advised, comforted, and fed by their friends, or scorned and taunted by their enemies, without interference.

For a long time the ward was without an occupant, and the Bailie let it to a vintner—Alexander Robertson, known as "Moreover"—for the storage of potatoes. The Fair o' Blair coming on, it was thought advisable to have the guard-house ready in case of need; and ere that day had gone a riotous Highlander was safely lodged within its precincts. After the freshness of his native glen, the odour of musty potatoes was too much, and with mighty energy he forced an egress from his prison by the window, but his freedom was of short duration. Speedily recaptured, he was brought before the Bailie (Whitson, 1827) on a charge of jail-breaking. Fortunately, for the credit of the town and the comfort of the accused, the case broke down with the first witness called in the prosecution.

Bailie (interrogating)—"Mr Robertson, did you see this man breakin' oot o' the jile?"

"Troth, sir, an' that is the very man 'at cam' oot o' my tawtie-hoose!"

It is needless to say that the answer revealed the absurdity of the charge.

Hung between two high wooden posts at the end of the guard-house was the "Auld Bell o' Blair," which was rung on stated occasions until the Han'sel Monday of 1832. The youngsters of the town had free permission to ring the bell on these festive mornings, and the violent tugging at the rope had probably so worn the fixings that on this Han'sel Monday morning, while being swung, it came down, and fell through the roof of an adjoining house, landing on the clay floor, to the great consternation of Leezie Saunders, who, fortunately for her personal safety, was at that early hour of the morning still an occupant of her box bed. After the dust had cleared away sufficient to show what was the cause of such a violent intrusion, Auld Leezie was heard to exclaim—"Preserve a' livin'! wha wad ha'e thocht ye wad ha'e been my first fit this mornin'!" The bell was never hung again. It may be seen in the Mechanics' Institute (see page 80.)

Lily Harris

Was an eccentric being (1730 to 1807), who would wander for days among the dens of Craighall in search of a bairn she alleged the fairies had stolen. She seldom failed to visit the house of mourning when informed of the death of any one known to her; but with all her eccentricities she did not fail, when occasion required, to show that she still retained a fair amount of practical shrewdness. She regularly attended the local fairs and markets, and if there was a calf or a stirk from the farm to be sold, Lily undertook the bargaining, and invariably held the best of it with the dealers.

Matthew Harris

Was the son of a crofter at the Muir, and was a hunchback, usually employed in running messages, or hawking goods about the country for himself. One day he had been out at Clunie, when a fellow-traveller meeting him accosted him—"Hullo, Matthaw, did ye come strecht frae Blair?"

"Aye."

"Weel, ye've gotten awfu' crookit on the road!"

Johnnie Eavlick

Was another old worthy, who kept a china shop in High Street, and hawked his dishes about the countryside in a bag slung over his shoulder. The Commercial Inn of our day was formerly a pie-shop, occupied by Tammy Mann. An eccentric couple, known as Rob and

May, lived up the hill, and also Jamie Orchar. An old rhyme went—

> "Some may mind o' Tammy Mann,
>   Wha sell't penny pies an' sugar bools;
> The place is noo a whisky shop,
>   For turnin' wise men into fools.
> Some may mind o' Jamie O———,
>   Wha carried beef sae lang tae Fell.
> When he wis asked whaur he wis gaun,
>   'Aha! I ken my lane.' He wadna tell."

Harry M'Intosh (1799-1858).

Daft Harry, as he was better known by, was of middle stature, round-shouldered, and considerably bent, walking with a slouching gait. All attempts to educate him were futile, and as he grew to manhood he was endowed with enormous strength, and found employment in Turnie Butter's works, turning a large fly-wheel with a crank handle to drive a drill for boring bobbins. From this occupation he was known to the youngsters as "Wheel," which never failed to irritate. Another name of equal power to produce effect was "Burgess," referring to Annie Burgess, a deformed and half-witted maid who was alleged to be Harry's sweetheart. Harry had set days for going the rounds of visiting the kitchens of well-to-do people who were kind to him, and he usually carried a bag for the bread and another one for bones and scraps of meat, which earned for him the term "Greasy Pouches." Saturday was aye a cruel day for Harry: it was shaving day, and the operation had to be performed on the stubbly beard of a week's growth, well greased with the picking of innumerable bones.

Oftentimes the shaving operation suffered interruption. When the barber's shop was at the Cross, those who went close to the window could see him at work, and the youngsters would creep up until they saw Harry arrayed in the white sheet and his face lathered; they would then suddenly shout, "Wheel! Wheel! Burgess!" which instantly brought Harry to his feet, and, if the barber failed to detain him, he would give chase, as he was, in his ghastly vestments.

Harry was ever in attendance at all funerals, and, judging from his own feelings, he must have regarded the honoured remains of the occupant with feelings of envy; for it was always a favourite theme to speak of the splendid arrangements that would attend on his own obsequies, and how much he would enjoy the procession on its way to the churchyard. Harry had very imperfect ideas of the future state; he was very decided about keeping clear of the nether regions, but equally resolved not to go to heaven, because the ministers sent "a' the puir fowk there, an' ye ken I never lik'it puir fowk," yet in many ways Harry was no simpleton, and could hold his own when any affront was offered him. One day, on entering the shop of one of the leading merchants of the town, and seeing him engaged talking with a stranger, he advanced in his usual over-familiar way, greatly to their annoyance. "Who is this?" asked the stranger. "Only a puir daft idiot," replied the merchant. "Na, na," said Harry, "it's yersel', min; ma faither wis a wise man, an' dee'd in's ain bed, but yours dee'd in an asylum." Harry knew a good deal more than was convenient for the merchant.

He had a curious habit when getting close to men—whether he knew them or not was all the same—by way of salutation, he began in the very best humour to pound each on the back between the shoulders with his fist, gentle at first, but harder and harder, until the sufferer called out, "O, liss, man!" when immediately the drumming ceased. Harry's anticipations of a grand funeral were realised through the kindness of David Brown, of Brown's Hotel.

JOHN COUPER,

Another worthy, was oftener in the "ale room" than was good for him. For a long time irregular in his habits, illness came upon him, and he lay dying tended by a kind sister. Rallying from a state of stupor, he asked that the pocket-book be taken from beneath his pillow, and the notes it contained exchanged for silver, which was done as quickly as possible, and the book put back to its place. After all was made right, his sister said—

"John, how are ye feelin' yersel' noo?"

"Juist wearin' awa'."

"Are ye no' a little better?"

"Ou, aye, but it canna last lang; it's awfu' unnat'ral."

"What did ye want wi' cheengin' the pound notes?"

"Siller's aye usefu'; it has ta'en me oot o' a' the ill scrapes ever I've been in."

"But if ye're no' expectin' tae get better, what gude can it dae ye?"

"Weel, I'm no sure whether I may tak' the richt road or the wrang. Siller's safer and aye usefu'."

John's sister, being an economical person, found "the siller aye usefu'," and allowed her lamented brother to take his chance of getting credit on his unknown journey.

A Quoit Club having been formed by a few of the merchants in town, about 1830, John Bruce gave a portion of his garden adjoining the "Whisky Roadie" for practising the healthful game, and on summer evenings many, through his kindness, were admitted to see the play.

An old woman, Candy Betty, who kept a small shop, near the old school, for the sale of candy and treacle beer, was frequently in trouble with her encroaching neighbours, and her shrill screeching voice went on steadily.

When Post Reid, the Town's Officer, failed to bring her to reason by a questionable application of the Queen's English, the last resort was a fierce explosion of Gaelic, which had the effect of silencing her.

"Smith Lamont" was another specimen of the belligerent native. One day he quarrelled with a customer, and they came out to the close to settle the matter by an appeal to the fists. "Posty" was at once informed of the affray, and, while endeavouring to separate the combatants, he received a dangerous kick in the abdomen, which, for a time, completely disabled him.

The severe pain caused him to howl piteously, and give utterance to all the doleful vocables of his native tongue. He was soon surrounded by many sympathisers of all ages, and a little girl, who became frightened at the result, ran home exclaiming, "Eh! mither, a wild man kickit Posty, an' he's greetin' in Gaelic."

The service of voluntary constables was instituted about 1840. Six householders took upon themselves the duties of guarding the peace each Saturday night, continuing from 11 p.m. to 3 a.m. By this plan a householder had only to act once a-year, and the town was saved a deal of expense.

George Constable was a wright in that shop now occupied by the Post Office (property still owned by his decendants.)

John M'Ritchie had also a wright trade in Mitchell Square, which is still carried on by his descendants.

Colin Mackenzie carried on a general trade in a building near the site of the Royal Bank.

Jeems Laird had an ale-house at the Royal Hotel pend.

Robbie Johnstone checked all merchandise at the weigh-house opposite 61 High Street.

William Davie (the elder) was an ironmonger.

"Laird" Forbes, a manufacturer in a small way.

Jeems Ross, printer.

William Robertson, bookseller.

William Culross, sawmiller.

William Cowan, wright.

John M'Nab had the ale-house "Dreadnought," where his curious sign may still be seen, &c., &c.

These, with other well-known characters of a bye-gone age, have passed beyond our ken; but familiar to this generation have been Robbie Porter, pawnbroker; Cripple Colin, with his wooden leg; Burlie Wull, the jail mason; John Jackson ("the General"), postboy; John M'Lachlan, the town bellman; &c., &c.

ABRAM LOW AND THE WELLTOWN BROWNIES.

Upwards of a hundred years ago, there was a small village named Welltown, about a mile south of Blairgowrie. Very little of it now remains, except some of the farm buildings, one part of which is in good repair, having above the lintel of the door a curious stone which has a peculiar history in connection with it. About the year 1730 there lived a blacksmith at Welltown, Abram Low (who also owned the farm). He was a very ingenious tradesman, and the stone is said to have been cut out by himself. He was generally believed by his neighbours to have obtained great wisdom from the fairies, and in his time it was a common saying, "I'll tell ye a tale of Abram Low and the fairies."

One night Abram was walking along the braes on his

farm, when they suddenly opened and showed him a company of these lightsome merry little elfins, with all the mirth and dancing imaginable, and they accosted him—

> " Welcome, welcome, Abram,
> For ever and for aye."
> " Never a bit," quoth Abram,
> "But for a night and a day."

And it is affirmed that during this night and day Abram got all his superior wisdom, which was discovered in answering the fairies at once and prescribing his terms. Their first word was their last, and according as they were answered, they held the stranger in estimation or not. So Abram became a great favourite with the fairies, and, it is stated, that he never needed a man to strike the forehammer. Having occasion to be from home one day, the journeyman asked him where he could get a man to strike the forehammer.

Abram whispered to him, " I'll tell you a secret, but you must not divulge it, nor speak to the two little men who will strike the hammer for you, as they won't bear to be spoke to, and if you in any way accost them we lose their service for ever. When you want them to come or want them to go, instead of speaking you must just give your hammer a purr on the studdy and they will start up and strike as long as you please; give your hammer another purr and they will disappear, but no words must be spoken." The foreman observed this rule throughout the day, and two little men, the one with a red cap and the other with a blue cap, started up and struck the hammer most powerfully. But, alas, for the faithless foreman! towards evening he exclaimed to his active assistants—

> " Weel strucken Red Cowl;
> Far better Blue."

They replied quickly, and disappeared never to return—

> " Strike here, strike there;
> We'll strike nae mair wi' you."

From that day the fairies departed from the Welltown for ever. Some time afterwards Abram Low had been dining with two trusty cronies—his brother lairds of

Carsie and Gothens. On his way home, alone, he bethought him to take a short cut, passing by the north side of the Black Loch. It was an eerie, lonesome place, covered with wood, and unfrequented save by smugglers and poachers. Night was coming on, and most men in those days gave such a place a wide berth. But Abram Low feared no one, and, as he passed along the gloomy solitude at the east end of the loch, he thought he saw, in the gathering gloom, a queer little object, with a blue cap on its head, sitting on the root of a fallen tree. Abram immediately recollected it must be Blue Cap, one of his long-lost fairies, and, forgetting the rule of silence, he shouted—" Hilloa, Blue Cap!" It was, indeed, Blue Cap, who, wroth at being recognised, replied, in an angry voice—

> " Blue Cap or Red Cap,
>   Whae'er I may be;
> Red Cap or Blue Cap,
>   Ye'll see nae mair o' me "—

Then vanished in the twinkling of an eye, and the fairy of the Welltown was seen no more.

Abram Low had a son named Isaac, who was a genius. For some time after the rebellion of 1745 there was a camp of English soldiery on the Muir o' Blair, hard by the Welltown, the soldiers under General Wade being engaged in the construction of the military road leading from Edinburgh to Fort George. Among the soldiers were several English tradesmen, and it is said Isaac was greatly indebted to them for insight to skilled workmanship. Nevertheless, he produced a very ingenious knife of goose dung. The plan he adopted was to collect all his filings of iron and steel, and mix them with leaven, which was given for food to the geese; then, preserving their dung and burning it, the steel came together in the forge. This knife he sent to London, with the following lines:—

> " I, Isaac Low, thee made
>   Of goose dung, heft and blade.
> O! London, for your life,
>   Mak' sic anither knife."

A Londoner attempted to make one like it, but Isaac,

not to be outdone, gave his knife a smart shake, and out sprung another knife concealed in the heft, and forced out by the heft, which made a spring that concealed it give way.

CHAPTER XI.

Sports, Pastimes, &c.—Angling—The Ericht as a Salmon River—Fishways on the Ericht—Fish Ladders for Loch Benachally—(Ardle—Blackwater—Ericht—Lornty—Lunan—Tay—Isla—Drimmie Burn—Fyall Burn—Lochs Benachally, Butterstone, Clunie, Marlee, Loch o' the Lowes, Stormont, Rae, Fengus, White, &c.)—Bowling—Cricket—Curling—Fair o' Blair—The Fair o' Blair 50 years ago—Football—Golf—Gymnastics.

ANGLING.

BLAIRGOWRIE as an angling resort is well known, situated as it is in midst of a famed fishing district where

"Salmon, trout, and pike abound
In loch, and stream, and mountain tarn."

On the 23rd March, 1840, a meeting was called for the purpose of forming an Angling Club in the district, which was numerously attended, and the Blairgowrie Angling Club was instituted. Rules for the management thereof were drawn up by W. S. Soutar, approved of and adopted.

The first competition of the Club took place on the rivers Ardle, Blackwater, and Ericht, which were divided into two sections each, and, drawing by lots for their fishing ground, gave each competitor fairness and justice, two members being spaced on each section.

According to the regulations, "the two members who shall respectively produce the greatest weight of trout at the annual competition shall act as Preses and Vice-Preses for the ensuing season."

At the Club meeting on 1st May, 1840, the members were enjoined "to prevent, as far as possible, the destruction of the parr, inasmuch as it is salmon fry in one of its intermediate stages previous to assuming the form and appearance of smolt; any member convicted of killing such shall be fined in amount as much as circumstances permit or may warrant."

The first annual competition took place on the 28th

June, 1840, when the greatest weight by two members was—

14 dozen trout,	=	17 lbs.
13 dozen trout,	=	16 lbs.

On the 1st May, 1863, David Cairncross presented to the Club a copy of his work entitled "The Propagation of the Eel, &c."

In 1878 it was resolved to have autumn competitions annually on Marlee Loch, all kinds of fish to count. However, as very few members turned up to compete, it was resolved at the annual meeting to enforce a rule, passed on 1st May, 1848—"that every member who fails to go out to the competitions shall pay a fine of one shilling," while on the 1st of May, 1846, it is recorded "that no member should be allowed to use a boat at the competition unless he worked the boat himself without assistance."

On the 3rd May, 1881, a proposal was made to hold an annual competition on Loch Leven, and on the 25th August eight members left for the loch at 4 a.m. A greater number of members would, no doubt, have joined in the competition had not this also been the day fixed for the grand review of Scottish Volunteers by Her Majesty the Queen at Edinburgh. The competition was considered very successful, 34 trout of 41 lbs. weight being taken, the heaviest basket weighing 9 lb. 12 oz. for 6 trout.

On the 24th May, 1882, James Crockart represented the Blairgowrie Club on Loch Leven at the National Angling Club's competition.

There are no records in the minutes of the doings or competitions, &c., of the Club from the 6th of May, 1882, up till the 18th of March, 1889, one sad mishap to the Club by the inattention and carelessness of an indolent Secretary and unworthy member of the Waltonian art.

The annual competition takes place about the middle of April, and the stream (open to any angler) and loch competitions about the middle of June; rule IV. providing that "the bait shall be fly, worm, or minnow, and all fish to be taken by rod and line and without assistance of any kind."

Various schemes have been made from time to time suggesting that the pike should be netted from Marlee Loch and it be formed into a trout loch on a plan similar to that of Loch Leven, but none of these schemes have come to anything.

The Ericht as a Salmon River.

The Ericht has always been noted for the variableness of its size, caused by the great declivity of its course and by the steepness of the hills where its branches have their source. In winter it comes down in terrible spate, while it summer it is nearly dry. In winter salmon spawn in numbers about and above the bridge, and in summer the river is swarming with parr, but from the state of the river an adult salmon rarely finds its way as far as Blairgowrie in the open season.

The first notice of the Ericht and its salmon fishings is contained in a Charter, granted by Robert the Bruce to the monks of Coupar Angus Abbey, and is as follows:—

"Carta Roberti I. regis Deo, Sanctae Mariae, &ca., de Cupro, nos de gratia speciali dedisse licentiam iisdem monachis piscandi et capiendi Salmones temporibus per statuta nostra prohibitis vicunque voluerint in piscariis suis aquarum de Thay, de Yleife, de Arithe . . . ad vsus proprios et pro potagio antedicti, &c. 5 Maii, 1326."

This document may be translated thus:—"Charter of Robert 1st, King through God, to the Holy Mary, &c. We, of our special favour, have given permission to the same monks of fishing for and taking salmon in times, prohibited by our statutes, whenever they wish, in their fisheries of the waters of the Tay, the Isla, the Ericht . . . to their own proper uses, and for the soup of the aforesaid convent."

In 1446 Drimmie was let for eighty salmon yearly, along with "arriage and carriage."

About the year 1750 the Duke of Athole was in the habit of coming to Blairgowrie to enjoy the pleasure of salmon fishing. On one occasion, when he had secured many fish, he sent the bellman through the town announcing that each inhabitant might have a salmon by coming to the house he stayed in.

In an old rental-book of the estate of Craighall the

following entry occurs:—"Charge Hawgh Cropt, 1750. James Falconer, Alexander Kinlock, M. Chapman, and Isack Low of Waltown, pays for ye salmon fishing £20 with 20 salmon fishes yearly." The rent was computed in pounds Scots, and amounted to £1 13s 4d of sterling money. These gentlemen seem to have held the fishing till 1754, and during their lease they never paid any rent.

In 1755, Invercauld took the fishings at the same rent, and paid the money part of it for some years. His rent, however, of 20 salmon was never paid. Invercauld was tenant of the Craighall salmon fishings till 1770.

In 1804, 336 salmon and 1 trout were taken by one haul of the net out of a pool near Erichtside Works. A fortnight afterwards 110 salmon were secured. The pool, which does not now exist, having been destroyed by the great flood of 1847, commenced near the northern extremity of Erichtside Works and continued down to the Skermy Tree (a plane tree which grows on the Welton Road, about 400 yards below the Bridge). From that point a croy extended obliquely across the river to divert the water to the lade which drove Cairncross' mill, nearly on the site of the Ashgrove Works.

The Keith, with the rocky gorge immediately below the waterfall, was a favourite scene of salmon netting. Where the river widens out into Powntrail and the Skellies, the salmon were only caught with the rod; but in the narrow and deep part immediately above, hand-nets on poles were used. About thirty yards below the waterfall, on the Rattray side of the river, there is a bay known as the "Kleice Kirn," which juts into the rocky bank. It was a favourite place with the salmon.

From 1740 to 1830 the Ericht was a very fine stream for rod-fishing. The salmon taken in the Ericht are not large. The heaviest ever known to have been captured in it weighed 24 lb., and was taken by James Crockart, the gunsmith. One weighing 18 lb. was secured in 1867, and another of 16 lb. was taken out of the Dookin' Hole above the Bridge of Blairgowrie, on the Rattray side. The average size of the fish was from 8 lb. to 10 lb.

The old fishers seem to have been a peculiar lot of men, and were equally ready to use the rod, net, or leister. There were Wully Bruce—a particularly good caster; Jamie Fenton, Peter Souter, and Rattray of Coral Bank. Of a later generation were Archie Irons, Samson Duncan, and Geordie Strachan; and of a still later race were Dr Rattray of Coral Bank and James Crockart, gunsmith, who, in his day, was the most eminent fishing authority of the district.

Fishways on the Ericht.

In 1870, when Frank Buckland and Young inspected the salmon rivers of Scotland, they found the Ericht at Blairgowrie, which had once been a famous salmon river, entirely blocked up by impassable dams, of which there were no fewer than six in the course of about 2 miles of water. The uppermost was not an insurmountable barrier, but the second at Westfields was entirely impassable, being twelve feet in height, and quite perpendicular.

The fourth and fifth dams were much lower, and the sixth, immediately above Blairgowrie Bridge, presented no great obstacle to the ascent of fish to the upper streams if there had been enough water flowing over it; but the intake lade from it was, and is, at least 12 feet wide and 4 feet deep, and absorbs and carries off the larger proportion of the water in the river in a dry season. At such times, the fine spawning bed below the dam is quite dry, so that any spawn which may have been deposited on it is liable to perish for want of water. And so it happens between impassable weirs and scarcity of water that what was at one time one of the finest stretches of salmon water in Perthshire is now absolutely unproductive, though about the former productiveness there can be no doubt whatever: for, about the middle of the 17th century, when salmon angling did not bring in a tenth of what it now does, part of the fishings between the highest and lowest weirs at Blairgowrie brought in a rental of £138 6s 8d, and there was a fishing lodge attached; and even so lately as 1835 they were worth £164 17s. There is much fine spawning ground on the Ericht above Rattray Bridge, and still more on its chief tributaries, the Shee and the Ardle; so that now, as the Tay District Board, with the consent and co-operation of the manufacturers at Blairgowrie, have constructed ladders, on the Macdonald system of fishway building, upon the impassable weirs at Westfields and Ashbank, it is to be hoped that the fishing, in course of time, in the Ericht and its tributary streams, may be restored to what it was about a hundred years ago, when the minister of the parish of Rattray wrote:—"Sportsmen look upon the Ericht as one of the finest rivers for rod fishing, both for trout and salmon;" and the parish minister of Blairgowrie:—"From the Keith for about two miles down the Ericht there is the best rod fishing to be found in Scotland, especially for salmon."

In the summer of 1884, the Tay Board, with commendable energy and enterprise, brought over Colonel Macdonald from the United States (whose system of fishway building has been adopted by the Government of that country, a grant of 50,000 dollars having been voted by Congress for placing Macdonald fishways on the great falls of the Potomac river, which are upwards of 70 feet high), who, during his visit to Perthshire, carefully inspected the impassable dams on the Ericht at Blairgowrie, and furnished plans for enabling salmon to surmount them, and these plans were fully carried out. In October, 1884, the completed fishways were inspected by the Tay District Board; Young, Inspector of Salmon Fisheries; several of the manufacturers of Blairgowrie; and Young, C.E., Perth, Col. Macdonald's representative and agent in Great Britain. Certain improvements were made by Col. Macdonald on the three lowest weirs with the view of concentrating the flow of water, and so facilitating the ascent of salmon; but the chief interest centred in the fishways which were placed on the inaccessible weirs at Ashbank and Westfields—the former ten feet and the latter 12 feet perpendicular—these being the first fishways of the kind ever placed on absolutely insuperable obstacles in a salmon river in Scotland.

When inspected, both ladders appeared to work beautifully when filled with water, and though the gradient of that at Westfields is so steep as 4·75 horizontal to 1 perpendicular, and the gradient of that at Ashbank is still steeper, being 4 horizontal to 1 perpendicular, both were filled with black and comparatively smooth water; whereas passes with so steep a gradient constructed on any other system of fishway building which has hitherto been applied in Scotland would have been filled with a mass of foaming white water, which no salmon would have been able to face. The cost of the improvements on the three lower weirs and of the Macdonald fishways at Ashbank and Westfields was about £400.

About half-way between the highest and lowest weirs there is a rapid or cascade on the Ericht where the river chafes and frets along between masses of rock, forming a series of fine pools and streams once famed as favourite haunts of salmon.

Fish Ladders for Loch Benachally.

In the Industrial Museum, Edinburgh, there are two model designs, by James Leslie, C.E., for a ladder for passing fish into Loch Benachally, proposed in 1870, but which has not been constructed. The first design is to accomplish the purpose intended by having a series of steps, with holes at the bottom, which are regulated by sluices in such a manner as to keep the difference of level of water on each side of steps constant; the velocity through the hole under stop will therefore be constant also, and if it be not greater than the velocity at which a fish can run, it is evident that they can pass into the loch by means of these holes. When the water in the loch falls to the level of the water in the first compartment, the first sluice is drawn full up and the water is regulated by the second sluice, and so on. The second design is intended to accomplish the same object by leaps and pools, the divisions between the pools being formed of stop planks, which can be taken out as the water falls in the loch. The upper division has a moveable sluice in front to regulate the water flowing over the stop planks.

The following are the principal fishings in the neighbourhood :—

The Ardle,

A first-rate trouting stream, which flows down Strathardle and, joining the Blackwater at Bridge of Cally, forms the Ericht. The Ardle is 11 miles long, and is generally open to all anglers. Some parts about Cally,

Blackcraig, and Woodhill are preserved, The trout average ¼-lb., but occasionally a 1-lb. trout is met with in the deep pools. From May to September is the best season.

THE BLACKWATER

Is a capital trouting stream, and May, June, and August are the best months. The trout run from 3 to 4 to a lb., and 10 to 20 lbs. may be caught in a good day. The whole of the Blackwater is open to the public.

THE ERICHT,

Formed by the junction of the Ardle and Blackwater at Bridge of Cally, flows down Glenericht for a course of about 10 miles and falls into the Isla at Coupar Grange. The whole river is open to the public, except opposite Craighall and in the policies of Glenericht. The best months for the Ericht are May up to September. On the upper reaches the trout run about 3 lbs. to the dozen, and on the lower reaches from 4 to 6 lbs. to a dozen. The lower parts do not fish well after May; but from the end of March up to that time 1-lb. trout are not at all uncommon, and sometimes a few of 2 lbs. or 3 lbs. are to be met with in the early summer with minnow. They are of the very best quality, and lovely shape.

Formerly the Ericht was a good salmon river, now salmon seldom come up save to spawn when they generally meet their death among mill wheels and other obstructions. It is said that as many as 300 salmon have been taken out at one shot from the Boat Pool of the Ericht, near the Bridge of Blairgowrie. Salmon are often killed in the lower part of the river after the nets have been taken off the Tay.

THE LORNTY

Rises in Loch Benachally, and, after a run of about 7 miles, falls into the Ericht about a mile above Blairgowrie. It contains good burn trout, about 4 to a lb., and fair baskets are often made. The best time is from April to September.

THE LUNAN

Rises in the Grampians, and flows through the lochs of

the Stormont, and, after leaving Marlee, has a run of about 4 miles, and falls into the Isla. It is all open to the public, and contains capital trout, which run heavy, about an average of 1 lb., while some may be got heavier. With a strong south-west wind ruffling the surface, good sport may be had.

The Tay

Is the chief salmon river of Scotland, and from an angler's point of view it is a magnificent river. It affords fair sport in spring and splendid sport in autumn, but in summer it is hardly worth fishing. The fishings are, however, all in the hands of the proprietors, from whom leave may sometimes be got.

The Isla

In its upper reaches is a first-rate trouting stream, and lower down salmon and heavy trout frequent it, but both are dour to rise. The trout in the lower reaches are of very fine quality, and run from $\frac{1}{2}$-lb. to 2 or 3 lbs., and, from the nature of the stream and feeding ground, they come into condition early in spring.

Drimmie Burn

Is a small stream, about 4 miles north, and contains trout, though of a very small size.

Fyall Burn

Also contains trout of small size.

Loch Benachally,

A good little loch for trout at the back of the hill of same name, is about three-quarters-of-a-mile long and half-a-mile broad. June and July are the best months. The trout run about 4 to a lb., and from 10 to 15 lb. is a good day's work. Permission to fish is usually given to anglers.

Loch Butterstone

Contains perch and pike, but few or no trout, and is about three-quarters-of-a-mile long by half-a-mile broad. About 20 lbs. of all sorts is a good basket. Permission to fish is necessary.

Clunie Loch

Lies about half-way between Blairgowrie and Dunkeld, is about three-quarters of a-mile long and half-a-mile broad, and contains pike and perch. Spoon bait and phantom minnow are the baits mostly used.

Marlee Loch, or Drumellie,

Is about 1 mile long and half-a-mile broad, with the river Lunan flowing through it. The Loch holds pike and perch, and trout of large size and fine quality, running from 1 to 4 lbs., are occasionally got with fly during the summer months.

Loch of the Lowes

Is about $1\frac{1}{2}$ miles long and half-a-mile broad, and contains pike, perch, and some heavy and very shy trout. Pike have been killed 30 lbs. and perch 4 lbs., and they take well all the summer season. A large peacock fly is a favourite bait, and phantom and spoon bait also do well. The perch are of excellent quality, and so are the trout; but the latter are rarely got save when netting for pike.

Stormont Loch, or Loch Bog,

Is about 2 miles in circumference, and contains large pike and perch. July and August are the best months, and spoon and phantom minnow are the best bait.

Rae Loch, or Loch of the Leys,

Contains perch and pike.

Fengus Loch

Contains perch and pike of fine quality, but not very large size.

White Loch,

Connected with Fengus Loch by a small stream, contains trout. It was netted in 1889 by one of the proprietors, and all perch and pike removed. The greater half of it is, however, preserved.

Black Loch, Monksmyre, Haremyre, and Saint Lochs

Are dark, sluggish lochs, containing pike and perch, but

seldom fished owing to the weeds. June, July, and August are the best months.

BOWLING

In the district can be traced back to the year 1554, when it is recorded that "Laird Drummond of Newton and his son were playing at the ba' att ye hie mercait green ₋o' Blair," at the time they were foully set upon and assassinated.

For several years previous to 1868 many endeavours had been made to get a Bowling Club formed in the town, but all efforts had been futile until by an advertisement in the "Blairgowrie Advertiser," of date 8th February, 1868 :—

"Blairgowrie and Rattray Bowling Club. The Committee will meet in the Royal Hotel, to-night, at 8 o'clock. All friendly to the movement are requested to be present."

At that meeting, attended by a number of proprietors, feuars, householders, &c., of Blairgowrie and Rattray, it was unanimously agreed to form a Club. After considerable trouble and delay a site was chosen at the west end of Lochy Terrace, and a bowling green and croquet green were formed, with walks around the same and with ornamental borders of flowers and shrubbery; a bowl-house was also erected at the east end of the green.

The ground embraced in the bowling green, &c., is about 130 poles. The green was opened on the 15th Aug., 1868, when the first game was played and heartily enjoyed by the members, and, on the 2nd of July, 1870, the first match with a foreign Club was played—Blairgowrie v. Spittalfield—resulting in a win for Blairgowrie by 28 points.

That the early bowlers were of a sympathetic nature may be inferred from a match played in September, 1870, on behalf of "the sick and wounded;" the defeated players had to forfeit 1s and the victors 6d, and at the close of the game 21s 6d was handed to the Treasurer on behalf of the sufferers.

CRICKET.

This purely Anglo-Australian game has been played in

Blairgowrie for a long number of years. It was instituted in 1867 by a number of gentlemen in town, mostly professional men. The ground was at the Welltown Rifle Range, where the game was played for several years; and their first match against the Meigle House C. C. was a decided victory of 7 wickets and 4 runs. At intervals Club succeeded Club until it was becoming a subject of history that no Club could outlive a season or two. In 1879 the promoters, in resuscitating the Club after it had been dormant for a few years, felt that the old difficulty of acquiring a field had to be met. By the kindness of W. A. M'Intyre, the "Haugh Park," which is the most convenient in the neighbourhood, became the local battlefield. In the beginning of 1881 a large piece of ground in the centre of the park was returfed in a highly-satisfactory manner, and is now one of the best pitches in the kingdom. In August, 1882, with the assistance of their lady friends, the Club got up a fancy fair, which realised a considerable sum, and put the Club in a more secure financial position.

For some years past it has been in the management of a younger generation, who have been very successful. The cricket "pitch" is beautifully situated.

CURLING.

The early records of the Blairgowrie Club are amissing, but the game of curling seems to have been a favourite winter pastime in the district over 170 years ago. The Rev. Mr Lyon (minister of the parish from 1723 to 1768), was so fond of curling that he continued to pursue it with unabated ardour even after old age had left him scarce strength enough to send a stone beyond the hog score; and on one occasion, having over-exerted himself in the act of delivering his stone, he lost his balance and fell on his back. Some of the bystanders ran to his assistance; and, in the meantime, one of the party placed the stone he had just thrown off on the centre of the tee. While still on his back, the minister eagerly enquired where his stone was, and being informed it was on the tee, exclaimed, "Oh, then! I'm no' a bit waur!"

A minute-book of the Club, containing records previous to 1783, is said to have been lost; but there is recorded in the minute-book of the Club, for the years 1796 to 1811, a reply to a challenge, which had evidently been sent from Coupar Angus to Blairgowrie, and is as follows:—

"To the Reverend Thomas Hill, Coupar Angus—The Curling Society of Blairgowrie present their respectful compliments to Mr Hill, and will do themselves the pleasure of meeting eight of the Coupar Society on the Loch Bog in terms of their challenge. Blairgowrie, Thursday forenoon, ten o'clock, 1784."

The minute-book of the Club has been very carefully kept by the different Secretaries from the time of James Duffus to that of the present one, James D. Sharp.

Blairgowrie and Delvine Clubs both claim an interest in the set of ancient stones, which had formerly been in the keeping of Blairgowrie, but presented or sold to the Delvine Club, in whose custody they have been for many years:—

"The Soo" measures $16\frac{1}{2}$ in. by 11 in., and weighs 79 lbs.
"The Baron" ,, $14\frac{1}{2}$ in. by 14 in., ,, 88 lbs.
"The Egg" ,, 17 in. by 12 in.. ,, 115 lbs.
"The Fluke" ,, $12\frac{1}{2}$ in. by 11 in., ,, 52 lbs.
"Robbie Dow" ,, 9 in. by 9 in.. ,, 34 lbs.

The last and least was called after one of the Baron Bailies, a son of the parish minister of the time. They were doubtless all taken in a natural state from the famous Ericht channel, and did a good deal of work in the hands of their strong masters; one peculiarity of them being their double handles. A metrical account of these and others is found in John Bridie's centenary ode:—

> "In early years the implements were coarse;
> Rude, heavy boulders did the duty then,
> And each one had its title, as 'the Horse,'
> One was the 'Cockit Hat,' and one 'the Hen,'
> 'The Kirk,' 'the Saddle,' 'President,' and 'Soo,'
> The 'Bannock,' 'Baron,' 'Fluke,' and 'Robbie Dow.'"

The rules of the Blairgowrie Club were framed in 1796 by the Rev. James Johnstone, minister of the parish (the President), and a Committee. An annual dinner is the first thing to receive attention in the rules, and this seems to have been of great importance. Members who sent an apology and did not dine were fined sixpence. Those who neither sent an apology nor came to dinner were afterwards fined one shilling, and as this did not secure a full attendance, a fine of half-a-crown was imposed on all absentees.

"The utmost harmony and conviviality," according to the common entry in the minutes, prevailed at these gatherings.

All were not eligible, for the rule as to membership was this:—

"No person can be admitted a member of the Society unless recommended by one of the members as a person of good character, who has formerly played on the ice."

But notwithstanding this protecting clause, it was still thought necessary to enact the following:—

"Rules for the Regulation of the Members while on the Ice and in Society.

"No member, while on the ice and in Society, shall utter an oath of any kind, under the penalty of two pence, toties quoties.

"No brother curler shall give another abusive or ungentlemanlike language when on the ice and in Society, or use any gestures or utter insinuations tending to promote quarrels: otherwise he shall be liable to be fined for the same at the discretion of the members then present."

The "utmost conviviality" mentioned above was scarcely consistent with the following rules as to the quantities of drink to be consumed on special occasions:—

"The members, when playing among themselves in a birled game, shall not spend more in a publick-house upon drink than sixpence each for one day. If, however, a regular challenge is given and accepted by one class of curlers to another, the expense on such an occasion may amount to but not exceed three shillings each to the losers, and the gainers half that sum."

Most of the earlier minutes record sundry fines for failing to observe the rule that each person "shall be bound, within three months from the date of his admission, to provide himself with two curling-stones, which must be approved of by the Society; or in case he fail to do this within the above period he forfeits five shillings that the Society may herewith provide stones for him, and he shall not be at liberty to carry them away as they are understood to belong to the Society."

A supply of stones, "not less than three dozen," was also provided and kept in repair at the expense of the Club. These were got from the Ericht when it was "in ply," and the work of finding them does not seem to have been very easy, for it is recorded on 15th July, 1799, that a Committee, at the command of the Preses—

"Proceeded up the water of Ericht, and they have to report that they found and laid aside a considerable number of stones out of which eighteen or twenty very excellent curling stones may be picked, and the Committee request, as they have been at considerable pains in searching out the stones, that another Committee should be named to bring them home."

The cost of "handling" them after their home-coming may be reckoned from the following account:—

To boring 24 stones, ...	£0	9	0
To handling do. with iron, ...	1	4	0
To lead, ...	0	2	6
To sorting the jumpers for boring,	0	2	0
	£1	17	6

An inventory of these stones is now and then recorded in the minute, and at one time their number is put down at "fourteen dozen." They would appear for a long time to have been protected by no covering, but simply to have been kept together by a chain. In the beginning of the 19th century, however, a house was erected for them at a cost of twelve shillings and elevenpence, from which cost four shillings fell to be deducted as "the price of the old chain sold." In 1819 a stone-and-lime house was built for £7. This was used also in 1859-62 as a magazine for volunteer ammunition. In 1881 a brick house was built, at a cost of £50.

No information is given in the earlier minutes as to the form of play; but in this the rink generally consisted of eight, and was presided over by a "director."

"Grips" were used for footing in delivering the stone, and Rule 8 prescribed that

"No member shall be seen on the ice as a player without a broom, under the penalty of twopence stg."

Prompted by a sympathetic spirit, the Blairgowrie Curlers, in their early years, organised "a charitable fund" for the benefit of members requiring occasional relief and for "other charitable purpose." The "fund" only continued for a few years, but while it lasted it seems to have done good service.

On the 25th July, 1838, Thomas Coupar represented the Club at a meeting of Curlers, in Edinburgh, in order to perpetuate and connect more closely the Brotherhood in the ancient national game. The outcome of this meeting was a Club, composed of different initiated Clubs of Scotland, formed under the name of the "Grand Caledonian Curling Club," latterly changed to "The Royal Caledonian Curling Club."

On the 25th January, 1841, on the way to Marlee Loch, where he and other members of the Blairgowrie Club were to compete for the point medal (a competition which originated at Duddingston in 1809), Mr Anderson, banker (President of the Club), remarked that he should not be surprised to see the greatest duffer carry off the trophy. "After a keen and exciting contest," says the Club minute of that date, "the medal was won by Mr Anderson, by a majority of one shot."

In the Royal Caledonian Club "Annual" for 1842 there is an account of the origin of the Blairgowrie Club :—

"In the course of 1782 an inhabitant of Coupar Angus, 'white-headed Jamie Cammell,' having occasion to be in Edinburgh in the prosecution of his trade as cattle-dealer, went out to Duddingston to see the play of the South-country brethren. During the game a very difficult shot occurred, on which all the curlers present tried their skill and failed; and Mr Campbell, having remarked that he thought he could take the shot, was invited to try, which he did and was successful. He afterwards continued to play during the remainder of the day with the Duddingston curlers, who were so pleased with his skill in the game that they invited him to dine with them, and initiated him a member of the Club by communicating to him the "word" and "grip." On his return to Coupar Angus he initiated the members of his own Club, from whom the Blairgowrie Club received the sign and secret in the following year."

The members of the Blairgowrie Club would appear to have been "initiated," though the above tradition finds no record in the Club's minute.

The London "Standard" of Wednesday, 6th October, 1883, thus commenced an editorial:—

"Blairgowrie is not in itself one of the most notable of Scottish towns, but it possesses a famous Curling Club, and this Club, according to a semi-official announcement, has just entered on the second century of its existence. Long before Sir Walter Scott had discovered the Highlands—in the days when a Celt in a kilt was considered as equivalent to a cattle thief, and when not one Englishman out of fifty thousand had ever heard the name of the place—the Perthshire villagers resolved to form a Club for the better pursuit of what Burns long afterwards designated 'the roaring game.' And ever since, so long as there was ice enough, the weavers of the Ericht braes have continued to play 'bonspiels' and add to their fame by feats of 'inringing' and 'rebutting.'

"In these days of ephemeral associations, which are no sooner formed than they begin to wane, the fact of a remote Scottish town being able to keep alive a curling meeting for more than a century speaks well for the good fellowship of the burghers."

On the 24th January, 1891, at the Annual Provincial Curling Match on Stormont Loch, Rink No. 1 Blairgowrie, skipped by J. D. Fell, won the silver jug, with a majority of 26 over the opposing rink.

The Ardblair Curling Club

Was in existence some fifty or sixty years ago, and reckoned among its members many keen and worthy curlers. Oft did the woods around Black Loch resound with their uproarious mirth. But, alas! the old Club is no more.

On the 30th of December, 1891, ten prominent gentlemen belonging to Blairgowrie and Rattray met within the Rectory, Blairgowrie, and formed themselves into a Curling Club—The Ardblair Curling Club. The Club owed its existence to the fact—the first in the annals of curling—of the expulsion of the Chaplain (Rev. F. W. Davis) from the Rattray Curling Club for "doing his duty."

The new Club started under the most favourable auspices. While scarce seven months old it numbered 35 members, and possessed fourteen trophies in silver cups, medals, &c.

P. K. Blair Oliphant of Ardblair and his lady became Patron and Patroness, with I. Henry-Anderson, S.S.C., as President, and the Club was kindly granted permission to use for curling purposes the two Muirton Ponds on the estate of Ardblair. On the death of his father, in 1892, Captain P. K. L. Oliphant became Patron. The Ardblair Club was admitted into the Royal Caledonian Club on 20th July, 1892.

The 4th of January, 1893, is a day to be long remembered by the Club. On that day, for the first time in its history, the Ardblair Club met a foreign foe on foreign ice (Stormont Loch), to compete for possession of the silver jug belonging to the Association of Clubs embraced in the Province of Strathmore. Twenty rinks entered the competition. Playing against the gallant curlers of Newtyle, for the honour of the Club and their own credit's sake, the Ardblair curlers carried off the trophy of the day by a majority of 13 points.

> " . . . The game is lost and won,
> And mighty deeds the Ardblair men have done
> Recounted are at night that table round,
> Where toasts, and mirth, and song, and glee abound.
> Again and yet again their shots they counted o'er,
> The guards, the wicks, the tees, they each had made,
> From time the *stoney* war began—to time
> When final stone by skip was laid and played.
> They ran the great encounter through and through,
> From gun to gun, from prime to final shot;
> Wherein they spake of most disastrous chances,
> Of moving accidents by snow and ice,
> Of hairbreadth 'scapes i' the imminent deadly breach,
> And portance in their first great foreign war."

Out of three Caledonian medals played for, the Ardblair Club has won two, which is exceedingly creditable.

John Panton. W. A. M'Intyre. Dr R. Lunan. John Bridie. J. D. Fell.
David Grimond.
BLAIRGOWRIE CURLERS IN 1888

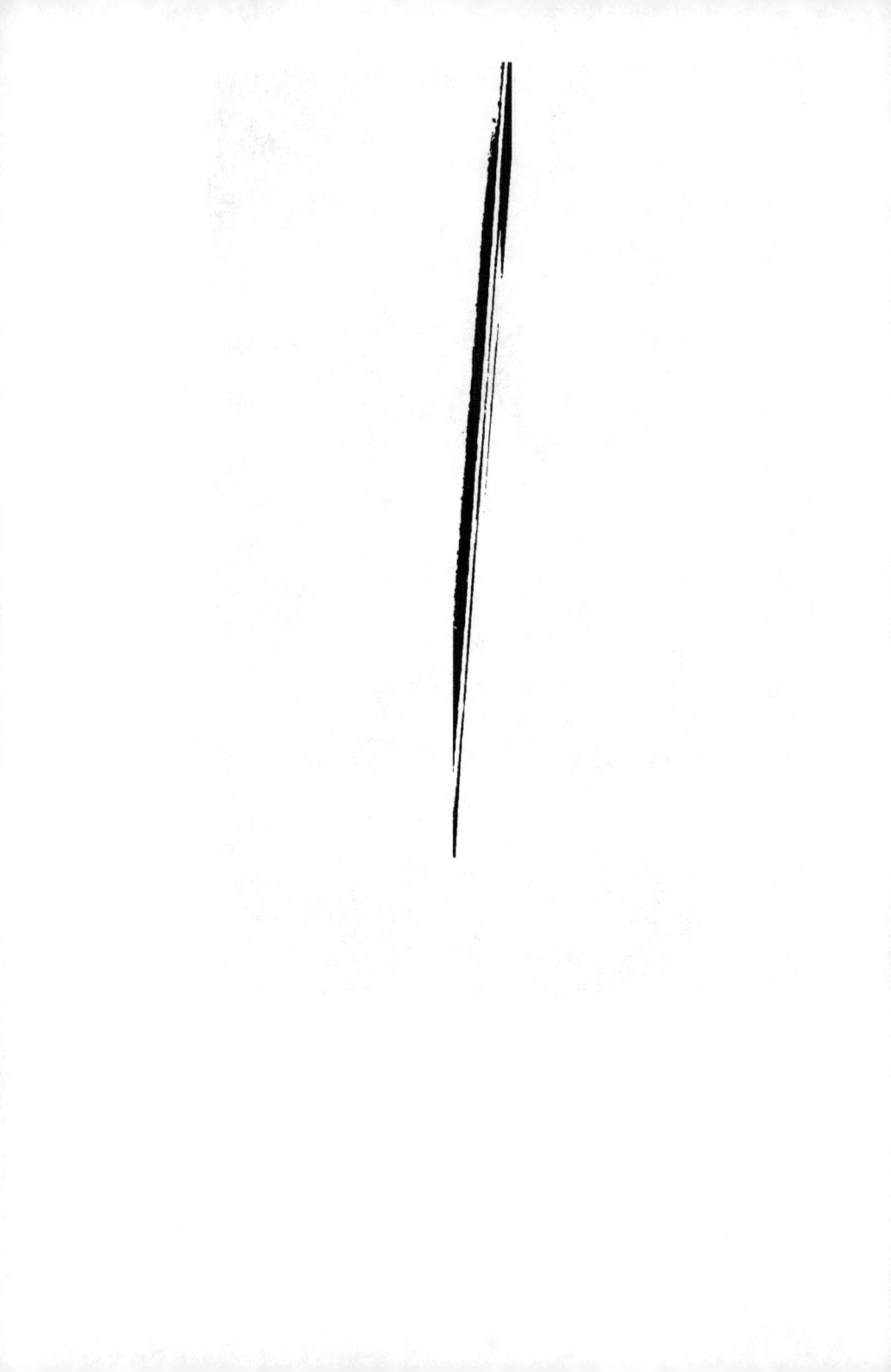

Cycling.

This favourite exercise is very much practised here, as elsewhere, by old and young of both sexes. Previous to 1875 the type of machine for the road was "the boneshaker" velocipede, which is now out of date. A Cycling Club was formed in the town in 1884, William Robertson being chosen first Captain, a position he held for nearly a decade. "Runs" are gone in for during the season, more especially on Thursday afternoons, to the neighbouring towns and places of interest.

In 1894, a union was formed with Alyth, Meigle, Newtyle, Coupar, and Blair, for the annual championship of the Strathmore District and a silver cup; the team from each section to be four in number, selected from among the members after test races, and the final race (of 16 miles) to count by points. Blairgowrie has won the cup on several occasions. The Club is in a very flourishing condition.

Fair o' Blair.

On the 1st of July, 1890, a public meeting of the inhabitants of Blairgowrie was held in the Public Hall, convened by the Baron-Bailie, to discuss and arrange the midsummer holidays. As the Dundee holidays fall to begin the last week of July, and the spinning mills of Blairgowrie are in dependence of those of Dundee, it was agreed that the holidays in Blairgowrie should begin on the last Saturday of July, and that the Annual Fair, formerly held on the 23rd of the month, be shifted to and held on the last Tuesday of July, which has continued to this day.

The Fair o' Blair Fifty Years Ago.

On the 23rd July the annual Fair o' Blair was held, but, however stirring a time it may appear to a younger generation, those who can recall this great day 50, or 60, or 80 years ago are apt to make comparison generally in favour of the "good old times." Then, from early morn, happy parties of all grades and in all sorts of conveyances were to be seen driving into the town from every quarter, while crowds of pedestrians thronged the roads. For days before the 23rd indications of some approaching gala day began to be manifest. Wandering hucksters of all sorts put in an appearance and appropriated the best sites for their stalls and fixtures. The great centre of attraction was the Wellmeadow, which at that time was a meadow covered with grass and possessing a well of pure spring water, both of which have now disappeared.

Down the eastern side of the Wellmeadow a row of whisky tents was pitched so close to each other that there was scarcely room to pass between. Behind, and next to the roadway, were the "sweetie stands," which were continued right up both sides of Allan Street and Leslie Street.

All sorts of merchandise were offered for sale, and the trade done on that day was a sufficient inducement to bring a "gingerbread man" from Kirkcaldy with his edible wares. The general briskness of trade was shared in by all the shops in the town, a liberal share, perhaps, falling to the dozen or so of public-houses which surrounded the Wellmeadow in addition to the whisky tents.

By noon the scene was of the most animated description, among the outstanding features being the white tents — the dark swinging mass of cattle — the bright dresses of the farm servants — the well-conditioned and sonsy farmers bargaining with the shrewd, canny cattle-dealers, and examining and judging cattle — swing boats and merry-go-rounds manned by jolly youngsters — with shows, cheap jacks, bawling balladmongers, scrapers of cat-gut, acrobats, &c.

During the day the special constables were always on duty, and scarcely found their office a sinecure, more especially toward nightfall. The rough manners and language of those days were the natural outcome of hearty life and labour, of outspoken frankness, and other qualities which those of a later generation, in view of their advanced condition, do not give too ample evidence.

The times are changed, and we change with them, and thus it shall always be. The young will prefer their own times, while the old people will aye dwell with most pleasure upon the recollections of their youth.

This has been a popular game since the days of John Ross, ye minister of Blair (1603), who proclaimed it from the pulpit in 1620, and afterwards joined in a game on the Sabbath with the players.

One day John Ross repudiated a Royal mandate by Charles I.:—"After divine service the people be not discouraged by dancing, either men or women, leaping, vaulting, or having May games, Whitson ales, or merry dances, or setting up Maypoles, and other sports therewith used," &c.

It seems then to have been the habit to hold their weekly market at the "kirke stile." With those John Ross had to do battle; but he found that his denunciations from the pulpit did little good.

"Weel, John, gin it wirna the day it is, what wad ye be seekin' for yer brockit quey?"

"Bein' the day it is, I canna tell ye; bot if ye wir tae offer me fourty shillin' the morn, I wad lat ye ha'e her."

"Weel, weel, I'll send the morn aboot it."

"Aye, aye, that will do, then, Jeems."

While this and such-like work was going on at the kirk stile, on the Sabbath, among the "auld folks," there was a game going on by "A Young Men's Association for the Promotion of Ba'-playin' on the Sabbath-day," to which, as soon as the blessing was pronounced, the indefatigable minister hasted to rout.

Levitically qualified, and of great muscular power and nerve, physically he had nothing to fear; morally, he had already, if not wounded some, made several heavy thrusts at them. Having divested himself of his sacerdotal robes, and put on his "guid un'erstanin's," staff in hand he cleared the market-place, and straightway proceeded to the ball-ground. His appearance quickly dispersed the hypocrites, while there remained a number who seemed resolved to stand by their "institution." The minister, on his part, determined if not to break its legs at least to peel the members' shins, thrust his staff into the ground, doffed his coat and hung it thereon along with his hat, and thus addressed that personification :—

> "Stand ye there,
> Minister o' Blair,
> Till I, John Ross,
> At the ba' get a toss."

To John Ross it was a matter of indifference in arranging as "to sides" who were his partners, as, win who might, he should make some good play, and so the game went on, John assuring his partners of his determined purpose to play well, while the other party were resolving to do their best for victory. The battle having begun, John Ross was at his post and played well. Not one opportunity did he let escape of missing the ba', and inflicting a merciless kick at the nearest rival—in fact, he broke through all the rules of the game, kicked right and left, chasing the cowards and hunting them down until he completely cleared the ground, having "routed them hip and thigh."

The first football club was formed in Blairgowrie in 1878. In April, 1881, "Our Boys" was formed, and was admitted to the membership of the S.F.A. Between other clubs in the district the matches were of an exceptionally keen nature, till the institution of the Perthshire Football Association in 1884-85, when Our Boys entered for the County Cup. In the 2nd XI. Perthshire competition in 1893-94, the 2nd XI. of the Club won the 2nd XI. county trophy. The Club held practice for some years on ground at the Haugh, then at Altamont Lane, removing to the South Haugh Park, and latterly to Cleekerinn. The 1st XI. of the Club was fairly successful during its existence, played some important matches with foreign Clubs, and was several times in the semi-final for the Perthshire Cup.

A Golf Club

Was formed in the district in 1889, and a course of about 60 acres laid out in the Muir of Blair, of nine holes, under the superintendence of the veteran Tom Morris, of St Andrews, who gave it as his opinion that "the Lansdowne Course was one of the best inland greens in Scotland."

The course is about $1\frac{1}{2}$ miles from Blairgowrie and half-a-mile west from Rosemount Station.

There are two splendid pavilions, with all conveniences,

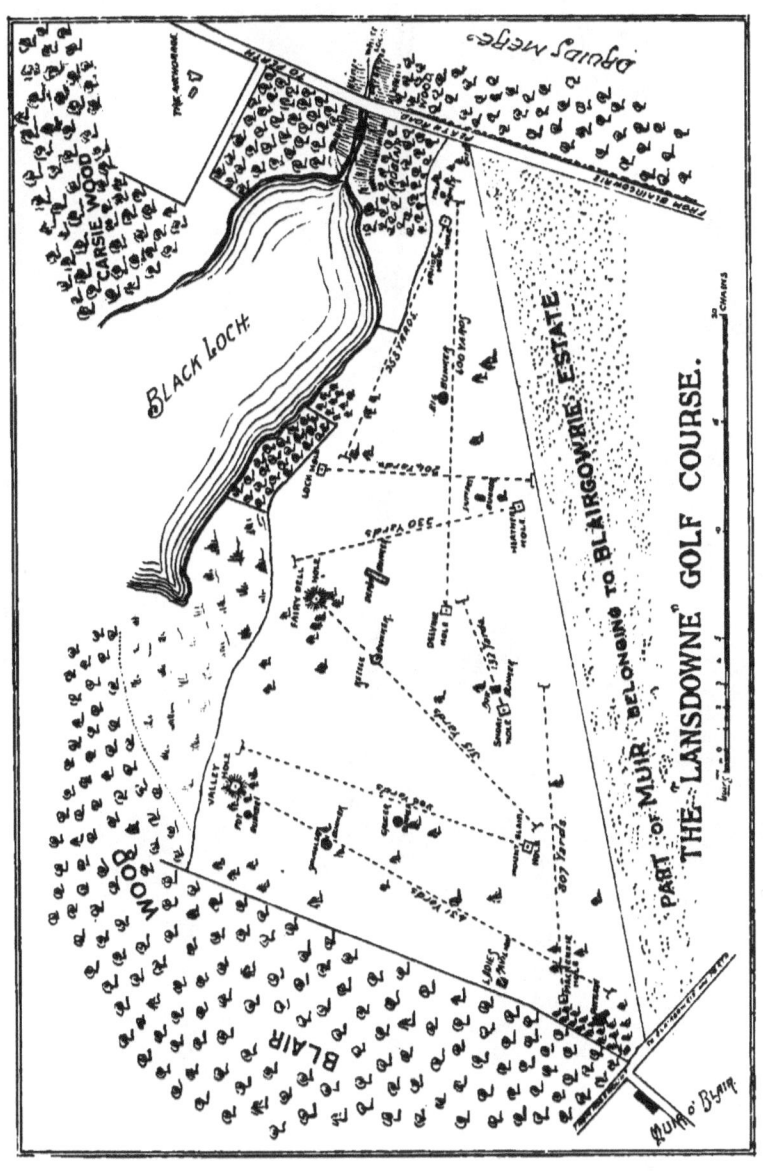

for the use of members, and the greens are beautifully placed. The membership is large, and many valuable trophies are annually played for.

The Gymnastic Club

Was formed in the winter of 1893 as the outcome of the evening continuation classes in Rattray Public School. In course of the season 1895-96, the Club entered the Dundee and District Junior Gymnastic Association, and while very creditable results have been obtained, the coveted honour is still out of their reach. This is accounted for principally from the want of a resident Instructor. E. M'Inroy, the present Instructor, comes from Dundee once a-week to instruct the members. They practised at first in Rattray Public School, afterwards in the Public Hall, and now in the Volunteer Drill Hall.

CHAPTER XII.

Eminent Men, &c.—Drummond of Newton—George Drummond—May Drummond—Blair of Ardblair—Mercer of Meikleour—Admirable Crichton—Thomas Graham (Lord Lynedoch)—Rattray of Rattray and Craighall—Grimond of Lornty—Professor Adams—Rev. John Baxter—Macpherson of Blairgowrie—Allan Macpherson—Dr James Neilson—Alexander Robertson—William Geddes—David C. Robb—John Bridie—Dr Robt. Lunan—Thomas S. Bisset—John Panton, &c.

DRUMMOND OF NEWTON.

THE family of Drummond of Newton is undoubtedly of great antiquity, but the race is now extinct in the district, their descendants being known by the name of Drummond of Blair Drummond. The family is traditionally traced to a Hungarian nobleman, who fled to Scotland in 1068, with Edgar Atheling, to avoid the hostility of William the Conqueror.

Sir William Drummond was knighted by James II., and died 1455. George Drummond and his son William were murdered in 1554 at the Paroche Kirke of Blair (see page 37). In 1634 George Drummond received charter from King Charles I. erecting Blairgowrie into a Burgh of Barony. A special lustre attaches to

GEORGE DRUMMOND,

Who was born at Newton Castle, 27th June, 1687. Receiving his education at Edinburgh, he was requested by the Committee of the Scottish Parliament in 1705 to examine and settle the national accounts preparatory to the legislative Union of the two kingdoms. In 1707 he was appointed Accountant-General of Excise. He fought at Sheriffmuir in 1715, and was the same year elected to a seat on the Board of Excise. In 1717 he was appointed one of the Commissioners of the Board of Customs, and elected Treasurer of the City of Edinburgh. From 1722-23 he was Dean of Guild, and in 1725 he attained to the dignity of Lord Provost. He was named one of the Commissioners and Trustees for improving the Fisheries and Manufactories of Scotland in 1727, and one of the Commissioners of Excise in 1737. He was one of the chief promoters of the Royal Infirmary of Edinburgh, and laid the foundation-stone in 1738. He took part in the '45, joining the Royal forces under Sir John Cope, and was present at the battle of Prestonpans. In 1752 he was appointed one of the Committee for the improvement of the City of Edinburgh. In 1753 he was Grand Master of the Freemasons in Scotland, and laid the foundation-stone of the Royal Exchange. In 1746 he was elected a second time Lord Provost, a third time in 1750, a fourth time in 1754, a fifth time in 1758, and a sixth time in 1763, in which year he laid the foundation-stone of the North Bridge. He died 1766, and was interred in Canongate Churchyard, where a monument has been erected to his memory. The inscription is as follows:—

> To the memory of
> GEORGE DRUMMOND, ESQ.,
> One of the Honourable Commissioners
> of His Majesty's revenues of
> Customs and Excise in Scotland
> and
> Six times Lord Provost
> of the City of Edinburgh,
> who died the 4th day of December, 1766,
> aged 79 years.
>
> This monument was erected
> by Archibald Drummond
> of Rudgeway, Esq., his eldest son,
> 1797.

This energetic individual was most strenuous in his support of religion and literature; was a member of the "Select Society," which contained among its members all the illustrious Scotsmen of the age.

To him the University of Edinburgh was indebted for the institution of five Professorships, viz.:—Chemistry, Theory of Physic, Practice of Physic, Midwifery, and Rhetoric and Belles Lettres. A few years after his death, the Managers of the Royal Infirmary placed a bust of Drummond by Nollekens in the hall of the building, with the following inscription written by his friend Dr Robertson, the historian:—"George Drummond, to whom this country is indebted for all the benefits which it derives from the Royal Infirmary."

During Provost Drummond's life, and especially when he was engaged in the preliminaries of founding and funding the Royal Infirmary, he was largely assisted by an eccentric sister—May Drummond—who adopted the tenets of Quakerism, and occasionally made tours through the kingdom, preaching to the people, who flocked in great multitudes to hear her, and so noted did her addresses become that Queen Caroline at length condescended to listen to one. In the "Scots Magazine" of June, 1773, is a poem written on a picture in which May Drummond of Newton was represented in the character of Winter—

> Full justly hath the artist planned
>   In Winter's guise thy furrowed brow,
> And rightly raised thy feeble hand
>   Above the elemental glow.
>
> I gaze upon that well-known face;
>   But, ah! beneath December's frost
> Lies buried all its vernal grace,
>   And every trait of May is lost.
>
> Not merely on thy trembling frame,
>   Thy wrinkled cheek and deafened ear,
> But on thy fortunes and thy fame
>   Relentless Winter frowns severe.
>
> Ah! where is now the innumerous crowd
>   That once with fond attention hung
> On every truth divine that flowed
>   Improved from thy persuasive tongue?
>
> 'Tis gone!—it seeks a different road;
>   Life's social joys to thee are o'er;
> Untrod the path to that abode
>   Where hapless Penury keeps the door.
>
> Drummond! thine audience yet recall,
>   Recall the young, the gay, the vain;
> And e'er thy tottering fabric fall,
>   Sound forth the deeply moral strain.
>
> For never, sure, could bard or sage,
>   Howe'er inspired, more clearly show
> That all upon this transient stage
>   Is folly, vanity, or woe.
>
> Bid them at once be warned and taught—
>   Ah, no!—suppress the ungrateful tale—
> O'er every frailty, every fault,
>   Oblivion, draw thy friendly veil.

The Admirable Crichton

Sir George Drummond, Lord Provost

Thos. Graham

Hon Mrs Graham

> Tell rather what transcendent joy
> Awaits them on the immortal shore,
> If well thy Summer's strength employ,
> And well distribute Autumn's store.
>
> Tell them, if virtue crown their bloom,
> Time shall the happy period bring,
> When the dark winter of the tomb
> Shall yield to everlasting Spring.

Provost Drummond's daughter was married to the Rev. John Jardine, D.D., one of the ministers of the Tron Church, Edinburgh, and was the mother of Sir Henry Jardine, at one time King's Remembrancer in Exchequer for Scotland, who died 11th August, 1851.

Blair of Ardblair.

The family of Blair are now extinct in the district. They were a branch of the family of Blair of Balthayock, descended from Alexander de Blair, who flourished in the reign of William the Lion.

William Blair was an Abbot of the Monastery of St Marie, at Coupar Angus, in 1430. In 1554 John Blair of Ardblair was the chief instigator of the murder of George Drummond and his son William, and one Patrick Blair of Ardblair was beheaded for his share in it. Sir Thomas Blair had the honour of knighthood conferred on him by Charles I. Rachel Blair of Ardblair was wife to Dr Joseph Robertson. Their only child, Christina Robertson, married, in 1795, Lawrence Oliphant of Gask (brother of the celebrated Lady Nairne), one of whose descendants now owns the estate.

Mercer of Meikleour.

Sir Andrew Mercer received a Charter for the Barony of Meikleour in 1440, and died 1473. His son, Sir Laurence, had a safe conduct to England from Edward IV. in 1473. Sir Henry Mercer was killed at the battle of Flodden, 1513, and regarding his son, Laurence Mercer, there is an inventory of his stock registered 26th May, 1581—"Twenty-two ky, each at £6; a bull at £3 6s 8d; seven young calfis at £1 each; and fifty drawand oxen at £8 each."

There is also in the glebe stocking of James Mercer,

minister of Clunie, included in his inventory in 1656, "a cow valued at £18."

Colonel William Mercer died June, 1790, had a daughter, Jane, who married Viscount Keith, a distinguished naval commander. They had an only child, Margaret Mercer Elphinstone, born 1788. She married, in 1817, the Count de Flahault de la Billarderie, in France, a General in the army of Napoleon I., and French Ambassador at the British Court in 1861. (This lady was granddaughter of the Hon. Robert Nairne, second son of Lord William Murray, 2nd Lord Nairne. John, the 3rd Lord Nairne, was attainted for his allegiance to the Stuarts in 1745, but the title was restored to his youngest son, William Murray Nairne, by Act of Parliament, 17th June, 1824. On the death of William, 6th Lord Nairne, without issue, 27th December, 1837, the title became extinct.)

The daughter of the Count de Flahault, Emily Jane Mercer, born 1819, was declared heir to the title of Baroness Nairne (dormant since 1837) by the House of Lords, 1874. She married in 1843, Henry, 4th Marquess of Lansdowne, in Ireland, and died 1894. The estate is now possessed by their son, Lord Fitzmaurice, 5th Marquess, at one time Governor-General of Canada.

ADMIRABLE CRICHTON.

The family of Crichton of Clunie, and Eliock in Dumfries, was collaterally descended from Murdoch, Duke of Albany, third son of Robert III., and uncle of James I.

James Crichton was born in the Castle of Clunie, 1560, his father being Robert Crichton, the Lord-Advocate of Scotland. He received his education at Perth, and at the University of St Andrews under the care of Professor Rutherford, his fellow-students being Buchanan, Hepburn, Robertson, and the future James VI. In 1572 he took his degree of Bachelor of Arts, in 1574 that of Master of Arts, and, before reaching the age of nineteen, had mastered ten different languages, which he could read and write to perfection. He practised the arts of drawing and painting, and improved himself to the highest degree in riding, fencing, dancing, singing, and in playing upon all sorts of musical instruments. At the age of twenty he set out upon his travels, first directing his course to Paris and then to Rome, where he disputed in presence of the Pope, and refuted every argument all the professors, masters, or doctors propounded to him. Arriving in Padua in 1581, the Professors of that University assembled to do him honour, and, journeying to Mantua, he challenged a prize-fighter who had foiled the most expert fencers in Europe, and who had already slain three persons who had entered the lists with him in that city. Crichton encountered his antagonist with so much dexterity and vigour that he ran him through the body in three different places, of which wounds he immediately died. The victor generously bestowed the prize—1500 pistoles—on the widows of the men who had been killed by the gladiator. The Duke of Mantua, struck with his talents and acquirements, appointed him tutor to his son, Vincentio di Gonzaga, a prince of turbulent disposition and licentious manners. One night, during the festival of the Carnival in 1582, while he rambled about the streets playing the guitar, he was attacked by six persons in masks. With consummate skill he dispersed his assailants and disarmed their leader, who begged his life, exclaiming, "I am your pupil, the Prince." Crichton immediately fell on his knees, and, presenting his sword to the Prince, expressed his sorrow for having lifted it against him, saying he had been prompted by self-defence. The dastardly Gonzaga, inflamed with passion or wine, plunged the weapon into his heart. Thus prematurely was cut off the "Admirable Crichton"—(for so was he named)—and his tragical end excited a great and general lamentation.

THOMAS GRAHAM (LORD LYNEDOCH).

Thomas Graham was born in Newton Castle, the family residence, in 1750. Succeeding to the estates of Newton and Balgowan, on the death of his father in 1766, he married, 1774, the Hon. Mary Cathcart, second daughter of Charles, 9th Lord Cathcart. From this period till 1792 he remained a private country gentleman, cultivating his two estates, indulging in classical studies and the enjoyment of elegant leisure. In 1792 his wife died, and his grief for her loss was so overwhelming as greatly to injure his health, and he was induced to travel. After visiting France he went on to Gibraltar and fell into the society of the officers of the garrison, and thenceforth determined on devoting himself to the profession of arms. Lord Hood sailing to the south of France, Graham accompanied him as a volunteer. In 1793 he landed with the British troops at Toulon, and served as extra aide-de-camp to Lord Mulgrave. On returning to Scotland he raised from among his own countrymen in Perthshire the first battalion of the 90th Regiment, of which he was appointed Colonel-Commandant, 1794. In 1794, 1796, 1802, and 1806 he was unanimously elected Member of Parliament for Perthshire, but was defeated in two contested elections of 1811 and 1812. In 1795 he was promoted to the rank of Colonel in the army. Obtaining permission, he joined the Austrian army, 1795, and continued in that service till the beginning of 1797. Attached to the Austrian army of Italy, he was shut up in Mantua with General Wurmser. During its investment, and the siege of the city continuing long and provisions getting scarce, a council of war determined that intelligence should be sent to the Imperialist General Alvinze of their desperate situation. This perilous mission Col. Graham volunteered to perform in person. Disguised as a peasant, he quitted Mantua on 29th December, and, after eluding the vigilance of the French patrols and surmounting numerous hardships and dangers, he arrived at the headquarters of General Alvinze at Bassano, 4th January, 1797. Joining his regiment at Gibraltar, he assisted at the reduction of the island of Minorca, and received high rewards from the King of Naples for his services in Sicily. From 1798 to 1800 he blockaded Malta, then held by the French, and obliged the garrison to surrender. The years 1801 and 1802 he spent in travelling through Europe. From 1803 to 1805 he served with his regiment in Ireland. In 1808 he acted as aide-de-camp to Sir John Moore in his unsuccessful mission to the assistance of the King of Sweden. He served in Spain during the campaign of 1808, and was in the disastrous retreat to Corunna. He was promoted in 1809 to the rank of Major-General; commanded a division at the siege of Flushing in the

Walcheren expedition, 1810; and was afterwards appointed to the command of the British and Portuguese troops in Cadiz, then blockaded by the French, with the rank of Lieut.-General. He was General in command, and defeated the French at the battle of Barossa, 1811, for which he received the thanks of Parliament, and was invested with the Grand Cross of the Order of the Bath, entitling him to the designation of Knight. In 1812 the siege of Cuidad Rodrigo was under his immediate direction; and in 1813 he commanded the left wing of the British army at the battle of Vittoria. During this year also he besieged and reduced San Sebastian. He commanded the left wing of the British army at the passage of the Bidassoa river. In 1814 he was appointed Commander of the Forces in Holland, and defeated the French at Merxem, for which he again received the thanks of Parliament. He was created a Peer of the United Kingdom by the title of Lord Lynedoch of Balgowan, but nobly refused a grant of £2000 per annum to himself and his heirs. In 1821 he was raised to the full rank of General; 1826, nominated Colonel of the 14th Foot; in 1834, removed to the Colonelcy of the Royals; and in 1829, appointed Governor of Dumbarton Castle. In his latter years Lord Lynedoch passed his time in Italy, but in 1842, when Queen Victoria visited Scotland for the first time, so anxious was he to manifest his sense of loyalty and his personal attachment to his Sovereign, that, though then in his 92nd year, he came from Switzerland for the express purpose of paying his duty to Her Majesty in the Metropolis of his native land. He died in London, 1843, when the title became extinct.

In the National Gallery of Scotland, the Mound, Edinburgh, is a full-length portrait of the Hon. Mrs Graham, and in the Catalogue is this notice:—

"Bequeathed by the late Robert Graham, Esq. of Redgorton, formerly of Balgowan and Lynedoch.—The Honourable Mary Cathcart, second daughter of Charles, ninth Lord Cathcart, was born in 1757, and died childless in 1792, after being married eighteen years to Thomas Graham of Balgowan, better known afterwards as Lord Lynedoch, one of the most daring of the heroes of the

Peninsular War. Inconsolable for the loss of his beautiful and amiable lady, the gallant Graham, at the age of 43, entered on the arduous and chivalrous career in which he achieved such high honours. He died in 1843, at the age of 94. After Mrs Graham's death, her husband, unable to look on her portrait, gave orders that it should be bricked up at the end of the room where it hung, and its existence was forgotten, and only discovered fifty years afterwards during alterations made on the house by another proprietor. It was exhibited in the British Institution in 1848, where it attracted very great attention, and again in 1857 at Manchester, among the Art Treasures, of which, by the general voice, it was pronounced one of the chief." (No. 304, by Gainsborough.)

On the 8th December, 1896, a monument to commemorate the deeds of the 90th (Perthshire) Regiment, raised in 1796 by Lord Lynedoch, was unveiled on the North Inch at Perth,

Rattray of Rattray and Craighall.

The Rattrays are one of our oldest families, and it is difficult to ascertain when first they settled in the district. It is assured that they were possessors of the Craighall estate before the reign of William the Lion, and long ere that owned the neighbouring barony of Rattray.

An old monumental slab above the doorway of the place of sepulture in the Rattray Churchyard bears date, "1066: Rattray of Rattray and Craighall."

It is certain that Alan de Rattrief lived in the days of William the Lion and Alexander II., his son, Thomas, being knighted by the latter sovereign. He got the lands of Glencaveryn and Kingoldrum with his wife Christian, the perambulation of said lands in 1250 being recorded in the Registry of the Abbey of Arbroath.

Sir Thomas left two sons, Eustace and John. In 1280 Eustatius de Rattrie gave to the monks of Coupar—"Omnenis habeo duarum Drimmies in tenements meo de Glenbethlac cum omnibus ritus." Adamus de Rattrie, son of Eustace, swore allegiance to Edward I. in 1292 and 1206, and in 1209 likewise gave to the monks of Coupar the third or West Drimmie.

The earliest existing charters of the Rattray family is a charter of inspexisse by Gilbert Hay, Constable of Scotland, dated at Dunkeld, 5th October, 1309, in which is recited a confirmation by King Robert Bruce, to the Abbot of Coupar, of all grants to the convent by Adam of Glenbathloch, of the lands of the two Drymmys, and of one by Eustace of Rattrief, dated at Dundee on Wednesday before the feast of St Clement, 1309, of right of commonty on said lands.

Adam died before 1315, and his son Alexander was one of the barons of Parliament held at Ayr in 1315, which settled the succession to the Scottish crown. Dying without issue, Alexander was succeeded by his brother Eustace, who was, in the Black Parliament held at Scone in August, 1320, charged with being accomplice in the conspiracy of Sir William Soulis and Sir David Brechin against the Bruce.

"King Robert summoned a convention, and because the vicissitudes of a long war had confounded the rights of property, he ordered every one to produce the titles by which they held their possessions. This demand was equally vexatious to the old as well as to the new; because brave men thought they held by the best right those estates they had taken by their arms from an enemy and the ancient possessors, as scarcely a house had escaped the calamity of war, had lost their written rights—if ever they had any—along with their other effects. They therefore took a bold step—bold in appearance, but desperate and rash in the result. When the King in Parliament desired them to produce their titles to their possessions, they all drew their swords, exclaiming that they carried their titles in their right hands. The King . . . concealed his anger for the time. Many of the nobility, conscious of the audacity of the action, entered into a conspiracy for betraying the Kingdom to the English. . . . Sir Eustace de Rattray, who, being invited to join with thes quho upon discontents against King Robert Bruce, conspyred to deliver him up to the King of England, refused, and quhen that treason was discovered, albeit they put in his name among the rest, yet his subscription and seal, being not found with the writ, he was cleared, quhen others that were found guiltie were punished. Sir David de Brechin and five other knights with three esquires, Richard Brown, Hammeline de Troupe, and Eustace de Rattray are the only persons whose names have come down to us as certainly implicated in the conspiracy. When the whole conspirators were apprehended a Parliament was summoned at Perth, where the letters were produced, and, every one's seal being recognised, Sir David de Brechin, along with Malherlie, Logie, and Brown, were convicted of treason by their own confession and executed. . . . Maxwell, Berklay, Graham, Troupe, and Rattray were also tried, but acquitted."

Eustace was succeeded by his son, John, who was also succeeded by a son of the same name. This latter died about the close of the reign of James I., leaving a son Patrick, who died in 1456, and was succeeded by his son, Sylvester, the most noted among his successors for generations, who in 1463 was appointed one of the Extraordinary Ambassadors sent to treat with Edward IV. about the affairs of the two kingdoms, and who negotiated with him the truce that was to last for fifteen years. By his wife, Alison Hepburn, he had a son, John, who was knighted by James VI., and married Elizabeth, daughter of Lord Kennedy. There were three sons of the marriage—John, Patrick, and Sylvester. On the 18th May, 1506, he was appointed Joint-Bailie of the Regality of Scone, with such salary and accommodation as were formerly enjoyed by Thomas Blair of Balthayock. John, who died in Holland in his father's lifetime, was an officer in the Dutch army, and, although married, left no issue.

The second son, Patrick, succeeded Sir John, and the only daughter, Grissel, became the Countess of John Stewart, 3rd Earl of Athole.

The following is an abstract from a copy MS. which refers to a disaster, which for a time marred the fortunes of the Rattray family of Craighall:—" Sir John Rattray quho was killed at Flodden (1513), with King James IV.; his eldest son called John had two daughters, bot he died before his father without heirs male. Always Sir John Rattray married for his second marriage Dam Elisabeth Kennadie, quho bar to him two sons, the one

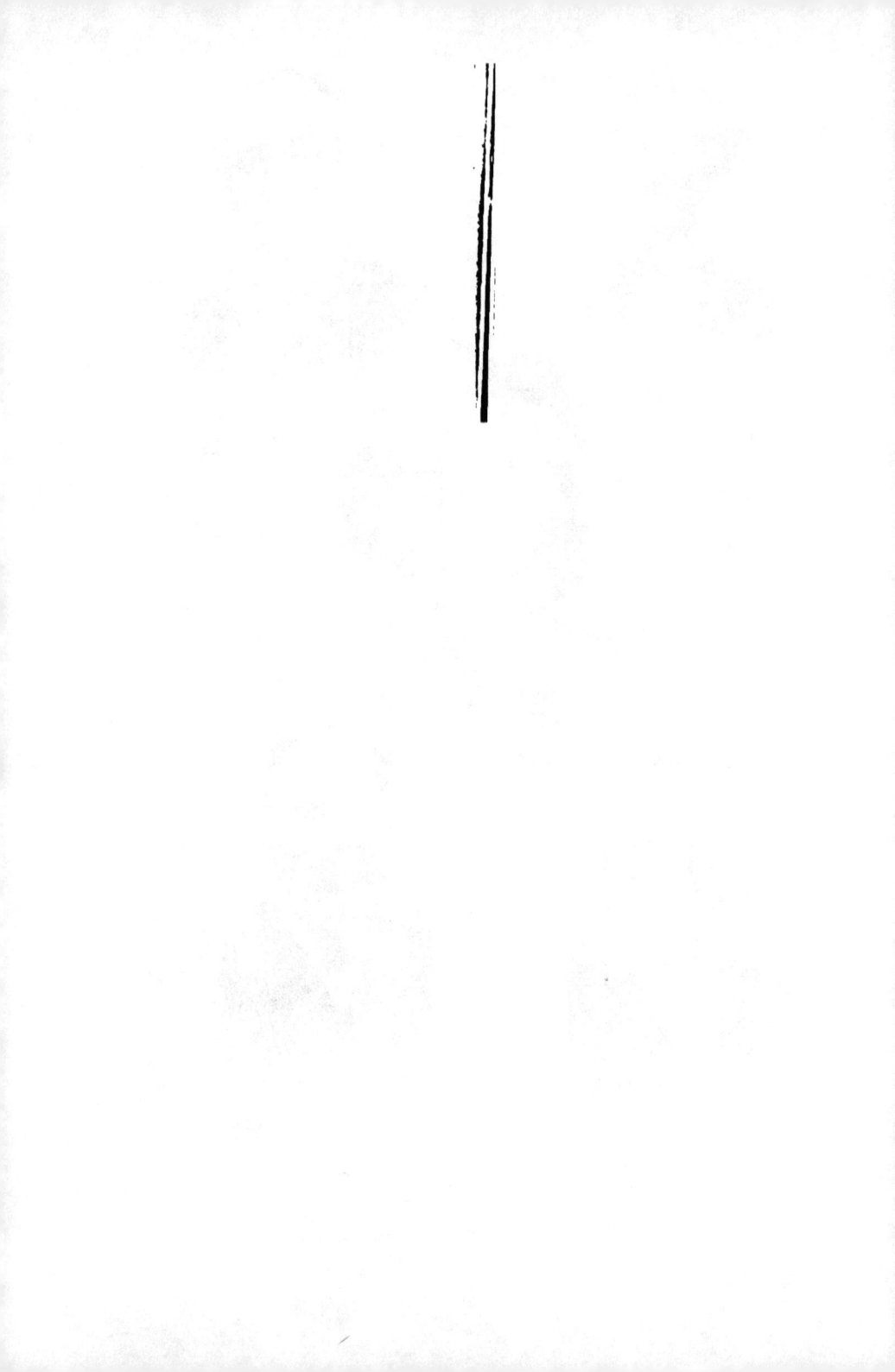

called Patrick, the other called Sylvester. Sir John Rattray being killed at Flodden, the Earl of Athol thought himself entitled to an equal portion of the estates of Rattray in right of his Countess, and this claim being resisted by his brothers-in-law, the Earl resolved to attain his end by force.

"Arraying a body of his clansmen, he marched down upon the castle of Rattray with the intention of carrying it by assault; Patrick, finding his few retainers unable to defend the place, made a timely retreat.

"The Earl broke into the old fortalice, ransacked and seized all the family documents on which he could lay hands. Also he took the two daughters, and married upon his son the oldest called Dam Grissell, and the other upon Sir James Stewart of Attemadies, in the north, and so possessed himself of the estate of Rattray and sundrie other lands belonging to that family."

This Dam Grissell had many children. Her son John was Chancellor of Scotland, and she had many daughters married to many honourable families.

"Dam Kennedie, for her and Sir John Rattray's sons, pleaded for the ryt of the lands of Rattray, bot they were overpowered by the Earl of Athol—the eldest, Patrick, being killed by the Leslies of Kinrorie (emissaries no doubt of the Earl of Athol), when he was building a strength of his owne securitie upon a rock that had bot on passage to enter be. Sylvester, the other son, got a warrant under the King's great seal to ye Lord Ruthven, Sheriff of Perth, to hold a court at Dundie (becaus of the Earl of Athol's power), when he was served heir to his brother and to his father, Sir John; but the Earl of Athol being Chancellor made out of the way the charter of Silvester Rattray, who could not recover his right oyet.

"This Silvester atteir with the Laird of Kinmonth of that Ilk assist and obtened by law the lands of Craighall and a fifth part of the barony of Rattray, becaus thes lands wer provyded to the children of Dam Elizabeth Kennadie by the said Sir John, whilk continue with that family till this day.

"At length, in 1533, Silvester petitioned the King for a commission to have the service completed at Dundee, narrating that for the space of 12 years he had been hindered from getting himself served as heir to his father's lands by the Earl of Athol and others, who slew his brother, Patrick Rattray, in the chapel of his house at Glenballoch, and he was informed that the Earl was meditating a similar fate for himself. The commission sought was granted under the great seal, 17th October, 1533, and the service accordingly took place under this special authority at Dundee. No proceedings appear to have been taken against Athol for the base part he acted, but the passing of the service at Dundee obviously brought about some amicable arrangement or compromise with him, for in December following, Grizella, Countess of Athol, granted a precept of clare constat in favour of Silvester Rattray as heir of Patrick Rattray, his brother, in the lands of Braidwalls and other parts of Rattray."

Next year Silvester was infeft at Dundee in the barony of Craighall and Kynballoch. He died in 1554, leaving two sons, David, his heir, and William. Both were implicated in the death of Robert Rollack, Polcolk, and David Donald, Grange, under circumstances which have not been recorded, but for which they compounded by money payment.

David had two sons, George, who lived to the beginning of the 17th century, and Silvester, who was minister of Auchtergaven and the ancestor of the Rattrays of Dalnoon.

In 1587 George Rattray of Craighall binds himself and his dependants "to serve the Earl of Argyle in all his actions and adoes, against al persons, the King's majesty only exceptit, and sall neither hear or see his skaith, but sall make him foreseen therewith, and sall resist the same sae far as in me lies, and that in respect the said Earl has given me his band of maintenance."

George succeeded his father in the reign of James VI. He was succeeded by Silvester, who was infeft in all his father's lands by a charter under the great seal 20th October, 1604. He died in 1613, and left two sons, David and Silvester. The latter, who was bred to the Church, was the progenitor of the Rattrays of Persie.

The elder son, David, did not long survive his father,

and left a son, Patrick. Upon his own resignation he got a charter under the great seal from King Charles I., of date 28th February, 1648, of the lands of Craighall, Kynballoch, and others, containing a novodamus and erecting them into a free barony to be called Craighall and Rattray for all time coming.

By his wife, Anne Drummond, daughter of John, 2nd Lord Madderty, he had a daughter, married to Ogilvy of Balfour, and a son, James, who also left a son, Dr Thomas Rattray, a man of singular piety and learning, who was served heir to his father before the Sheriff of Perth, 13th July, 1692. He was a Bishop of the Scottish Episcopal Church, and distinguished himself by his literary abilities, and especially by his writing on liturgical subjects. He married Margaret Galloway, daughter of Thomas, Lord Dunkeld, and died in 1743, leaving two sons and three daughters.

The eldest daughter, Margaret, married the celebrated John Clerk of Pennicuik, for four years President of the Royal College of Physicians, Edinburgh, and more than thirty years first medical practitioner in Scotland. He died in 1757. James Clerk, his eldest son, succeeded to the Clerk-Rattray estates in right of his grandmother, and assumed the surname of Rattray in addition to his own. He was an eminent member of the Scottish Bar, and was constituted a Baron of the Scottish Exchequer. He died 1831, and was succeeded by his son Robert, who died 1851, leaving four daughters and two sons—James, his successor (the present proprietor), and Adam, an officer in the Gordon Highlanders.

James Clerk-Rattray entered the army in 1851, and served with great distinction in the Crimean and Indian Mutiny campaigns, having been wounded in the Redan, and engaged in the relief and defence of Lucknow. In 1871 he was created a Commander of the Bath, and has held rank as Hon. Lieutenant-General since 1879. In 1897 he had the honour of knighthood conferred on him by Her Majesty the Queen. (See chapter XIV.)

GRIMOND OF LORNTY.

The family of Grimond have long been resident in the district. David Grimond was one of the pioneers of the flax-spinning trade. His brother, James Grimond, who died in 1862, was the first spinner Watt got to make trial of jute fibre. David Grimond of Oakbank was born at Lornty, in 1816, and received his education at Blairgowrie. His father dying in 1835, he succeeded him, and carried on a successful and extensive business. In 1843 he built Brooklinn Mill, and in 1862 he succeeded to the business of his uncle, James Grimond of Oakbank, with which mill his name was mostly associated. He was extensively known as an energetic, enterprising, and trustworthy gentleman. He died 18th June, 1889.

Joseph Grimond, fourth son of David Grimond of Lornty, was born in 1821, and received the rudiments of his education at the Parish School of Blairgowrie. While but a youth he entered the service of a company of cloth merchants in Dundee, and, after serving his apprenticeship, proceeded to Manchester, where he founded a business—one of the most successful and extensive in Scotland. Returning to Dundee in company with his brother, Alexander, he erected the Bowbridge Mills, which, with Maxwelltown Carpet Factory and Dyeworks, employ over 3000 hands. The newest machines and best appliances were constantly added, and the comfort and health of the work folks were always cared for as of prime importance. He established offices in London and New York for the sale of the varied productions of their looms; founded in Manchester an important industry for the manufacture of oil cloth for packing purposes; and to have a careful selection of the raw material, he visited Calcutta and established an office with staff for the purchase and selection of the fibre. In the course of his business he visited nearly every capital of Europe and America, and brought home some object of beauty and of interest. His leisure he devoted to his friends and his flowers. In politics he was an ardent friend of John Bright whom he knew and loved. He was for many years a Director of the North British Railway; a Deputy-Lieutenant for the County of Dundee; a Magistrate for Forfarshire, with residence at Kinnettles, and took a warm interest in the public business of the county. He died 2nd November, 1894.

Professor Adams.

David Laird Adams was a native of Blairgowrie, where he was born in 1837. He received the rudiments of his education at the Parish School, studying afterwards at the Church of Scotland Training College, Edinburgh, and at the University there. He also studied abroad, chiefly in Germany. Taking the degree of M.A., he acted for some time as teacher in Dollar Academy, Merchiston Castle School, and Anderson's College, Glasgow. Graduating B.D. in 1871, he was ordained to his first charge, St David's, Edinburgh, and in 1875 elected minister of Monimail, Fife. From 1874 to 1880 he acted as Examiner for the degree of B.D., and in 1880 was elected to the Chair of Hebrew and Oriental Languages in the Edinburgh University, which position he occupied till his death in 1892.

John Baxter, D.D.

John Baxter was born in Blairgowrie in 1800, receiving his education at the parish schools of Blairgowrie and Rattray; then in Dundee under Mr Campbell (afterwards Dr John Campbell of London); and subsequently at the Grammar School of Dunkeld under Mr M'Culloch (afterwards Dr M'Culloch of Greenock). He matriculated at the University of St Andrews, 1822-23, and took his M.A. degree in 1826; licensed by the Presbytery of Meigle in 1831, he was ordained to his first charge in Persie; transferred to Hilltown Church, Dundee, in 1838, "came out" with his congregation at the Disruption, 1843; and in 1858 accepted a call to the First Free Church, Blairgowrie, where he continued till his death in 1893. In 1881 he received the degree of D.D. from St Andrews University, and in 1887 was proposed for the Moderatorship of the Free General Assembly.

Macpherson of Blairgowrie.

This family is descended from Donald Macpherson of Noid (or Nuide), who in 1635 married Isabel, a daughter of Alexander Rose of Clova. They were the common ancestor of the following families of Macphersons, viz.:—Cluny, Ralia or Glentruim, Blairgowrie, Belleville, and Philadelphia.

ALLAN MACPHERSON.

Allan Macpherson, who was a Colonel in the East India Service, bought the estate of Blairgowrie in 1792 and built Blairgowrie House, dying in 1817. His son, William (born in 1784 at Barrackpore, near Calcutta), succeeded to the estate, and continued to reside at Blairgowrie House till 1829, when he left for New South Wales, having been appointed by Sir George Murray, then Colonial Secretary, as Collector of Inland Revenue for that Colony, from which he succeeded to other and higher appointments. He died 1866.

During the time he resided at Blairgowrie he took an active interest in the progress and advancement of the town and district, making himself very popular by many acts of kindness to the community, of which he was feudal superior. He gifted to the town the large market square known as the Wellmeadow, along with the market customs of the burgh, and the "Waulk Mill," besides other properties and privileges to assist the town's revenue.

Allan Macpherson was born at Blairgowrie House in 1818, and journeyed to New South Wales in 1829 with his father, and received his education in that colony. He came home in 1851, and returned in 1856 to New South Wales, where he resided many years. Being repeatedly elected representative of one of the divisions of the colony as a member of the Legislative Council, he took a leading part in the proceedings of that body.

ALLAN MACPHERSON.

In 1866 he became proprietor of the estate of Blairgowrie on the death of his father, and in 1869 took up residence in the family mansion. He was a Justice of the Peace and a Deputy-Lieutenant for Perthshire, and acted upon nearly all the executive Committees of the County of Perth. In politics he was formerly a Liberal, but latterly he became associated with the Conservative party. He died 6th November, 1891. In 1892 a memorial fountain was erected to his memory, by Mrs Macpherson and family, in the Wellmeadow.

JAMES NEILSON, M.D.

This gentleman was born in Blairgowrie in 1841, and received his early education in the Free Church School. After a distinguished academical career at Edinburgh University, he assisted Professor Simpson for some time, and afterwards was appointed resident surgeon of Maternity Hospital, and while there he took his degrees of M.D. and L.M., 1862. In that year he settled down in Blairgowrie.

In his professional capacity he had all the requisites for a successful doctor; his great skill in grappling with disease and his deep knowledge of the technicalities of his profession caused his patients to have unbounded confidence in him.

He took a deep interest in all that appertained to the moral and social advancement of the community. At the election of the first School Board he was returned at the head of the poll by a large majority; he was also Chief-Magistrate for more that one term. He was an ardent and pronounced Liberal. The assiduous attention which he paid to his very large practice, and the exposure to which he was at all times and in all weathers subjected, hastened his untimely death, 8th February, 1886.

ALEXANDER ROBERTSON.

This gentleman was born in Blairgowrie in 1813, and died in Edinburgh, 12th November, 1880. His father was originally a merchant and afterwards a banker in the town.

Having been educated to the law, he carried on an extensive and successful practice, as well as the agency for the Bank of Scotland. For many years he held the office of Town Clerk, in which capacity he was very useful to the burgh and the community. He was an active and available public servant, and took considerable part in all the local affairs of his time. As a speaker he was able and successful, and several of his happy public appearances are still remembered.

For more than twenty years he was President of the local curlers, and, by his skilful management and scientific playing, he was perhaps the means, more than any other, of bringing the Club into the proud position of one of the foremost, if not actually the most successful, in Scotland.

Of the 22 silver medals won by Blairgowrie a large proportion were gained under his renowned Presidency.

He was the principal promoter of the Blairgowrie Gasworks, and to him the town was largely indebted for enjoying this great boon of modern civilisation long before its neighbours.

He was one of the leading members of St Mary's Parish Church, and rendered much valuable service in connection with the building of the new place of worship.

He was a man of much tact and good sense. He had a generally well-stored and cultivated mind, and was of an agreeable, genial, and obliging disposition.

WILLIAM GEDDES.

This well-known artist was born in Blairgowrie in 1840, and was trained to the house-painting business, but the bent of his mind was always towards the Fine Arts, to which he assiduously devoted his leisure time and ultimately all his efforts. His early studies were of the genre class, mostly figure groups illustrative of Scottish life and manners, many of them containing fine touches of humour. To these and kindred subjects, still life and groups of trout and salmon, with an occasional landscape, his time and talent were devoted, and in some of these departments—notably those of fish painting—while he had many imitators, he had no rival. His genius was conspicuous in many directions; as a sculptor he would undoubtedly have excelled had he chosen, and he was possessed of literary ability of a high order. Socially he was a genial and brilliant spirit, original and sometimes eccentric, a clever mimic, and kindly-hearted fellow. His pictures were exhibited and admired for many years in Edinburgh and elsewhere. He died 31st October, 1884.

JOHN BRIDIE: FIRST PROVOST OF BLAIRGOWRIE.

David C. Robb.

This gentleman was born in Blairgowrie, 7th February, 1851, and was educated at the parish schools of Rattray and Blairgowrie. After completing a course of study at the High School of Dundee, he entered the University of St Andrews in 1866. Here he concluded a highly-successful curriculum by graduating M.A. in 1870, and at the same time gained by competition the much-coveted honour of being appointed Guthrie Scholar, the Scholarship being £250. From St Andrews he went to Worcester College, Oxford, where he graduated in due course, securing first class honours in Classics; but, though thus proving himself an excellent classical scholar, the bent of his mind led him towards natural science, and he selected Chemistry. In this new work he soon distinguished himself so much that he was appointed Assistant Professor of Chemistry, a post which he occupied for about seven years. In 1879 a translation of Pasteur's "Studies on Beer" was published for Frank Faulkner, of the Brewery, St Helens, under Robb's editorship, and at the time of his death he was similarly engaged upon Dr Landolt's work, "The Optical Rotation Power of Organic Substances." He possessed a superior knowledge of botany and natural science generally. He died 2nd June, 1881.

John Bridie.

This gentleman settled in Blairgowrie in 1855, and for over 30 years was identified with public life. In 1867 he became a member of the Town Council, and under the old regime he rose to the position of Baron-Bailie. In the Police Commission he was for several years a Junior Magistrate, then Senior Magistrate, and when the Act of 1892 came into force he obtained the title of Provost. In November, 1893, while re-elected a Commissioner he retired from the Provostship, and was re-elected Baron-Bailie. He took a hearty interest in everything connected with the welfare and happiness of the community, and devoted much time and thought to public business.

A discriminating judge of pictures—who could himself sketch and paint with no mean ability—he, for several years, criticised the Royal Scottish Academy Exhibition in the columns of the "Dundee Advertiser." To the local press he wrote much in the form of vigorous articles on current topics, happy paragraphs and graphic accounts of travel, and clever sketches. Of his poetical pieces several have obtained a well-merited place in the volume, published 1893, of Edward's "Modern Scottish Poets." John Bridie had a keen appreciation of the beautiful, and these varied qualities gave to the works of his hands grace and beauty, and among the best painters in Scotland he was respected. His genial temper and *bonhomie* made him friends everywhere, and he was altogether a man of wide and varied sympathies, and no question of human interest came to him amiss. He died 26th June, 1894.

ROBERT LUNAN, SURGEON.

DR ROBERT LUNAN.

After a highly-distinguished career at the University of Edinburgh, a few years' practice with his uncle, Dr Smith, Provost of Forfar, and a six months' voyage on board a whaler in Davis Straits, Robert Lunan came to reside in Blairgowrie in 1836, and from the first gave evidence of that energy and independent outspokenness which characterised everything he did ever after. In his early years he was one of the best rifle shots of the county, and succeeded in winning the £30 Challenge Cup for Fife and Kinross at the St Andrews Wapenschaw of 1862. In connection with his shooting exploits he had a splendid record, trophies of one kind and another having fallen to his lot at nearly every competition in which he took part. On one occasion when, with an ordinary Enfield rifle, he came very nearly beating the cracks with their Winchester rifles at Montrose, he was presented on his return with a rifle and case. On another occasion he was presented with a silver snuff-box, with a eulogistic inscription on a gold plate on it, from the ladies of the Stormont.

On the 22nd January, 1891, he had special honours paid him by the Blairgowrie Curling Club, of which he had then completed his fiftieth year as a member. He was entertained to a banquet in the Queen's Hotel, and presented with a massive silver dinner service, together with an illuminated address. The address spoke of the Doctor's "fifty-five years of unremitting attention to his professional duties, and the desire of the subscribers to recognise specially his unwearying kindness to the poor of the district, and the manner in which, without consideration of self, he had always been ready to devote his time and skill to those in distress." The tureen of the dinner service bore the inscription—"Presented to Dr Robert Lunan, Blairgowrie, by the public, as a token of the universal esteem in which he is held, and in grateful recognition of his valuable professional services, and his invaluable kindness to the poor during the last 55 years. Blairgowrie, 1891."

As a judge of violins Dr Lunan occupied a foremost place, and owned a splendid collection, including a valuable Gaspar di Salo. His opinion on the merits of a violin were highly valued, and the possessor of more than one valuable violin is indebted for it to the Doctor's discriminating judgment. He laboured for 58 years in Blairgowrie, and died 24th April, 1894, aged 82.

Thomas S. Bisset.

This gentleman was born at Marlee, near Blairgowrie, in 1839. After receiving the rudiments of education at the Parish School, he was trained to work in iron, and early in life he gave evidence of an intellectual interest and practical skill in mechanics. As the result of a visit to the Exhibition in London, 1862, he designed his first self-acting back-delivery reaping machine. In 1867 he patented the steel-lined fingers for reapers and mowers which are now used by every maker.

In 1868 he constructed a bicycle, and claimed to be the first maker and rider of these machines in Britain. In 1878 the firm, finding their premises at Marlee too remote from railway transit, acquired ground at Greenbank, and erected extensive buildings thereon for the carrying on of business. In this year (1878) the firm constructed their "Scotia" mower—the first machine with enclosed gear made in Britain—and in 1880 the now famous "Speedwell" was designed. In 1887 Mr Bisset commenced the manufacture of self-binding reapers, realising that they would soon come into general use. The perfecting and practical manufacture of these machines cost Bisset much labour and attention, but he had unlimited courage and perseverance.

He was for a number of years a member of Blairgowrie School Board, and took a keen interest in all branches of education. He died 27th August, 1896.

JOHN PANTON.

This gentleman was born at Blairgowrie in 1834, his father, William Panton, being overseer for many years on the Blairgowrie estate. Receiving his education at the Parish School, and choosing the law as a profession, he served his apprenticeship in the offices of Duncan & M'Lean, Perth. Returning to Blairgowrie, he commenced practice along with Dallas, writer, but the partnership was of short duration. From this humble start his energy soon developed itself, and he extended his operations in every direction. He was appointed factor on Blairgowrie estate in 1855, and retained the office till his death.

JOHN PANTON.

In 1857 he opened a branch of the Royal Bank at Millbank House (transferred to present buildings on their erection in 1872). His law offices, in connection with the Royal Bank, were the centre of a wide and varied activity, the moving spirit of which was "The Factor." This term was the usual form in which he was addressed, and arose from the large number of properties he was agent for—Blairgowrie, Bamff, Parkhill, Glenericht, Drumore, Coupar Grange, and Clayquhat estates, &c. He was agent for the Royal Bank; a Director and Valuator of the Royal Insurance Society; Director of Blairgowrie Gas Company; Director of Westfields Spinning Company; Chairman of Blairgowrie Water Commission; a County Councillor, Parish Councillor, and member of other bodies. He engaged in extensive concerns as maltster at Blairgowrie Arbroath, Craigie, Perth, Stirling, and other places; and carried on a successful cattle mart in Blairgowrie.

He bought the estates of Dalnagairn in Strathardle; Inchmartine (2800 acres) in the Carse of Gowrie; and Buttergask (1250 acres), and Carsie in Strathmore. He also farmed Blacklaw and Gormack. He rented the extensive sheep grazings of Glenfernate, Dalmunzie, and Old Spittal of Glenshee. He was one of the leading partners in Newtyle Chemical Works; was Superior of Rattray; and owned a large number of properties in Blairgowrie, Perth, Glasgow, &c.

In 1868 John Panton took an active part in the political campaign which broke up the Tory yoke in the shire. In recent years business rather than politics occupied his brain, but his sympathies and his vote were in the Conservatives' favour. He was for long a Free Churchman, but a good many years ago he joined the Established Church, of which he was a regular attender.

As a solicitor a large share of the business of the district fell into his hands, and, in difficult arbitrations and in the management of trust estates, his skill and strong common sense made him an indispensable adviser. In the midst of his extensive and varied business John Panton found time for much kindly social intercourse. He was a keen curler and a genial friend, and was ever inspired by a simple desire for the public welfare and the general good. He died 29th September, 1898.

Of whom shall I further write? To sketch shortly the lives of the worthy citizens—natives of the town and district—would fill a volume alone.

James Anderson of Bleaton (1797-1868), solicitor and banker.

George B. Anderson, son of the former (18 -1868)—a banker and popular Captain of the Volunteers.

John Baxter of Ashbank (1799-1869)—flaxspinner.

John Bisset of Marlee (1808-1890)—farmer and agricultural implement maker; the founder of the world-famous firm of Bisset & Sons, makers of reapers and mowers.

David Brown of Thorngreen (1800-1865)—lessee of the principal hotel in town, then Brown's Hotel; proprietor of a coach, "Braes of Mar," which ran between Perth and Braemar; who also ran stage-coaches to Coupar Angus and Dundee; carried on distilleries at Blairgowrie, Ballied, and Pitcarmic; and farmed Marlee, Thorngreen, Grange of Airlie, Auchteralyth, besides having sheep grazings in Inverness, &c.

Peter Chalmers (1799-1887) of Gowanlea—for over fifty years leader of psalmody, first in the Parish Church and afterwards in First Free Church.

Robert Cowpar of Falcon House (1822-1887), J.P.—a distinguished officer in the service of H.M.E.I. Company, rising gradually from Ensign to honorary rank of Lieut.-Colonel; who farmed Wester Essendy, Drummellie, and Cottarton.

William Culross, native of Welltown (1798-1889) wood-merchant.

James Leslie, the Thorn (1808-1894) (after whom Leslie Street is named)—a very successful breeder of black polled cattle.

Jacob Low, of Welltown (1809-1883)—an extensive sheep farmer in Queensland, and for several years member of the Legislature.

William M'Farlane (1854-1886)—journalist, occupied important positions on the staff of the "Scotsman," on the press in China and Japan, published a book on Chinese character, which was much appreciated, sub-editor of the "Portsmouth Times."

James Peters (1766-1860)—appointed first postmaster in Blairgowrie about 1810.

William Robertson (1810-1879)—bookseller, who set up the first printing press in the town about 1838.

James Ross (1789-1875)—bookseller, started in 1855 the first newspaper in town, under the title of "Ross's Compendium of the Week's News."

James Struth (18 -1894)—began life as a mill lad, with a natural bent for mechanics fostered by his employers, rising step by step until he was chief of one of the largest and best jute industries in India.

Peter M'Intosh (17 -1831)—spinner, the first to introduce spinning by machinery into the district.

Thomas Clark of Heathpark—publisher in Edinburgh.

William S. Soutar—solicitor and banker.

James Crockart—angler, gunsmith, and a crack rifle shot.

James Chalmers of Boglea (18—-1897) J.P.—draper, farmer, and Provost of Blairgowrie.

William Craigie (1821-1897)—slater, Town Councillor, &c.

Thomas Mitchell of Greenfield (1820-1884) — draper, Baron-Bailie.

William Panton of Maryfield—farmer and maltster.

George Saunders (1807-1873)—manufacturer.

George P. Cochrane—teacher.

William Cowan (1806-1989)—wright.

John Fleming (1807-1876)—builder, a member of Town Council, and Bailie in 1859 and 1863.

. . . .

George G. MacLaren—a distinguished military surgeon, served over 22 years in India; for many years Medical Supervisor of the important Civil Station of Dehra Doon, N. W. Province, who performed in 1880 a successful operation on the right eye of Yakoob Khan, ex-Ameer of Afghanistan; retired on a pension with honorary rank of Lieut.-Colonel.

James F. MacLaren (brother of the above)—appointed, 1881, Surgeon to Her Majesty's 2nd (Prince of Wales' Own), Goorkha regiment, permanently stationed during peace at Dehra Doon, N. W. Province. (It was this regiment who so markedly distinguished itself along with the 92nd Highlanders, at the battle of Candahar, under Sir Frederick Roberts, during the Afghan War.)

Charles Templeman, M.D., B.Sc., Medical Officer of Health, Dundee.

Alexander M'Farlane, M.A., B.Sc., D.Sc., LL.D.—acted as Assistant Professor of Mathematics in Edinburgh University, 1879-1881; in 1885 appointed Professor of Physics in University of Texas.

James Isles, J.P., F.S.A., Scot.—wine merchant, antiquarian, and art connoisseur.

James Stewart, coal merchant, ex-Provost.

Isaac Henry-Anderson of Druidsmere, S.S.C.; factor on the estates of Ardblair, Craighall, Marlee, &c.; Clerk of Eastern District Road Trust; for many years agent of Commercial Bank.

Robert Robertson, solicitor and banker, for many years Town Clerk.

Peter Chalmers—a distinguished soldier, saw active service in the Crimea, Adjutant of the Stirling Volunteers, retired on a pension with honorary rank of Major.

David Chalmers, timber and coal merchant, for nearly 30 years an enthusiastic volunteer and popular Captain.

William Davie, ironmonger and seedsman, donor of the Public Park to Blairgowrie.

David Farquharson, A.R.S.A., artist.

William Dickson, artist.

John Craigie, M.A., LL.B., advocate.

Thomas Steven, J.P., wright, for many years a Bailie and Chief-Magistrate.

James Ogilvy, brewer, a County Councillor, and proprietor of Parkhead estate.

William Robertson, baker, first music teacher of James Durward Lyall (Durward Lely) Scotland's famous tenor.

Thomas T. M'Laggan, M.A., teacher of Classics, High School of Edinburgh.

James Moncur, Superintendent of Scottish Prison Stores, Edinburgh.

James C. Anderson of Aikenhead, late Resident Magistrate, Bengal Civil Service, India.

James Moir, Professor of Conveyancing, Glasgow.

David Templeman, flaxspinner, Provost of Blairgowrie.

James Kynoch, Chief Engineer, Canadian General Electric Company.

Sir William Laird of Gartsherrie, &c., &c.

1

KEITH FALL: ON THE ERICHT

CHAPTER XIII.

Walks and Drives around Blairgowrie—To Lornty and the Heughs—Round Knock-ma-har—Round the Golf Course—Places of Interest near Blairgowrie—Distances from Blairgowrie—The Royal Route—Blairgowrie to Dunkeld—To Alyth—To Coupar Angus.

To Lornty and the Heughs.

ON a ramble up the river side we enter Lower Mill Street from the Wellmeadow, at the Victoria Hotel. Immediately before us, on a low-lying tract, are the Grain Mills, belonging to the representatives of the late John Panton. Next to them, after passing a jute store, are the buildings long known as the "Plash Mill," now the property and works of John Abercromby, millwright. Next is the "Muckle Mill," and on the north side of the road are Ericht Linen Works. On the heights to the left are the Parish Manse and part of the Glebe, and further up, on the summit, is "Mount Zion"—the Parish Kirk o' Blair—the back wall of which forms almost a plumb line to the side of a grassy wooded ravine in which runs the Cuttle Burn. A short distance from this, the Ericht rushes impetuously down a gorge, forming a cascade known as "The Keith." Tradition points out this as the scene of Cargill's leap, when he was pursued by the dragoons of Claverhouse. Pleasantly situated on the opposite side is Linnkeith house, and further up, the residence and works of Keithbank. We now pass through Oakbank, with its works, warehouses, and workers' dwellings, while the residence of the same name is seen nestling among the trees on the high ground to the left. Near this is Ashbank, and on the opposite side of the river the house and works of Bramblebank. We now pass Brooklinn, with its mill standing on the face of the ravine of Lornty, at its junction with the Ericht. Turning by a curve to the left, the road leads us to Lornty Bridge, where the north road from the

"Cross" of Blair, up by the "Hill" and Burnhead, joins in. The bridge of Lornty has been three times built, one structure over the other—the lowest one attributed to the Romans about the year 80. Two nice walks branch off here—one on each side of the Lornty. The one on the left leads past Lornty Cottage and the old mill of Lornty, through the policies of old Lornty House on to the Dam and Falls. The Dam has been artificially constructed for storage of water to Lornty Mills. Beyond this, the walk ascends gradually the rugged heights, and abruptly descends to the water's edge, where a rustic seat has been erected overlooking the placid waters of the Dam. The walk on the north side leads up to "Prince Charlie's Well" and the old castles of Glasclune and Drumlochy.

Having crossed the bridge and traversed a very rough road for about a fourth of a-mile, we strike a path to the right, and pursue our way to the "Heughs." The track is a zig-zag but well-beaten one, through a deep hollow, then ascending a steep ridge to a grassy flat, where a rustic seat enables the traveller to rest. Near this is the Heugh mineral well, possessed of valuable therapeutic medicinal properties. The walk may be continued up the acclivity to the summit of the "Heughs," turning to the right and gradually descending along the crest till we enter on the highway at Bridge of Craighall, crossing which and pursuing our way southwards, we pass through Westfields and Rattray, and re-enter Blairgowrie at the Bridge.

ROUND KNOCK-MA-HAR.

A pleasant walk may be had from the Cross of Blair, ascending the Hill by the Parish Manse and the Hill Kirk, through Hill Terrace—the High Street of Blairgowrie of 200 years ago—and turning to the right at Stormont Lodge, cross bridge over the Cuttle Burn, on to the "Board of Health." A fine stretch of country is here brought into view, from Mount Blair in the north to Kinpurnie in the south, and Benachally in the west. Several seats have been erected to allow the traveller to enjoy the scenes at his leisure.

The road to the right leads down to Lornty, passing

several gigantic specimens of beech trees. We pursue the Knockie Road to the left, passing Knockie Quarry. Right down below us, stretching east and west, is the ravine of Lornty, while away to the north are the Carnashic Woods and Muir of Cochrage. To the west are the lochs of the Stormont and the hills around Dunkeld. By a keen eye a distant view of Glasclune Castle may be had. Entering a wicket gate, we turn southwards, cross the summit of Knockie, and descend by Maryfield and Newton Castle to the town. Splendid views of the Howe of Strathmore may be had from various points of vantage on the descent.

Round the Golf Course.

This is the favourite Sunday promenade during the summer season. Leaving the town by the south at Bankhead, we pass the old Tollhouse and the entrance to Altamont House. Close by is Blairgowrie Quarry, producing a hard rough stone of gravelly formation. To the left is the home farm of Blairgowrie, with the Mansion House and policies of the same—the residence of the Superior of the town. This demesne was built in 1792, and is pleasantly situated. For upwards of half-a-mile from the Toll, southwards on the left, the path is delightfully shaded by the overhanging branches of the trees which, when in full leaf, presents a glorious appearance. Woodlands House on the right marks the site where the "Bloody" Cumberland camped on his way to Culloden. Adjoining this is Heathpark (built by Thomas Clark, the famous Edinburgh publisher), and Brownsville, both desirable residences. After passing through the muirland hamlet known as the "Green Tree" we come to the cross roads at Rosemount Station. The main road leads south-east to Coupar Angus and Dundee. The road to the left leads to Rosemount House, Parkhead, and Coupar Grange, also to the Welton and up the riverside to Blairgowrie. The road to the right leads west to the Golf Course and "Dark Fa's." By the great storm of November, 1873, a large tract of Rosemount Wood was blown down, but the road is still lined with a row of beautiful silver birches which withstood the storm.

About half-a-mile west is the Golf Course, laid out in 1889, which extends on to the Perth Road near "Drybriggs" at Druidsmere. Coming to the "Dark Fa's" we join the main road leading from Blair to Perth via Cargill, and turning to the right, facing north, pass by the Cemetery and Falcon House. To the left, at a distance, is the pretty little hamlet of Muirton of Ardblair—a frequent and well-known resort of artists and lovers of the picturesque. The Essendy Road branches off here, leading to Lethendy, Delvine, and Dunkeld, passing the Druidical Circle about a mile down. From Cleekerinn on the left a fine view is had of the slope on which the town of Blair is situated.

There are many other pleasant and favourite walks in the immediate neighbourhood, of which mention might be made, as "Along the Loon Braes," "Round the Coontlie," "The Hatton Hill," "Castle Hill," the "Gallowbank," down by "The Welton," &c., &c.

Places of Interest near Blairgowrie.

The Hatton Hill, 2 miles east, through Rattray.
The Castle Hill, 2 miles south-east, through Rattray.
Craighall, 3 miles north, through Rattray.
The Heughs, 2 miles north, by Oakbank.
Glasclune Castle, 2 miles north, by Maryfield.
Newton Castle, at the back of the town.
Ardblair Castle, 1 mile west, via Dunkeld.
Marlee Loch, 2 miles west, via Dunkeld.
Druidical Circle, 1 mile west, Essendy.
Muirton of Ardblair, 1 mile south-west.
Golf Course, 1½ miles south.
Stormont Loch, 2 miles south.
Beech Hedge, 4½ miles south, via Meikleour.

Distances from Blairgowrie.

Alyth,	...	5 miles.	Forfar,	...	20 miles.
Birnam,		13 "	Forneth,	...	5 "
Braemar,	...	35 "	Glamis Castle,		15 "
Bridge of Cally,		6 "	Glenshee,	...	20 "
Bendochy,	...	4 "	Kinclaven,	...	5 "
Blair Athole,		32 "	Kirkmichael,		13 "
Cargill,	...	6 "	Kirriemuir,	...	14 "

Carsie,		2½ miles.	Lethendy,	...	4 miles.
Clunie,	...	6 ,,	Meigle,	...	8 ,,
Caputh,	...	6 ,,	Meikleour,	...	4½ ,,
Coupar Angus,		4¾ ,,	Persie,	...	8 ,,
Den of Airlie,		10 ,,	Pitlochry,	...	26 (24) ,,
Dundee,	...	19 ,,	Rattray,	...	1 ,,
Dunkeld,	...	12 (13) ,,	Spittalfield,	...	5 ,,

THE ROYAL ROUTE.

Before the extension of the railway system by Aberdeen to Ballater, the road from Blairgowrie to Glenshee and Braemar was on two occasions taken by Her Majesty the Queen, Prince Consort, and suite, on their way to Balmoral.

This was in the years 1842 and 1857; but since then many other Royal personages have journeyed thereon, hence its term, "The Royal Route."

On leaving Blairgowrie the road crosses the Ericht by a handsome bridge, up the Boat Brae, and, turning to the left, we enter Balmoral Road, passing some beautiful cottages and villas. Now and again we have a view of the Heughs of Mause. Passing the entrance to Craighall House, we come to the Bridge. It was built in 1810, and is very passable, but the accesses to it are abrupt and dangerous. In the olden days vehicles and passengers to the north had to ford the river by what was known as the "Rough Ford." The building of the bridge was followed by an advantageous and better executed work in the cutting of a new road to Cally, several miles of the way taking a lower altitude and escaping the steep ascent of the old road up by Mause. The road is cut along the face of the left side of the Ericht, and at openings of the trees brings the eye in more immediate command of the opposite side, with views of the famed house of Craighall. As we journey on for nearly a mile, the scenery is of the most romantic and magnificent description, and can scarcely be excelled, not only as an enchanting, but a perfect embodiment of all that constitutes the essential elements of beauty and grandeur. Wood, water, chasm, and rock are finely intermingled in all the light and shade so dear to the lover of Nature in her grandest displays of panoramic sublimity. Through a deep ravine of savage rock and crag, rugged and bare, or clothed with dense foliage of hazel and oak coppice, here and there relieved by tall and graceful trees, imparting to the view the most delightful sylvan beauty, dark and sullen flows the "ireful" river. In the depth of its abyss the water rushes along its stony bed, filling the solitude with a ceaseless roar. To those who wish to have the incomparable scene at its best, let them go to its enjoyment during the summer months when it is decked by Nature in the mantle of green. Passing onward we round the heights of Mause, losing the track of the river and its rocky banks, while a new panorama is exposed to view. On the other side of the river, near the crest, is Rannagulzion, and almost below, near the river side, on a beautiful site, amid charming surroundings, stands Glenericht House.

A former proprietor of this estate, Sir William Chalmers, a Waterloo veteran, was knighted by the Queen on her first journey north this route to Balmoral in 1842.

A little further on is the Barony of Cally, which at one time included a considerable extent of country, from the revenues of which a monastery and nunnery connected with Dunkeld Cathedral were maintained. There were wont to be two Chapels in the Barony— one with burying-ground at Wester Cally, which has disappeared, and the other at Steps of Cally. This one had also a burial-place attached, which has been put in order and is still used.

Bridge of Cally, from the stone bridge spanning the Ardle, may be regarded as a leading entrance to the Highland Glens. The main road splits off into two here. One, striking to the right, leads to Clayquhat and Ashmore; to Persie; up the Blackwater and Glenshee to the Spittal of Glenshee; then up Glen Beg, round the Devil's Elbow, over the Cairnwell (3039 ft.), and down Glen Clunie to Braemar, distant from Blairgowrie, 35 miles. The other road strikes off to the left up Strathardle, passing many desirable shooting lodges and mansions — Blackcraig with its house-bridge and castellated mansion, Woodhill, &c.—on through Ballintuim to Kirkmichael, the capital of Strathardle, distant from Blairgowrie, 13 miles. The road continues onwards

BRIDGE OF CALLY.

through Enochdhu, along Glenbrierachan, over the hill at Badvo, and down through Moulin to Pitlochry.

BLAIRGOWRIE TO DUNKELD.

Distance by the Upper Stormont—12 miles.
Distance by the Lower Stormont—13 miles.

Proceeding westward from the Cross of Blairgowrie we diverge to the right at Stormont Inn. Near by are the extensive agricultural engineering works of J. Bisset & Sons, Ltd. Beautifully situated is Ardblair Castle, an old fortress, of date 1668, but recently restored and modernised. The Rae Loch, or Loch of the Leys, is immediately to the west, while half-a-mile to the north is Craig Roman (600 ft.) A short distance further on are the Parish Church and School of Kinloch, and Marlee Hotel, and to the left are Marlee House and homestead. A field-breadth to the south is Marlee Loch, a beautiful sheet of water, which abounds in trout, perch, and pike. Proceeding along, we pass on our right Kinloch House and the entrances leading to the mansions of Ballied and Logie. At the double turn of the road we pass Clunie Cottage on the left, with the farms of Tullyneddie on the right. We now approach Clunie Loch, having in its centre an island, on which, it is alleged, the Admirable Crichton was born. The scenery around the loch is extremely beautiful. On the high ground to the north of the loch is Forneth House. Just below the road and two miles further on is the residence of Laighwood. Near this part, we observe to the right Benachally (1594 ft.) A short distance from it is St Crux Well, to

SPITTALFIELD.

which pilgrimages were wont to be made. We now pass a succession of very beautiful lochs with a rich diversity of scenery—Lochs Butterstone, the Lowes, and Craiglush —and, turning abruptly to the left, strike south-east down hill to Dunkeld.

This town occupies a site of rare beauty on the banks of the Tay, and is surrounded by hills—one the classic Birnam (1580 ft.) and another Craig-y-Barns, both well worth ascending. There are many interesting sights in this quaint old town worthy of a visit.

The road from Dunkeld to Blairgowrie by the Lower Stormont is also famed for its scenery. For a few miles after leaving Dunkeld the road winds along the romantic banks of the river Tay.

Close to the road is the mansion-house of Stenton, with Stenton Craig to the north, while on the other side of the river may be seen, embosomed amid the trees, the old and new Castles of Murthly. In a short time we pass through Caputh and Spittalfield, the latter one of the prettiest villages in Perthshire. Near by is the mansion-house of Delvine, with traces of a Roman station. The picturesque Tower of Lethendy may be seen to the north-east. The next place of interest along the route is the charming village of Meikleour, which was in former times a place of considerable importance. In the middle of the village stands the Market Cross, bearing date 1698, in good preservation. In a field almost opposite is the "Tron" of former days, with an iron necklet, doubtless used as "the jouggs." The entrance to the mansion of Meikleour is directly off the Market Square. On this estate, along-

TRON AND JOUGGS.

side the main road from Blairgowrie to Perth, is the famous "Beech Hedge," one of the arboreal wonders of the world. The length of the hedge is about 580 yards, and it has an average height of 90 feet. It is believed to have been planted in 1746. For over half-a-century the hedge has been regularly cut on the side next the road, in order to 'keep the road clear and give to the row a truly hedge-like character. The operation of pruning is carried out every five years, and, from the height and extent of the hedge, the work is of no ordinary labour. Turning to the left, the road passes through the woods of Meikleour, up by and through the woods of Carsie to the Muir of Blair. On the right may be seen the Golf Course, and on the left the beautiful residence of Druidsmere. Rounding the bend of the road at "Dark Fa's," and passing the Cemetery and Falcon House, we enter the west end of the town. Pretty little cottages and villas dot the side of the road from Falcon House right in for nearly half-a-mile.

On the road which strikes off to the west at Falcon House, about half-a-mile away, is a Druidical Circle, arranged as a hexagon, with a block of stone at each angle point. The road passes directly through the centre of two opposite sides. To the south is the village of Muirton of Ardblair, where a famous Admiral in the Russian service was born about the year 1769.

Blairgowrie to Alyth, &c.

Crossing the Bridge of Blair we climb the Boat Brae, in Rattray, at the top of which the road divides, one leading off to the left to Kirkmichael and Glenshee, the other to Alyth, Kirriemuir, &c. We pursue our way along the latter to the Cross of Old Rattray. Another road branches off to the left to Alyth and Glenisla. About half-a-mile along this road is the mansion of Parkhill, commanding a magnificent view of the Valley of Strathmore. Getting clear out of Old Rattray, in a short time we pass through Bevershire, a small village near the Littleton of Rattray. Immediately east of this the road descends and again ascends the Hollymill Brae. Driving along this road eastwards a very fine view is had of the Howe of Strathmore, which has been compared to the scenery along the banks of the Rhine.

About 5 miles east from Blair is the town of Alyth, the old part of which is irregularly built on a steep declivity of the Grampians. Several miles to the northeast are the "Reekie Linn,' the Den of Airlie, and Airlie Castle, the ancient seat of the Ogilvies, Earls of Airlie —"The Bonnie Hoose o' Airlie" of Jacobite song. Southeast from Blair about 7 miles is Meigle, a small village, and seat of a Presbytery. In the churchyard are several upright pillars adorned with emblematical figures, which are of great interest, particularly to archæologists.

This route goes down Reform Street, along to the right at Bankhead, and, turning to the left at foot of William Street, enters on the Coupar Angus Road at the old tollhouse. A short distance down is the entrance to Altamont House on the right and that to Blairgowrie House on the left. The road leads down a fine stretch to Rosemount Station, past several interesting residences, in a district almost given up to the cultivation of that most luscious of all fruits—the strawberry. The road crosses the railway at Rosemount Station, goes away south-east by Moorfield, Mayriggs, Couttie, and Bridge of Isla, to Coupar Angus, distant from Blairgowrie about $4\frac{1}{2}$ miles. The chief attraction of this place is the ruins of the once-famous abbey of St Benedict, founded with great ceremony on Sunday, 12th July, 1164, by King Malcolm IV. A fragment only of this building now remains, having survived the storm of iconoclastic fury which broke over Scotland at the Reformation.

CHAPTER XIV.

CURIOUS, INTERESTING, AND AMUSING.

A Blairgowrie in America—A Curious Despatch from India—A "Blair Chiel'" Mayor of Dunedin—A "Blair Highlander" in Russia—Pennant's Description of Blair—Copy of a Burgess' Circular—Waterloo Heroes connected with Blairgowrie—An Interesting Operation on the Ameer—Blairgowrie in 1800—Blairgowrie 50 Years Ago—Statistics of Death Rate—"Blair Watter Curlin' Stanes"—Blairgowrie Instrumental Band—The Hymn Tune, "Blairgowrie"—Forest of Clunie Farms—The Catty Mill—Carsie Scutching Mill—Baldornoch Slate-Merchants' Pic-nic—St Fink—Benachally Monument—Parish Kirk Elders—Copy Letter from the Young Chevalier—The Bridge of Craighall—The Priest's House—The Ash Trees—Parish Church—Illuminated Clock—Athletics—An Inducement to Feuars on Blairgowrie Estate — Montrose Disbands his Army near Blairgowrie—Genealogy of the Family of Blair—Blairgowrie Volunteers in 1804—Interesting Despatches from India, 1858—A Local Violin Maker, &c.

A BLAIRGOWRIE IN AMERICA.

IN a pamphlet issued in 1882 by the Scottish American Land Company, descriptive of the State of Iowa, it is stated that "at Blairgowrie, a farm owned by Mr Adamson, of Pitlochry, Scotland, we saw a lot of steers, about 600 in number, in good condition."

There is also a place named Blairgowrie near Chicago.

A CURIOUS DESPATCH FROM INDIA.

"We hereby certify that the 'Neilsonian' cauliflower, produce of the seeds supplied by Mr Neilson, merchant, High Street, Blairgowrie, are very fine. These vegetables have of late daily graced the *Worshipful Festive Board*, and their great size, beautiful whiteness, and delicacy of taste and appearance, have invariably called forth complimentary comment.

"Given under our *Worshipful* hand and holograph, at

our Castle of Tarooshek, in the province of Scinde and Valley of the Indus, this fifteenth day of February, one thousand eight hundred and fifty-nine.

> "R. Cowpar, Captain, H. M.'s 1st Bombay Fusileers, Dep. Commissioner of Hydrabad, and Her Majesty's Justice of the Peace for the island of Bombay and its dependencies, &c."

A "Blair Chiel'" Mayor of Dunedin.

The "Otago Guardian" of 2nd July, 1874, says:— "After one of the sharpest contests ever known in Dunedin, Mr Keith Ramsay has been elected Mayor of this city. . . In the year 1862 Mr Ramsay emigrated from Blairgowrie to New Zealand, and that he had in so short a time risen to the highest municipal dignity in the City of Dunedin speaks volumes for his industry, perseverance, and sterling worth, and reflects honour on his native town of Blairgowrie."

Again, the "Otago Guardian" of 29th July, 1875, reports that at a meeting of the City Council, on 28th July, the following resolution was, on the motion of Councillor Walter, the Mayor-elect, passed unanimously:—

"That this Council desire, on the eve of the retirement of Mr Ramsay from the Mayoral Chair, to thank him for the courtesy and impartiality he has always manifested during his term of office, and wish that at no distant period he may be found taking an active part in the affairs of the city."

Mr Ramsay was entertained to a banquet in the Free Church School, James Street, by his old schoolfellows, while on a visit home in 1898.

A "Blair Highlander" in Russia.

On the occasion of the coronation of the Czar in 1856, at Moscow, John Saunders (MacAlister), a native of this district, attended as piper and valet to the Duke of Sutherland, who represented the Queen. The "Daily News" correspondent states that "MacAlister, the Duke's piper, was in attendance in the ante-room at Lord Granville's ball in full uniform, kilt and philabeg, it being the intention of the noble host that, in some interval of the dance, the Russian guests should be made acquainted with the peculiar characteristics of Highland music; but the bardic soul of MacAlister was impatient of restraint. He shouldered his pipes and, striking up a pibroch, marched into the centre of the brilliant ring, round which Dukes and Duchesses were at that moment dancing.

"I watched the effect (says the correspondent) of this strange music on the unaccustomed ears of the Russians with great interest. They were at first evidently astounded, the officers putting their hands to their ears, and the ladies crossing their hands and gazing on the kilted Aeolus in mute surprise. But soon it became evident that there was a sympathy between the warlike race on the one hand and the warlike music on the other; and when the Grand Duchess Constantine, one of the most beautiful women in Russia, retired to another apartment, she sent for MacAlister, who played 'The White Cockade' in a manner that elicited Her Imperial Highness' commendation. From that moment he became the fashion, and several times in the course of the evening played again to admiring audiences. MacAlister, since his arrival, has been quite a lion among the Russians, who follow him in crowds through the streets, thinking him to be the chief of all the foreign ambassadors, and that, with a fastidious refinement of hauteur, he prefers walking on the ground, as none of the carriages are grand enough for his notions of personal dignity."

Pennant's Description of Blair.

Pennant, on his Scottish tour, states that in passing through the district of Blairgowrie, it was a proverbial remark that "the inhabitants wanted fire in winter, water in summer, and the grace of God all the year round."

Copy of a Burgess Circular.

"Blairgowrie, *20th Nov., 1863.*

"Sir,—As you are, by the Titles of your Property in the Barony of Blairgowrie, bound to contribute to the

Town's Funds; and, as you appear to be in arrear, to the extent undernoted, I have to request that payment of this arrear be made to me within ten days. No further notice will be sent. One year at 1s.

"I am, Sir,

"Your most obedient servant,

"Pro ALEXANDER ROBERTSON,
"Town Clerk.

"JNO. HERON."

WATERLOO HEROES CONNECTED WITH BLAIRGOWRIE.

Lieutenant-General Sir William Chalmers, eldest son of William Chalmers of Glenericht, served in Sicily, in the Walcheren expedition, and throughout the Peninsular War, being present at seventeen engagements. He commanded a wing of the famous 52nd Foot at Waterloo, and had three horses shot from under him. He was knighted by the Queen on her first journey to Balmoral through Glenericht in 1842, was created a C.B. and K.C.B., and Colonel-in-Chief of the 78th Highlanders. He died in 1860.

Colonel Sir Colin Campbell, 5th son of John Campbell of Melfort, by Colina, daughter of John Campbell of Achalader, was educated at Perth Academy, and first served as a midshipman on board of an East Indiaman. Two years later he was serving as a Lieutenant in the 3rd battalion of the Breadalbane Fencibles, and in 1799 was appointed Ensign in a West Indian regiment. Again, Campbell exchanged to the Ross-shire Buffs, and displayed great gallantry at the siege of Ahmednuggur, under Sir Arthur Wellesley. He was severely wounded at Assaye, and afterwards accompanied Wellington to the Peninsula, where he got a staff appointment. For his services in Spain he obtained the Gold Cross with six clasps, and was made a K.C.B. He accompanied Wellington to Belgium, and at Waterloo was commandant at headquarters.

John Young served as a trooper in the 6th Inniskilling Dragoons, and took part in the glorious charge of the Union Brigade at Waterloo. He had the Waterloo and two other medals, and after leaving the army settled down in Blairgowrie as a porter. "Watery," as he was familiarly called, appeared occasionally at Masonic processions bearing a rather lengthy sword. On the 18th of June he used to decorate the windows of his house in Tannage Street with laurel. He was buried in Blairgowrie Cemetery with military honours.

William Tyrie, son of James Tyrie, farmer, Milton of Clunie, enlisted in the 42nd Highlanders and served in Spain. At Quatre Bras, Tyrie received two severe wounds from a Lancer, but his assailant was almost immediately killed by a mounted British officer.

An Interesting Operation on the Ameer.

In 1880 Dr G. G. MacLaren (now of Falcon House, Blairgowrie), Civil Surgeon at Dehra Doon, India, achieved a successful operation on the right eye of the ex-Ameer of Afghanistan, Yakoob Khan, at Mussoorie. A fleshy excrescence of some years' gathering was removed, by which complete recovery of his imperilled vision was secured.

Blairgowrie in 1800.

Blairgowrie, a village and parish in the County of Perth. The village was created into a Burgh of Barony in 1634, of which Colonel Macpherson is Superior. The parish extends in an irregular form, in length about 11 miles, and about 3 in breadth. It is divided into two districts by the Grampians, which form the northern boundary of the Valley of Strathmore. The hills are covered with heath, and there are considerable tracts of muir, moss, and natural wood. The arable soil is generally a stiff loam, and part is gravelly. The Isla, Ericht, and Ardle are the rivers, which abound with trout and salmon. The Ericht is a very rapid river, and has some very fine cascades; its banks are highly ornamented, and many gentlemen have put down summer quarters in its vicinity. There are many lakes of different sizes, some of which when drained have yielded great quantities of excellent marl. There are two freestone quarries, but the stone is of inferior quality; and muirstone abounds in every part. There are several chalybeate springs, one of which is particularly resorted to. Considerable quantities of household linen are manufactured. The new method of husbandry is practised here with great success. Newton House, the birthplace of the justly-celebrated George Drummond, Esq., six times elected Lord Provost of Edinburgh, is a fine old mansion, commanding an extensive prospect. There are several cairns and druidical circles in the parish. Population returned to Sir J. Sinclair, 1651.—"Gazetteer of Scotland," 1803 : Printed in Dundee.

BLAIRGOWRIE 50 YEARS AGO.

The old town existed at the Hill, but at the beginning of the century a move was made to the low ground. High Street, Allan Street, and the Croft were laid out, and formed the first streets of the new town. There had been many houses alongside the High Street (part of the old turnpike road from the south country to the north), for nearly a century before. The High Street at this time extended from the Cross to Rorry Street. There was nothing beyond this but land, except M'Nab's ale-house (the Dreadnought). All north from the High Street was land. The old Parish School was the first building in John Street, and Geddes' house the first in James Street. The houses in High Street and Allan Street were small, with no mutual gables in those days, but built with narrow slits between each. Leslie Street was all garden ground, and the Wellmeadow in grass for grazing purposes. From the top of what is now David Street a broad belt of old oak, plane, and elm trees extended west beyond the Castle of Newton to the march of Ardblair, and returned by the Gallowbank, where only a remnant of that sylvan grove remains to remind us of departed scenes. An old avenue of beech and elm, which formed the approach from Perth Road to the Castle, has also been swept away.

STATISTICS OF DEATH RATE.

Year.	No. of Deaths.	Estimated Percentage Over 60 Years.	Highest Age Attained.
1890	69	30	86
1891	88	50	90
1892	97	39	89
1893	96	46	96
1894	88	35	101
1895	103	56	94
1896	84	46	96

"Blair Watter Curlin' Stanes."

These mineralogical treasures are found in the Ericht from the Red Brae up to the Strone Brig. Belonging to the trap family, they usually consist of quartz, hornblende, and augite; felspar and iron pyrites are also sometimes detected. The stones are generally in small blocks, and it is a rare occurrence to get a block to yield a pair of stones. The colour, when freshly broken, is dark green, with a bluish tinge running through, but when the stone has been polished, the colour becomes a very dark green. These curling stones, though now not so much sought after as formerly, form a grand tool on which a curler may rely. They possess many virtues which every good curler wishes his own curling stones to have; they are hard, tough, have fair specific gravity (neither too heavy nor too light), are not "sookin'" stones (a grave objection open to almost all curling stones), take a grand polish, give grand "chappin'" blows, and receive them equally well. On the ice they are unequalled.

Blairgowrie Instrumental Band.

This band was organised about the year 1829, and was composed of the following members:— William Scrimgeour (Leader), James Heron, Andrew Davie, John Clark, James Robertson, John Saunders, William Buttar, William Chalmers, John Small, John Robertson, Robert Duncan, and Andrew Mitchell. The instruments used were:—Clarionets, key bugles, flutes, French horn, bassoon, serpent, trombone, and bass drum. As to the uniform, it consisted of white trousers, blue jacket with scarlet facings, and a blue bonnet with red band, surmounted by a bunch of feathers.

For nearly 30 years this band continued to exist, and on the institution of the Volunteer force in 1859, the members then were patriotic enough to enlist, and the band—men and instruments—was at once made available for the local corps. Over these Joseph Simpson was appointed band-sergeant, a position he held for 16 years, when he resigned. At that time there were some four clarionets and two flutes in the band, besides the usual brass, some 16 in all, the intention having been to shape itinto a reed band. "Joe" Simpson played the euphonium, at which he was a recognised adept.

Alexander Ambrose joined the corps in 1859 (although the books only credit him at 15th September, 1861), and was in the band up till June, 1885, when he retired, after being band-master for eight years.

William Hebenton joined the band in October, 1864, and was associated with it for nearly 30 years, 8 of which he was band-master.

Several years ago, however, the Volunteer Band was broken up and a Pipe Band instituted for the Volunteers.

In 1894 a Town's Band was organised, and Mr Hebenton undertook the duties of leader and instructor. He is a good player of the clarionet. He continued in office for about two years, when Mr Neill was appointed.

THE HYMN TUNE "BLAIRGOWRIE."

In "The Life and Letters of the Rev. Dr Dykes," published 1898, there appears the following (page 157):—
"On February 22nd he wrote a tune for the marriage of a friend, to the words—

'The voice that breathed o'er Eden.'"

The friend was Rev. F. W. Davis, of the Rectory, but the hymn tune, which Dr Dykes named "Blairgowrie," was written for the marriage of the Rector's eldest sister to Lieut. A. R. Davis Tosswill, of the old 75th Regiment of Foot, now known as "The Gordon Highlanders." Dr Dykes presented the copyright of the tune to Rev. F. W. Davis.

THE FOREST OF CLUNIE FARMS.

Over fifty years ago there were quite a lot of farms and crofts in that district now known as the Forest of Clunie. The old folks were wont to sum up a few in the lines—

"Easter Bog, Wester Bog,
Dullater
Bog, and Bog Mill,
Whistlebare, an' Shirra' Muir,
An' bonnie Birkin' Hill."

The farm of Dullater was tenanted by one Donald Keir, whose daughter (Charlotte Keir), kept a public-house in Balmoral Road, Rattray, for many years.

The Catty Mill.

A short distance off the main highway to Dunkeld, near the entrance to Ballied, existed a distillery known as Catty Mill. David Brown, farmer of Marlee, was the last distiller in occupancy, about the year 1849. The buildings were very extensive, with a long range of malt barns, several worms, and a large number of stills, while a ganger resided permanently. Traces of the ruins may still be seen.

Carsie Scutching Mill.

Was in the occupancy of Donald M'Intosh in 1800; the remains of the lade are still visible. The mill was afterwards turned into a sawmill by William Culross. A Farina Mill, occupied by James Ogilvy, of Blairgowrie, now stands near its site, but on the other side of the burn.

Baldornoch Slate.

For many years prior to 1850 a famous slate quarry was in operation at Baldornoch, in the vicinity of Forneth. The slates were of excellent quality, and had in large sizes. One building, at least, in Blairgowrie is covered with them—the First Free Church. One day, while the workmen were at dinner, the sides of the quarry fell in and covered up all the working plant, rendering the quarry useless, as it was never afterwards worked.

The Merchants' Pic-nic.

In 1864 the merchants of Blairgowrie convened and successfully carried out, along with their friends, a pic-nic to Glamis Castle; again, in 1865, to Meikleour; and the last, in 1866, to Murthly Castle. The writer has before him an interesting photo. of the group on the last occasion. Many of the familiar faces are with us to-day, but, alas! the majority have "crossed the bourne which knows no returning."

St Fink.

About half-way between Blairgowrie and Alyth, to the north of the highway, lies a small estate known as St Fink. About the year A.D. 720 a chapel existed here, dedicated to Saint Fyncan, Fyncana, or Phink, one of the nine virgin daughters of Saint Donevald of the Den of Ogilvy. They were known as the nine maidens, although Boece only gives seven as their number. Boece thus writes:—"Donevald had vii dochteris, quhilk levit with him in gret penance, on beir breid and wattir. They eit nevir bot anis on the day: and the residew thairof occupyit in continewal labour and orison. Thir holy virginis efter deceis of their fader . . . (came to) . . . Abernethy, whare thay leiffit ane devote life, and wur buryit at the rute of ane aik, quhilk is halden yit in gret veratioun amang the pepil." Saint Fincana's day was 21st August. Several sculptured stones have been unearthed from time to time at St Fink, but whether or not they belonged to the chapel cannot be determined.

Benachally Monument.

On the summit of Benachally stands a cairn, erected in 1830 by Messrs M'Intosh for Sir John Bisset of Reichip. On taking out the "found" the workmen unearthed a skeleton of a man over six feet in height. It was generally believed to be the remains of an English trooper who was reputed to have been murdered there in 1715 or 1745. His horse was observed for several days saddled and bridled wandering in the Forest of Clunie. He was on his way to the north with gold to pay the English soldiery when he met his fate, and it is said that the gold of the murdered trooper went to purchase an estate in the Stormont, which passed into the hands of many proprietors in the course of a century, every one of whom failed to prosper.

Parish Kirk Elders

Ordained in 1821:—William Macpherson, Blairgowrie House; David Kidd; *Thomas Soutar, Netheraird; *George Chalmers, Hillton of Mause; *Thomas Soutar, schoolmaster; and *John Baxter. Those marked * were in office at the Disruption, 1843. Ordained in 1841 :—Robert Chalmers, Nether Clayquhat; James Low, Muirton; George Playfair, Parkhead; Robert Johnstone, schoolmaster; Peter Chalmers, precentor; James Cowpar, M.D.; John Connacher (afterwards missionary at Constantinople).

Letter from Young Chevalier.

Copy of letter from the young Chevalier to the laird of Craighall, dated Blair in Athol, 2nd September, 1745:—

"It is now some weeks since I arrived in this country, with a firm resolution to assert His Majesty's right, and as I am now got so far into the country, with a good body of the King's loyal subjects, I now require you may join the Royal Standard with all the expedition possible, when you may depend upon meeting with my favour and friendship.

"Charles, P. R."

The summons did not, however, meet with the expected response from the young laird.

The Bridge of Craighall.

In 1613 Silvester Rattray, then minister of the parish of Rattray, petitioned the Privy Council for the erection of a bridge at Craighall. The petition was granted, and an order was issued for a subscription to build the bridge; but the matter went no further. Travellers to and from the north had to ford the river at the Coble Pule and again at Craigmill until the bridge was built in 1810.

The Priest's House.

This domicile, occupied by the hereditary beadles of the Parish Church, stood in the south-east corner of garden at James Street House. The low house on opposite side of street was built for the beadle after "The Priest's House" was demolished by Robert Robertson, nearly fifty years ago. The old beadles, John MacLachlan and his father, resided here many years. At the south-west corner of the garden stood another small house, long occupied by Allan Heron, the first letter carrier in the town.

THE ASH TREES.

Before James Street was formed, there was a path leading from the Hill of Blair westwards to Brown Street, passing the front of "The Priest's House." The south side of the path was marked by a high bank, and a row of beautiful ash trees, long since removed, but still remembered by many old inhabitants.

PARISH CHURCH.

Rev. J. W. Foyer, elected assistant minister of Parish Church, May, 1867; transferred to Kilry, August, 1877.

ILLUMINATED CLOCK.

In September, 1869, a new clock with transparent dials was set up in spire of South Free Church. It was lit with gas at night for several years.

ATHLETICS.

Early in May, 1869, the Athletic Games Association was formed, with James Small, President; James Playfair, Vice-President; James Isles, Secretary. The first games were held in July in a park near Altamont, which were a great success. The surplus revenue amounted to over £92.

AN INDUCEMENT TO FEUARS ON BLAIRGOWRIE ESTATE.

TOWN FEUS.

As a special inducement and benefit to the Feuars on Blairgowrie Estate, all parties building a dwelling-house thereon of the value of £400 will be entitled (in terms of an arrangement between the late Allan Macpherson and the Railway Company), to a free first class pass over the Caledonian Railway from Blairgowrie to Perth and Forfar and intermediate stations.

MONTROSE DISBANDS HIS ARMY NEAR BLAIRGOWRIE.

In 1646, King Charles I., having surrendered to the Scottish army, immediately thereafter wrote to Montrose commanding him to disband his forces. Montrose refused to obey the first order, but to a second and more peremptory one he yielded a reluctant consent. Preparatory to disbanding his army, Montrose appointed it to rendezvous at the Haugh of Rattray, near Blairgowrie, at which place, on the 30th July, 1646, he discharged his men after addressing a feeling and animated oration to them, in which, after giving them due praise for their faithful services and good behaviour, he told them his orders and bade them farewell, an event no less sorrowful to the whole army than to himself, and, notwithstanding he used his utmost endeavours to raise their drooping spirits and encourage them with the prospect of a speedy peace, and assured them that he contributed to the King's safety and interest by his present submission no less than by his former military attempts, yet, falling on their knees, with tears in their eyes, they beseeched him that he would take them along with him wherever he should go. They were, however, disbanded as Montrose had then enough to do to provide for his own safety. The reason is not given why Rattray was chosen for this last rendezvous of his army, but probably he was actively supported by Rattray of Craighall, which may account for the scene of his valedictory address, and he seems to have been marching and countermarching between Brechin and Perth, looking for a favourable opportunity of attacking that portion of the Parliamentary army which was commanded by General Baillie of Jerviswoode.

Genealogy of Family of Blair.

Alexander de Blair
(Flourished in the reigns of William the Lion and Alexander II.)

Sir William de Blair (son of)
(Steward of Fife, Knighthood conferred on him by Alexander II.)

Sir Alexander de Blair (son of)
John de Blair (son of)
David de Blair (son of)

Patrick,
1st of Balthyock.

Thomas
(Progenitor of the Blairs of Ardblair).

THOMAS (son of),
2nd of Balthyock
(Received grant of lands of Ardblair, 1399).

THOMAS (grandson)
(died beginning James IV. reign).

ALEXANDER (son)
THOMAS (son)
(succeeded 1509).

LAURENCE,
　THOMAS (2nd son),
　　PATRICK (3rd son)
(Progenitor of the Blairs of Pittendriech, Glasclune, &c.)

BLAIRGOWRIE VOLUNTEERS IN 1804.

Lieut.-Col. Macpherson.
Capt. Hogg.

1st Lieut., James Scott.　　　2nd Lieut., James Dick.

Sergeants—
Thomas Johnston, Robert Douglas, Duncan Keay.

Drummer, George Drummond.

Corpl. John Fleming.　　　Pvt. David M'Lagan.
Pvt. Jas. Anderson.　　　 „ John Anderson.
 „ John Bisset.　　　　　 „ Robert Butter.
 „ Chas. Cameron.　　　　 „ Alex. Crighton.
 „ Geo. Chalmers.　　　　 „ David Chalmers.
 „ Peter Chalmers.　　　　„ James Dick.
 „ Wm. Duncan.　　　　　 „ Peter Drummond.
 „ Robt. Dow.　　　　　　 „ John Davie.
 „ Hugh Fraser.　　　　　 „ Jas. M'Nab.
 „ James Fenton.　　　　　„ Sam. M'Dougal.
 „ D. Farquharson.　　　　„ John M'Intosh.
 „ Alex. Fleming.　　　　　„ Andrew M'Donald.
 „ Alex. Falconer.　　　　 „ Alex. M'Omie.
 „ Jas. Gow.　　　　　　　„ Andrew M'Gregor.
 „ Geo. Gilruth.　　　　　 „ Alex. M'Gregor.
 „ Jas. Galloway.　　　　　„ Adam M'Gregor.

Pvt. Geo. Gorrie.
„ John Hutcheson.
„ John Hood.
„ Andrew Lindsay.
„ John Leslie.
„ Jas. M'Kenzie.
„ Jas. Robertson (1st).
„ Jas. Robertson (2nd).
„ John Robertson.
„ Wm. Stratton.
„ Robert Stratton.
„ James Stratton.
„ John Stewart.
„ John Douglas.
„ Wm. Cowan.
„ James Maxwell.
„ Donald M'Pherson.

Pvt. Thos. Mitchell.
„ Wm. Mitchell.
„ Robt. M'Dougall.
„ John M'Dougal.
„ John Pennycook.
„ Thos. Rattray.
„ James Sime.
„ Thomas Soutar (1st).
„ Thomas Soutar (2nd).
„ W. D. Stewart.
„ David Williamson.
„ Daniel Scott.
„ James Laird.
„ Geo. Lamb.
„ Wm. Gow.
„ Andrew Saunders.
„ George Fife.

Interesting Despatches from India.

Copy of despatch from Sir James Outram, India, of 17th January, 1858, in which is the following honourable mention of Capt. (now Lieut.-Gen. Sir) J. C. Rattray of Craighall :—

. . . "Much credit is also due to Capt. Rattray (of Her Majesty's 90th), commanding the infantry, to Lieut. Gully, commanding the battery of No. 1 advanced outpost, and to the officers and men of their post, for their vigilance and alertness in checking and punishing the enemy at every opportunity."

In the "Homeward Mail" of August 19th, 1858, we find the following record of the distinguished services of Capt. Rattray :—

"We are glad to chronicle an important success gained by Captain Rattray, on the 5th of July, at Kusma, six miles N.N.E. of Dinapore, over 400 rebels led by Judar Sing. Our force consisted of 150 Sikhs and 50 cavalry, and, with the loss of only two wounded, cut up upwards of 100 of the enemy.

"The present mail brings us additional particulars of the capture of Gwalior and the pursuit of the rebels; we also learn that Capt. Rattray has defeated the rebels at Kusura in the Benares district, and that General

Roberts had caused the enemy to vacate Jeypore, and was marching in pursuit."

The following is a copy of Capt. Rattray's despatch after the action:—

"After a march of six hours I came up to Judar Sing's force at Kusma, consisting of about 400 men; they awaited our approach very steadily. I immediately attacked them with 150 Sikhs and 50 cavalry. I completely routed them, killing upwards of 100 of them, a great many of whom were sepoys. We pursued them until nearly dark. The cavalry cut up nearly fifty. Judar Sing escaped with difficulty. The country was entirely under water, otherwise none would have escaped. Only two of my men wounded."

A Local Violin Maker.

James M'Intosh was born in the year 1801 at Carsie, near Blairgowrie, at which place his father, Donald M'Intosh, was a lint-miller. He was the grand-nephew of Robert M'Intosh ("Red Rob"), the famous Edinburgh violinist and composer (1745-1807). Coming of a good stock of violin players and violin makers, it is not surprising that his work should be much above average. There is nothing of the amateur noticeable about even his early works; the cutting is all done with a firm hand as if the maker knew exactly what he wanted, and had the skill necessary to produce the effect. His early violins (1842) are rather high and Stainer-like in build, the sizes being 14, 8, $4\frac{1}{2}$, $6\frac{1}{8}$. The narrowness of the upper bout is there very noticeable. These violins are marked with imitation purfling, the scroll is well cut, and the back generally in one piece, and cut "on the slab." The tone is large and telling, with something of the sharpness of the Stainer quality. His later violins (1869) are nearer the Stradivari model, neatly purfled, and more artistic in appearance. All his violins are covered with spirit varnish, thinly laid on, and of a grey colour. The wood is always good, and frequently of fine figure. Altogether M'Intosh made 204 violins, 10 violas, and 35 violoncellos, the last also having whole backs of well-marked maple, and being fitted with pegs and tail-pieces of his own making. His violins have a label printed from types on white paper, with the last line hand-written:—

"JAMES M'INTOSH,
Violin maker, Blairgowrie,
March, 1842."

M'Intosh, who was a skilful violin player as well as a violin maker, died at Blairgowrie in 1873.

His son, James, tenanted the farm of Boatlands, near Coupar Angus, and William for many years carried on a successful business as draper in Allan Street.

APPENDIX.

ARCHÆOLOGICAL RELICS

In NATIONAL MUSEUM OF ANTIQUITIES OF SCOTLAND, EDINBURGH, from the District:—

(For Letters and Numbers refer to Catalogue, 1892.)

A.F. 56. Axe of green mottled stone, 8 by $3\frac{1}{2}$ inches, finely polished, found on the bank of the Ericht at Rattray. Deposited 1873.

A.B. 480. Portion of flint knife.—1879.

B.E. 139, 140. Whorl of lead, $\frac{3}{4}$ in. diameter; of slate-stone, 1 in. diameter; from Kinclaven.—1880.

D.G. 43. Lance head, $2\frac{3}{4}$ in. long, from Blacklaw.—1832.

E.Q. 1, 2, 3, 4. Fragments of urn; small lozenge-shaped piece of worked bone, perforated; burnt bones; from sepulchral deposits at Murthly.—1870.

H.D. 61, 62-68, 69, 70, 71, 72, 73, 74. Rubbing stone of blue granitic stone, 28 by 24 by 12 in.; round balls of quartz, from 3 to 5 in. diameter; whetstones or polishers of greenish stone, 3 and 5 in. long; whetstone of greystone, 4 in. long; stone whorl, $1\frac{3}{4}$ in. diameter; circular disc of mica-schist, 2 in. diameter, perforated; long handled comb, $4\frac{3}{4}$ in. long; from hut circle at South Persie.—1866.

E.A. 2. Cinerary urn of clay, $15\frac{1}{2}$ by 12 in., finely ornamented, from Glenballoch.—1881.

E.C. 5, 6. Incense cup, $1\frac{3}{4}$ in. high, within larger urn (6) 1878. (See page 78.)

H.D. 75, 76, 77. Fragment of bronze pin, 5 in. long, from hut circle; block of granite, 12 by 12 by $3\frac{1}{2}$ in. with shallow cup-shaped cavity; flat, circular disc of

chlorite schist, 4½ in. diameter, pierced in centre, from the "Grey Cairn," Balnabroich.—1866.
I.B. 101. Slab of sandstone, 44 by 24 by 5 in. with figures of men and animals in relief, from Gellyburn, Murthly.—1887.
M.A. 31. Brass cooking-pot, 8 in. high, lip broken, handle 7 in. long, and ornamented with double concentric circles and central dots, found at Blairgowrie.—1856.
O.B. Medal of George Drummond of Blair.—1882.

RELICS

In possession of JAMES ISLES, J.P., F.S.A., Scot.

Bronze pot from Blackloch. (See page 78.)
Bronze celt or axe, found at Ballied.
Iron door knocker, dated 1682, found at Meikleour.
Iron studs from door of Glasclune Castle.
Key found in debris at same place.
Coin tester of brass from old shop in Blair.
Tinder box, steel, and flint.
Three flint arrow heads from Marlee.
Shell found in coffin at Gourdie.
Hour-Glass from Parish Church of Lethendy.
A peer-man found near Greenbank Works.
A stone, inscribed I.R., 1617, found at Rosemount.
Stone cup from Roman camp at Delvine.
Stone seal, inscribed R.I., found at old weigh-house in High Street.
Piece of wood rafter from Donald Cargill's house at Hatton.
Wood plough socket found at Rattray.

RELICS

In possession of JAMES M'LEVY, Librarian, Mechanics' Institute.

Stone axe found near Roman camp at Meikleour.
Silver medal, ornamented and inscribed—"Presented to Parochial School, Blairgowrie, by Robert Geekie, Esq., of Rosemount. Annual medal. Elizabeth Gray, 1st Class, Dux, 1869."
Silver medal, plain and inscribed as above, but no date.

CHURCH TOKENS,

Formerly in use in Blairgowrie, Rattray, Clunie, and Kinloch, from the collections of G. S. DUNCAN, F.S.A., Scot., and JOHN REID, Ogilvie Arms Inn. (See Illustration.)

BLAIRGOWRIE.

No. 1, 2. M.: I. L.   Minister: James Lyon (1720) and (1762)
3. M.: W. D.   „   William Dow (1782)
4. M.: J. J.   „   James Johnstone (1817)
5. A. O. G.: Minr.   Archibald Ochiltree Greig: Minr.

RATTRAY.

6. M.: R. B.   Minister: Robert Bowis (1708)
7. PARISH OF RATTRAY, 1849.   William Herdman

CLUNIE.

8. M.: A. M.   Minister: Alex. M'Culloch (1731)
9. A. O.   Alex. Ogilvy, A.M. (1722)
10. CLUNIE CHURCH, 1840.   George Millar

KINLOCH.

11, 12. M.: I. G.   Minister: James Gray (1697)
13.   1751.   Robert Anderson
14.   L. B.   „   Laurence Butter
      1821.

A]Wag-at-the-Wa' Clock, dated 1710, said to have belonged to Lord Lynedoch, may be seen at the office of Robert Nelson, Solicitor, Wellmeadow.

A beautiful model of the Celestial Globe, used in teaching by Miss Murray in the Dames' School, Meadow Bank Cottage, is now the property of Miss Robertson, James Street House.

William Dickson, Maybank, has a Curiously-Shaped Stone, which was found several years ago in the Moss of Cochrage. It resembles the shape of a pike, is 28 inches in length, tapering from $4\frac{1}{2}$ inches to $2\frac{1}{2}$ inches, from $\frac{1}{2}$-inch to 2 inches thick, with regular markings on both sides, and weighs 10 lbs. Antiquarian authorities in Edinburgh are of opinion that it is a war-club used by the early Britons, which supposition is borne out by the fact that it is similar to war-clubs in use at the present time by some of the hill tribes in India.

William Grant, Chemist, and George Cunnison, Burgh Surveyor, have a copy of Feuing-Plan of Blairgowrie estate, dated 1854, which shows a curious illustration of the town at that period.

Blairgowrie Cottage Hospital.

To commemorate the Queen's Jubilee, 1887, the erection of a Cottage Hospital was proposed, but through lack of interest the suggestion fell flat. It was, however, quietly worked up by the late John Panton, and, since his death, by Lieut.-Col. G. G. MacLaren, M.D., of Falcon House, with such success that about £2500 has been raised by subscription (Lieut.-General Sir J. C. Rattray, £1000; Sir William Laird of Gartsherrie, £500, &c.), and ere long the noble aim of the promoters will be accomplished.

Blairgowrie Whisky.

"Blairgowrie—The Royal Scotch Whisky" has had a large consumption in and around London for the last 20 years, and was so named in remembrance of a very pleasant visit to Blairgowrie. It took the highest award at Rochefort Exhibition. The label is printed on a ground of Royal Stewart tartan. The whisky is bottled by the sole proprietors, Nicholls, Piper, & Co., Glasgow.

Another whisky known as "Blairgowrie Blend" (10 years old) is sold by J. L. Webster, wine merchant.

"Change Here for Blairgowrie."

As Blairgowrie is situated at the terminus of a branch line of the Caledonian Railway, travellers have generally to change carriages at Coupar Angus (4½ miles distant). At this station, John Robertson, porter, has been for over 40 years the most prominent figure, with his well-known cry, "Change here for Blairgowrie."

In "Industry and Invention," by Samuel Smiles, LL.D., appears the following :—

> " From early morn till late at e'en,
> John's honest face is to be seen,
> Bustling about the trains between,
> Be't sunshine or be't showery ;

CHURCH TOKENS

And as each one stops at his door,
He greets it with the well-known roar
   Of 'Change here for Blairgowrie.'

" Even when the still and drowsy night
Has drawn the curtains of our sight,
John's watchful eyes become more bright,
   And takes another glow'r aye,
Thro' yon blue dome of sparkling stars,
Where Venus bright and rudy Mars
   Shine down upon Blairgowrie.

" He kens each jinkin' comet's track,
And when it's likely to come back,
When they have tails, and when they lack—
   In heaven the waggish power aye ;
When Jupiter's belt buckle hings,
And the Pyx mark on Saturn's rings,
   He sees from near Blairgowrie."

. . . . .

With the 19th century on the wane, and the 20th looming into view, may Blairgowrie go on and prosper. Some day in the near future we look for the Electric Light, Municipal Buildings, a New Town Hall, the Public Park utilised, and many other improvements carried out, which would tend to make this favourite resort still more popular, and not content to " Rest and be Thankful."

" FLOREAT BLAIRGOWRIE."

INDEX.

A.

Abbey of Cambuskenneth, 34, 35.
Abbey of Coupar, 33, 34, 37, 88, 89, 185.
Abbey of Scone, 34, 35, 80, 81, 92.
Abercromby, John, 170, 233.
Aberdeen, 92, 93, 237.
A Blair Chiel', 245.
A Blair Highlander, 245.
Abbotshall, 81.
Achalader, 54, 140, 161, 247.
Act Anent Brydals, 104.
Acts of Parliament, 66, 67, 68, 82, 149.
Adams, Professor, 221.
Adamson, D., Ironmonger, 147.
Adamson, John, 169.
Adamson, of Pitlochry, 244.
Address to Earl Russell, 59.
A Disputed Victory, 29.
Administering the Lord's Supper (1719), 105.
Admirable Crichton, 37, 131, 210.
Admiral, a Famous, 242.
Adventure Schools, 112.
Advertiser, Blairgowrie, 160.
Advertiser, Dundee, 62, 217, 226.
Advertiser Office, 19.
A Generous Merchant, 106.
Agreements, 80, 81.
Agricola, Julius, 14, 25, 26, 140.
Agriculture, 125.
Agricultural Engine Works, 170.
Aikenhead, 77, 232.
Airlie Castle, 242.
Airlie, Den of, 242.
Airlie, Earl of, 66, 131, 242.
Airlie, The Bonnie Hoose o', 242.
Albin, 25.
Alexander II., 33, 80, 214.
Alexander III., 132.
Alexander, Earl of Mar, 35, 132.
Alexander, Wolf of Badenoch, 35.
Alexandria, 100.
Allan Street, 16, 17, 19, 21, 67, 148, 158, 172, 174, 202, 249, 260.
A Local Violin Maker, 259.
Along the Loon Braes, 236.
Alpin, King of Scots, 31.
Altamont, 255.
Altamont House, 140, 235, 243.
Altamont Lane, 204.
Altamont Quarry, 22, 235.
Alyth, 12, 34, 68, 81, 98, 99, 133, 166, 201, 236, 242, 253.

Amberley, Lord, 61.
Ambrose, Band-Sergt., 163, 251.
Ameer, Operation on, 248.
America, 62, 63, 243.
Amusing Notes, 244.
Analysis of Water, 65.
Ancient Trade, 171.
Anderson, Geo. B., 59, 163, 230.
Anderson, I. Henry, S.S.C., 139, 147, 200, 232.
Anderson, James, of Bleaton, 147, 162, 198, 230.
Anderson, James C., of Aikenhead, 232.
Angling, 183.
Angling Club, 183.
Annual Fair, 201.
An Old Account, 108.
Antiquarian Museum, 78, 262.
Antiquities, 76, 77, 78, 79, 80, 128, 262, 264.
A Peer-Man, 263.
Appendix, 262.
Arboriculture, 24.
Arbroath, 229.
Ardblair, 33, 37, 48, 78, 93, 116, 121, 122, 127, 200, 209, 232, 249, 257.
Ardblair Castle, 33, 129, 236, 239.
Ardblair Curling Club, 199, 200.
Ardblair Family, 33, 34, 38, 93, 129, 256, 257.
Ardblair, Muirton of, 88, 236, 242.
Ardle, The, 12, 183, 187, 189, 190, 248.
Argentine, 37.
Arms, Coat of, 61.
Army of Montrose Disbanded, 255.
Argyle, Earl of, 218.
Ash Trees, The, 255.
Ashbank, 169, 188, 189, 230, 233.
Ashgrove Works, 186.
Ashmore, 238.
Associate Antiburgher Church, 94, 95.
Aspect, 74.
Athletics, 255.
Athole Street, 20.
Athole, Duke of, 57, 64, 84, 185.
Athole, Earl of, 216, 217.
Auchmithie, 96.
Auchteralyth, 230.
Auchtergaven, 218.
Auction Mart, 19, 80.
Auld Bell o' Blair, 19, 80, 174.
A Wag-at-the-Wa', 264.

B.

Badenoch, Wolf of, 35.
Badvo, 239.
Bailies, 51, 63, 66, 72, 74, 75, 82, 84, 88.
BAILIES OF BLAIR—
 Ayson, W. J., 75.
 Ayson, Robert, 75, 148.
 Bridie, John, 75.
 Brown, John, 75.
 Brown, George, 75.
 Buchan, Alexander, 75.
 Chalmers, David, 67, 75, 161, 163, 231, 232.
 Chalmers, James, 21, 75, 231.
 Craigie, William, 75.
 Constable, George, 75.
 Dick, James, 75, 169.
 Dow, Robert, 75.
 Fell, John D., 75.
 Fleming, John, 75, 162, 231.
 Johnstone, Thos.; Kidd, David; Low, Thomas; Lunan, Robert; Mitchell, Thos.; M'Nab, James; Neilson, Dr James; Robertson, George; Robertson, Robert; Robertson, William; Scott, James, 75.
 Stewart, James, 75, 232.
 Stewart, William, 150, 171.
 Steven, Thomas, 75, 232.
 Whitson, Thomas, 75, 174.
 Wilson, David, 75.
 Young, James, 75.
Bailzies o' Blair, Ye, 144.
Bailie Depute, 84.
Bailie. General, 43, 256.
Balcairn, 77.
Baldornoch, 252.
Balfour, R. A., 162.
Balgowan, 49.
Ballads, 141.
Ballater, 237.
Ballied, 230, 252, 263.
Ballied House, 140. 240.
Ballingall, Dr Geo., 140.
Ballintuim, 238.
Balmoral, 52, 54, 238.
Balmoral Road, 237, 238.
Balnabroich, 262.
Balthayock, 83, 129, 209, 216, 256, 257.
Balude, 92.
Banff, 53, 61, 68, 94, 229.
Bamilie, 82.
Bands, 55, 56, 57. 59, 156, 162.
Band of Manrent, 37, 40, 81, 83.
Bandoch, 82.
Bank Buildings, 18.
Banks, 16, 17, 18, 19, 21, 147, 148, 150, 171, 179, 223, 229, 232.
 Bank of Scotland, 147, 223.
 Blairgowrie Deposit Co. Bank, 148.
 Cheque Bank, 150.
 Commercial Bank, 147, 232.
 National Security Savings Bank of Perth, 148.
 North of Scotland Bank, 148.
 Perth Banking Co., 148, 149.
 Royal Bank, 148, 171, 179, 229.
 Union Bank, 18, 148.
 Western Bank. 147.
Bankhead, 235. 243.
Bankhead Toll. 16, 19, 235.
Bank Street, 21, 98.
Bannock. The, 195.
Bannockburn. 34.
Baron, The, 195.
Baron Bailies, 195, 201, 225, 231.
Barony of Blair, 246.
Barony of Cally, 238.
Barony of Craighall, 218, 219.
Barony of Meikleour, 209.
Barony of Rattray, 217, 219.
Baron Clerk-Rattray, 52.
Barony Court. 42. 51.
Barber of Blair. The, 171.
Barty, George, 150.
Barty Mortification, 150.
Battle of Glasclune, 14, 36, 131.
Baxter, John, 253.
Baxter, John, of Ashbank, 169, 230.
Baxter, Dr John, 97, 221.
Baxter, Capt. John, 163.
Bayly, Lieut.-Col., 26.
Beeches. The, 16.
Beech Hedge, 47, 140, 236, 241.
Bell o' Blair. 19, 80, 174.
Bellman. 173.
Bell, Patrick. 81, 89.
Benachally, 13, 64, 65, 189, 234, 240.
Benachally Monument, 253.
Bendochy, 16, 68, 82, 92, 141, 150, 236.
Benedict XIII., 35, 81.
Bennett, A. W., 147.
Bennet. Robert. 105.
Ben-y-ghloe. 13.
Bernham, David de, 33.
Bevershire, 242.
Bhlair-gobhainn-righ, 71.
Birds, 119.
Birds o' Benothy, 141.
Birnam, 12, 236, 240.
Birkin Hill, 251.
Births, 115.
Bishop Brown, 37, 130, 141.
Bishop of Orkney, 85.
Bishop of Rattray, 45, 141, 142.
Bishop of St Andrews, 33, 34, 35, 80.
Bissats o' Ferold, 141.
Bisset, John, of Marlee, 170, 230.
Bisset, Sir John, 253.
Bisset, Thomas S., 170, 227.
Bisset, Works of, 20, 170, 230, 239.
Blaar, 116.
Blackcraig, 68, 190, 238.
Blacklaw. 229, 262.
Blackloch, 13, 78, 180, 192, 199, 263.
Black, R. Robertson, 149.
Black Parliament. 215.
Black Watch. The, 163.
Blackwater, The, 183, 189, 190, 238.
Blair, 89, 90.
Blair Athole, 236.

INDEX.   269

Blair in Athole, 236, 254.
Blair of Ardblair, 33, 34, 38, 93, 129, 256, 257.
Blair of Balthayock, 209, 256.
Blair of Balude, 92.
Blair of Glasclune, 131, 257.
Blair of Gowrie, 116.
Blair of Pittendriech, 257.
Blair Drummond, 81, 83, 85, 206.
Blairs, 16, 17, 78.
Blair, Church of, 33, 35, 37, 44, 80, 81.
Blair, Curlers of, 14, 46.
Blair, Estate of, 43, 48, 49, 51, 222, 228, 229, 255.
Blair, Farm of, 235.
Blair, Feuars of, 48, 82.
Blair, Muir of, 14, 33, 34, 47, 48, 49, 79, 80, 81, 82, 148, 175, 180, 204, 242.
"Blair Watter Curlin' Stanes," 250.
Blair, Quarry of, 235.
Blair, 50 Years Ago, 249.
Blair, Abbot, 37, 209.
Blair, Alex. de, 33, 209, 256.
Blair, Sir Alex. de, 256.
Blair, Andro, 38.
Blair, Crest of, 71.
Blair, David, 38.
Blair, David de, 256.
Blair, Gilbert, 92.
Blair, John, 33, 38.
Blair, John de, 256.
Blair, James, 92.
Blair, Patour, 38.
Blair, Patrick, 38, 40, 256.
Blair, Rachel, 209.
Blair, Thomas, 38, 216, 256.
Blair, William, 38, 50.
Blair, Sir William de, 256.
Blair, de Bargillo, William, 88.
Blairgowrie Advertiser, 160, 193.
Blairgowrie to Alyth, 242.
Blairgowrie Annual, 158.
Blairgowrie Arms Hotel, 18.
Blairgowrie Blend, 265.
Blairgowrie Chiel' in Dunedin, 245.
Blairgowrie to Coupar Angus, 243.
Blairgowrie Deposit Company, 148.
Blairgowrie District Photographic Association, 150.
Blairgowrie Highlander in Russia, 245.
Blairgowrie House, 73, 139, 140, 170, 222, 235, 243, 253.
Blairgowrie in America, 243.
Blairgowrie Monthly, 158.
Blairgowrie News, 160.
Blairgowrie Parish Church Literary Association, 157.
Blairgowrie Volunteers in 1804, 257.
Blairgowrie Waterworks, 63.
Blairgowrie Whisky, 265.
Blairgowrie, Parish of, 67, 68, 95, 96.
Blairgowrie, Town of, 15, 42, 49, 50, 52, 54, 57, 58, 61, 63, 64, 65, 67, 68, 69, 70, 71, 74, 77, 78, 81, 82, 91, 95, 96, 97, 99, 100, 106, 122, 124, 127, 129, 130, 131, 132, 134, 135, 137, 139, 140, 147, 148, 150, 152, 153, 154, 156, 157, 159, 160, 161, 163, 165, 167, 168, 169, 171, 173, 175, 179, 183, 185, 187, 188, 192, 193, 194, 195, 198, 199, 200, 201, 203, 204, 206, 220, 221-232, 234-239, 241, 243-246, 248, 251-253, 255, 256, 259, 260, 263-266.
Ancient Trade, 171; Angling, 183; Burgh of Barony, 42, 66, 71, 81, 82, 124, 206, 248; Burgh Charters, 42; Burgh Seal, 70; Bailies, 51, 63, 75; Banquets, 59; Burns Centenary, 55; Bowling, 193; Curling, 120, 194, 200; Cross of, 18, 19, 59; Description of, 17, 137, 246; Distances from, 236; Etymology, 16; Ecclesiastical State, 91, 122; Evening Classes, 154; Eminent Men, 128, 206; Earthquake, 52; Fossil Plants, 23; First Bailie, 51; French Revolution, 53; First Newspaper, 53; Fair o' Blair, 173, 174, 201; Founding of Public Hall, 57; Field Club, 151; Football, 203; Franchise Demonstration, 67; First Provost, 70; Gift of Public Park, 69; Gas, 52; Golf, 204, 235; Improvements, 17, 66; Interesting Notes, 244; Institutions, 147; Macpherson Fountain, 19, 71; Military Service in, 50; Mons Grampius, 12, 17, 26; Old Worthies, 171; Opening of Railway, 14, 53; Quarries, 23; Rifle Corps, 56, 58; Situation, 11, 12, 15, 91; Soil, 21; Sewage System, 73; Schools, 106; School Boards, 66, 156, 228; Schoolmasters, 103; 108; Walks and Drives around, 233.
Blair's College, 99, 100.
Blairhill, 78.
Blairloch, 78.
Blairgowrie Statistical Account—
Antiquities, 128; Births, 115; Bleachfield, 117; Birds, 115; Bridges, 127; Character, 115; Climate, 118; Disadvantages, 128; Diseases, 118; Ecclesiastical State, 122; Eminent Men, 128; Farm Rents, 125; Gentlemen's Seats, 127; Improvements, 125; Islands, 120; Inclosures, 124; Labour, 117; Markets, 124; Manufactures, 121; Minerals, 121; Poor, 123; Prices, 117; Produce, 125; Professions, 114; Provisions, 117; Religious Persuasions, 115; Rent, 115; Rivers, 119; Stock, 115; Stamp Office, 117; Schools, 122; Scenery, 119; Situation, 116; Soil, 116; Springs, 121; Surface, 116; Woods, 121.
Bleachfield, 117.

Bleaton House, 17, 148.
Bloody Inches, The, 33, 78.
Board of Health, 20, 234.
Board of Supervision, 73.
Boat Brae, 49, 237, 242.
Boatlands, 260.
Boatman of Blair, 105.
Boat Pule, 190.
Boetius, 30.
Bog, 251.
Boglea, 231.
Bogmill, 251.
Bog, Thomas, 50.
Boundary Commission, 68.
Bowling, 18, 84, 193.
Braemar, 230, 236, 237, 238.
Braes of Angus, 35.
Braes o' Mar, 230.
Braidwalls, 218.
Bramblebank, 162, 233.
Brass Coin Tester, 263.
Brass Cooking Pot, 263.
Breadalbane, Earl of, 95, 157, 164.
Brechin, 83, 98, 256.
Brewery, 19.
Brewing, 171.
Bridge, 71, 73, 186, 187, 190, 234, 242.
Bridges, 127.
Bridge of Blair, 16, 19, 52, 71, 140, 145.
Bridge of Cally, 189, 190, 236, 238.
Bridge of Craighall, 234, 237, 254.
Bridge of Isla, 243.
Bridie, John, 55, 60, 67, 69, 70, 73, 75, 144, 146, 150, 154, 195, 225, 226.
Brisbane, Tinsmith, 172.
Brooklinn, 168, 220, 223.
Bronze Celt, 78, 263.
Bronze Pin, 263.
Bronze Pot, 263.
Brown, David, 177, 230, 252.
Brown, John, 18, 21, 75.
Brown, John, Writer, 94.
Brown, George, 75.
Brown Street, 21, 94, 147, 151, 171, 255.
Brown Street Chapel, 93, 94.
Brown's Hotel, 177, 230.
Brownsville, 48, 235.
Bruce, John, 173, 178.
Bruce, King Robert, 185, 215.
Bruce, Wully, 186.
Brude, King, 31.
Buchan, Alex., 75.
Burgess Circular, A, 246.
Burgesses, 66, 82.
Burgh of Barony, 42, 66, 71, 81, 82, 124, 206, 248.
Burgh Charters, 42, 81, 206, 248.
Burgh Police Act, 70.
Burgh Seal, 70.
Burlie Wull, 179.
Burnhead, 64, 234.
Burns Centenary, 55.
Burrelton, 12.
Business of the Town, 174.
Butler, Sir James, 33.

Buttergask, 229.
Butterstone, 32, 191, 240.
Butter, Turnie, 176.
Buttir of Gormok, 39, 40, 132.
Buzzard Dykes, 78.

C.

Cairnbutts, 77.
Cairncross, David, 184, 186.
Cairnie, 32.
Cairnmoor, 77.
Cairns, 77.
Cairnwell, The, 238.
Calady, 88, 89.
Caledonia, 13, 25.
Caledonian Camp, 78.
Caledonian Railway, 255.
Cally, 43, 88, 89, 189, 237.
Cally, Bridge of, 189, 190, 236, 238.
Camera, Thomas de, 88.
Cammell, Jamie, 198.
Campbell, Archibald, 38.
Campbell, Captain, 54.
Campbell, Sir Colin, 247.
Campbell, John, 247.
Campbell, J. L., 161, 162, 163.
Campbell, Major, 140.
Campbell, Miss, 147.
Campy, 81, 90.
Campsy, 89, 90.
Candy Betty, 178.
Caoill-daoinn, 13.
Caputh, 141, 237, 241.
Caputh Bridge, 32.
Caractacus, 25.
Cargill, 12, 14, 43, 83, 236.
Cargill, Daniel, 84.
Cargill, Donald, 263.
Cargill Leap, 233.
Carnashic Woods, 235.
Carnegie, Andrew, 159.
Carrington, 35.
Carse of Gowrie, 229.
Carsie, 48, 81, 180, 229, 237, 242, 259.
Carsie Farina Mill, 252.
Carsie Scutching Mill, 252.
Cascades, 119.
Castles, 129.
Castlehill, 130, 136, 162, 236.
Castle of Rattray, 136.
Castle Street, 20.
Caterans, 35.
Cattle, 116.
Catty Mill, 252.
Celestial Globe, 264.
Cemetery, 236, 241, 248.
Cennethy, 15.
Centenary of Burns, 55.
Chalmers, David, 75, 161, 163, 231, 232.
Chalmers of Drumlochy, 38, 39, 81, 83.
Chalmers Family, 88.
Chalmers, James, 21, 75, 231.
Chalmers, Major P., 232.
Chalmers of Mause, 253.

INDEX. 271

Chalmers of Nether Clayquhat, 254.
Chalmers, Peter, 230, 254,
Chalmers Street, 21.
Chalmers, William, 38, 41, 83, 88, 90.
Chalmers, Sir William, 52, 238, 247.
Chalmer, Thomas. 88.
"Change Here for Blairgowrie," 265, 266.
Character, 115.
Charles I., 42, 71, 81, 124, 203, 206, 219. 255.
Charles II., 92.
Charlie, Prince, 14, 18, 47, 130.
Charlie's Well, 47.
Charters, 42, 51, 74, 81, 82, 83, 84, 185, 209, 219.
Chawmer, John, 90.
Chawmyr, Robert, 88, 89.
Cheque Bank, 150.
Chief-Magistrates, 60, 66, 67, 69, 70, 71, 73, 75, 225.
   Bridie, John, 75, 154.
   Doig, Thomas, 70.
   Fleming, John, 162, 231.
   Neilson, Dr James, 75, 223.
   Steven, Thomas, 75, 232.
Children's Rhyme, 172.
Choral Society, 151.
Choral Society Conductors—Hirst, Neale, Smith, 151; Fisher, Howells, Parker, 152.
Church of Blair, 33, 35, 37, 44, 80, 81.
Church Tokens. 90, 264.
City Fathers, 74.
Clackmannan, 34, 80.
Clark, Bailie, 74.
Clark, Thomas, 231. 235.
Clayquhat, 37, 46. 229. 238.
Claverhouse, 14, 210, 233.
Cleaven Dykes, 78.
Cleekerinn, 204, 236.
Clerk-Rattray Estates, 219.
Clerk, John, of Penicuik, 219.
Clerk-Rattray, Sir James, 219.
Cleansing Department, 173.
Climate, 118.
Cloth, 117.
Cloves of Mause, 121.
Clunie, 13, 15, 34, 37, 78, 81, 141, 175. 192, 210, 237, 240, 264.
Clunie Cottage, 240.
Coble Pule, 49, 142, 143, 254.
Cochrage, 15, 44, 68, 77, 78, 82, 235, 264.
Cochrane, George P., 231.
Cockade, The White, 246.
Cockit Hat, The. 195.
Coffin, The, 172.
Collection for Glasgow, 103.
Colonsay's Lord, 36.
Commendator of Scone, 84.
Commercial Bank, 147, 232.
Commercial Bank House, 147.
Commercial Inn, 175.
Commercial Street, 18, 67.
Commissions of Volunteers, 162.
Commissioners, 51, 52, 66, 69, 72, 73, 74, 225.

Commissioners, Seal of, 70.
Common Muir, 49, 80. 82.
Communion Cups, 106.
Communion Tokens, 90, 264.
Compendium of News, 160.
Conditions of Life, 114.
Condy, 41.
Congregational Church, 20, 100.
Connacher, John, 254.
Constable, George, 75, 178.
Constable Lane, 21.
Constitutional Club, 18. 152.
Coontlie, The, 236.
Corbie Stane, 142, 143.
Corrydon, 81.
Cottage Hospital, Blairgowrie, 265.
Cottarton, 230.
Cottershade. 77.
Councillors, 82.
Council, County, 67, 229, 232.
Council, Parish, 229.
Count Dauide, 80.
Count Gillebryd, 80.
County of Perth, 61.
Coupar, Andrew, 135. 141.
Coupar, 12, 80, 89, 90, 214, 215.
Coupar Angus, 17, 33, 52, 53, 61, 80, 88, 127, 150, 166, 168, 185, 195, 198, 199, 201, 209, 230, 235, 237, 243, 260, 266.
Coupar Grange, 82. 190, 229, 235.
Coupar, James, M.D., 254.
Coupar, Thomas, 198.
Couper, John, 177.
Courthouse, 42, 82.
Couttie, 243.
Cowan, William, 50, 179, 231.
Cowan, William, student, 155.
Cowan, John, 162.
Cowpar, Col. Robert, 230, 245.
Crago, John of, 90.
Craighall, 14, 24, 74, 133, 136, 137, 138, 175, 185, 190, 214, 216, 218, 219, 232, 234, 236, 237, 254, 258.
Craigie, 229.
Craigie, John, 232.
Craigie, William, 75, 231.
Craigliach, 133, 134, 138.
Craiglush, 240.
Craig Roman, 78, 239.
Craig-y-Barns, 240.
Crechton, John, 40.
Creuchies, 68.
Crichton, Admirable, 37, 131, 210, 240.
Crichton, Bishop, 131.
Crichton of Eliock, 131, 210.
Cricket, 193.
Cripple Colin, 179.
Crockart, James, 161, 184, 186, 187, 231.
Crockart, William, 57, 172.
Croft, 19, 249.
Croft Lane, 67, 171, 172.
Cromwell, 14, 43, 136.
Cross, 147, 176.
Cross of Blair, 18, 19, 59, 234, 239, 249.
Crown Inn, 19.

Culross, William, 179, 230.
Cumberland, 14, 47, 235.
Cunnison, George, 265.
Curious Despatch, A, 244.
Curious Notes, 244.
Curiously-Shaped Stone, 264.
Curlers' Dinner, The, 146.
Curling, 120, 194, 200.
  Account of Origin, 198; Ardblair, 199; Blair Curlers, 14, 46, 146, 198, 224, 226; Centenary Ode, 195; Curling House, 197; Charitable Fund, 198; Early Records, 194; Ericht Water Stanes, 195, 250; Form of Play, 197; The Greatest Duffer, 198; Jamie Camnnell, 198; A London Editorial, 199; Match in 1782, 198; Minute Books, 196; Minister's Fondness for, 194; Metrical Account, 195; Prince Charlie, 14, 46, 146; Royal C. C. C., 198; Rules of, 195; Supply of Stones, 197; Winter Pastime, 194.
Cuttle Burn, 20, 233, 234.
Cycling, 201.
Cycling Club, 201.

D.

Daft Hary, 176.
Dalmunzie, 229.
Dalnagairn, 229.
Dames' Schools, 111, 264.
Dark Fa's, The, 59, 77, 161, 235, 236, 242.
Darroch, 76, 162.
David II., 34, 129.
David Street, 249.
Davie's Pend, 19.
Davie, William, 179.
Davie, William, 55, 69, 70, 232.
Davie Park, 69.
Davidson, Sergt., 164.
Decreet Arbitral, 48, 82.
Deed of Demission, 93.
Delvine, 14, 30, 78, 140, 195, 236, 241.
Den of Airlie, 237, 242.
Den of Ogilvy, 253.
Description of Seal, 70.
Description, Pennant's, 246.
Devil's Elbow, 238.
Dewar, Dean of Guild, 61.
Dick, Bailie James, 75.
Dick, Lieutenant, 51, 257.
Dickson, D., R.W.M., 156.
Dickson, George, 155.
Dickson, William, 232, 264.
Diocese of Dunkeld, 99.
Disadvantages, 128.
Diseases, 118.
Disruption, 94, 95, 96, 97.
Distances from Blair, 236.
Doeg, Jeems, 172.
Doig, Thomas, 69, 70.
Donald Cargill, 263.

Donaldson, John, 50.
Dookin' Hole, The, 186.
Douay, 99, 100.
Doune, 99.
Dow, Robbie, 195.
Dow, Robert, 75.
Downie, James, 50.
Dramatic Society, 152.
Dreadnought, The, 179, 249.
Drill Hall, 18, 164, 205.
Drimmie, 86, 185, 191, 214.
Druids, The, 76.
Druidsmere, 139, 232, 236, 242.
Druidical Circle, 236, 241.
Drumlochy, 14, 37, 38, 39, 40, 41, 45, 83, 88, 131, 134, 234.
Drumlochy Castle, 131.
Drummellie, 192, 230.
Drummond of Blair, 14, 34, 37, 38, 42, 71, 81, 83, 84, 206, 209.
Drummond, Crest of, 71.
Drummond Charters, 42.
Drummond, Massacre of, 14, 37, 84, 131, 193.
Drummond Summons, 38.
Drummond of Cargill, 83, 84.
Drummond, George, of Blair, 37, 38, 42, 81, 206.
Drummond, George, Lord Provost, 78, 85, 86, 128, 157, 206, 249, 263.
Drummond, Sketch of his Life, 206.
Drummond Monument, 207.
Drummond Bust, 207.
Drummond Medal, 263.
Drummond Place Names, 20, 21.
Drummond, David, 84.
Drummond, John, 83.
Drummond, May, 208.
Drummond, Sir Walter, 83.
Drummond, William, 37, 38, 40.
Drummond of Ledcrief, 38, 39.
Drummond, Millowner, 169.
Drummond, Moray, 81.
Drummond, Thomas, 38.
Drummond of Blair Drummond, 81, 83, 85, 206.
Drumore, 229.
Drwmy, 88.
Drybriggs, 236.
Drymmys, 215.
Dryomie, 82, 88.
Duddingston, 198.
Duffus, James, 50.
Dullater, 251, 252.
Dunblane, 99.
Duncan, Comes, 80.
Duncan, son of Donald, 80.
Duncan, G. S., F.S.A., Scot., 78, 264.
Duncan, Justiciario, 80.
Duncan, James, 50.
Duncan, Samson, 187.
Duncrub, 41.
Dundee, 43, 50, 53, 54, 61, 65, 80, 97, 121, 128, 166, 225, 230, 231, 235, 237.
Dundee Advertiser, 62, 217, 226.
Dundee Blairgowrie Association, 152.

INDEX.

Dunkeld, 12, 37, 43, 83, 99, 130, 192, 215, 235, 236, 237, 239, 240, 241, 252.
Dunkeld Cathedral, 238.
Dunkeld Road, 18, 159.
Dunsinane, 12.
Dwly, Master Antonio, 90.

E.

Earl of Gowrie, 79, 128.
Earl of Mar, 35.
Earl Russell, 59.
Earthquake, 52.
East Banchory, 50.
Easter Bog, 251.
Easter Rattray, 76.
Eavlick, Johnnie, 175.
Ecclesiastical State, 91, 122.
Edinburgh, 41, 65, 78, 81, 93, 97, 128, 184, 198, 206, 259.
Edinburgh Review, 56.
Edinburgh University, 93, 226.
Edinburgh Blairgowrie Club, 154.
Edward I., 33, 130, 133, 214.
Edward III., 133.
Edward IV., 216.
Edward, Doctor, 172.
Electric Light, 266.
Elliot, Hon. Mrs. 61.
Emma Terrace, 18.
Eminent Men, 128, 206.
Emperor Hadrian, 77.
English Army in Scotland, 103.
Enochhdu, 239.
Enrolment Returns, 50.
Episcopacy, 42.
Episcopal Schools, 111.
Eppie Clark's Ale-House, 14, 47, 146.
Ericht, The, 12, 13, 15, 18, 24, 62, 73, 79, 119, 120, 121, 124, 137, 138, 167, 168, 173, 183, 185, 186, 187, 188, 189, 190, 197, 233, 237, 248, 250, 262.
Ericht Lane, 19.
Ericht Linen Works, 19, 169, 170, 233.
Erichtside Works, 169, 186.
Erichtvale, 12.
Errochy, 82.
Erskine, John, 43.
Essendy Road, 76, 236.
Essendy, Wester, 230.
Established Church, 66, 95, 229.
Establishment, 94.
Etymology, 16.
Evening Classes, 154.
Evidences of Battle, 30.
Extent of Parish, 116.
Extracts, Parochial Registers, 100.

F.

"Factor," The, 229.

Fairies, The, 179.
Fair o' Blair, 173, 174, 201.
Falcon House, 20, 140, 230, 236, 241, 265.
False Alarm, A, 51.
Farina Mill, 252.
Farm Rents, 125.
Farquharson, David, A.R.S.A., 232.
Fasts, 91, 102.
Fell, John D., 49, 75, 176, 199.
Fengus Loch, 13, 162, 192.
Fenton, Jamie, 187.
Fenwick, Mr, 65.
Fercade, M. Eugene, 63.
Feu, The, 20.
Feuing Plan, 265.
Field Club, 151.
Filter House, 73.
Finegand, 81.
First Bailie, 51.
First Free Church, 16, 18, 96, 97, 221, 230, 252.
First Free School, 110, 223, 245.
First Free Literary, 158.
Fish, 119.
Fishings, 88, 90, 119, 183.
Fish Ladders, 188.
Fishways, 187.
Flaskhill, 84.
Fleeming, John, 50.
Fleming, John, 75, 162, 231.
Flint Arrow Heads, 263.
Flodden, 209, 216, 217.
Floreat Blairgowrie, 266.
Fluke, The, 195.
Flute Band, 56, 57.
Forbes, Laird, 179.
Forest of Clunie, 15, 251, 263.
Forest of Clunie Farms, 251.
Forfar, 11, 12, 36, 86, 98, 226, 236, 255.
Forneth, 22, 236, 252.
Forneth House, 240.
Fort George, 127.
Fothringham of Fothringham, 135.
Franchise Demonstration, 67.
Fraser, Sir Wm., 83.
Free Church School, 57.
Free Masonry, 57, 59, 156.
Free Manse, 96.
Free Press, 160.
Free Secession, 93.
Free South Church, 97.
French Revolution, 52.
Football, 203.
Fossils, 23.
Fyall Burn, 191.

G.

Galdus, 25, 26.
Galgacus, 13, 25, 26, 140.
Gallowbank, 20, 42, 79, 236, 249.
Gallowsknowe, 42, 142.
Gammell, Col., 134.
Garrick Club, 152.
Gartsherrie, 232, 265.

274 INDEX.

Gas, 52.
Gas Brae, 17.
Gas Work, 17, 19, 52, 224, 229.
Gask, 93, 130.
Geddes, James, 21.
Geddes, William, 224.
Geekie, Alexander, 150.
Geekie, Dr, 23.
Geekie, Robt. of Rosemount, 148, 263.
Gellately, Geo. 148.
Gellately, Corporal, 163.
Gellyburn, 23, 263.
Genealogy of Blair Family, 256, 257.
General, The, 179.
Gentlemen's Seats, 127.
Geology, 21.
George Street, 18, 21, 94, 98.
Ghost of Mause, 43.
Gillies, Bishop, 99.
Glamis, 12, 236.
Glamis Castle, 153, 252.
Glasclune, 14, 36, 68, 131, 234, 235, 236, 257, 262.
Glasclune, Hering of, 40, 84.
Glasclune, Burn of, 64.
Glasgow, 93, 96, 97, 229, 232, 266.
Glebe, 66, 91, 96, 233.
Glenballoch, 76, 77, 218, 262.
Glenballow, 46.
Glenbathloch, 215.
Glenbeg, 238.
Glenbethlac, 214.
Glenbrierachan, 239.
Glencairn, 43.
Glencaveryn, 214.
Glenclunie, 238.
Glenericht, 52, 55, 88, 190, 229, 247.
Glenericht House, 238.
Glenfernate, 229.
Glenisla, 242.
Glenshee, 229, 236, 237, 238, 242.
Globe, The, 61.
Glower-ower-im, 13, 15.
Golf, 204, 235.
Golf Club, 204.
Golf Course, 204, 235, 236, 244.
Good Story, A, 54.
Goorkha Regiment, 221.
Gorblair, 78.
Gordon of Lesmore, 40.
Gordon of Scheves, 40.
Gordon of Straloch, 81.
Gormack, 12, 14, 37, 38, 39, 77, 78, 82, 132, 229.
Gorthy, Laird of, 85.
Gothens, 180.
Gourdie, 78, 262.
Gowanbrae, 77.
Gowanlea, 230.
Gowrie, 16, 17, 229.
Graham of Gormok, 41.
Graham of Montrose, 14, 42.
Graham, Hon. Mrs. 213.
Graham, Thomas, 14, 20, 49, 74, 82, 93, 211, 264.
Grain Mills, 233.
Grampians, 11, 12, 15, 190, 242, 248.
Grange, 218.

Grange of Airlie, 230.
Grant, Wm., Chemist, 265.
Grant, Private, 154.
Greenbank, 77, 78.
Greenbank Works, 16, 170, 263.
Greenfield, 55, 231.
Green Lady o' Newton, The, 142.
Green Tree, The, 235.
Grey Cairn, 262.
Grey, Gilbert, 40.
Grimond, Alex. D., 220.
Grimond, David, 165, 168, 219.
Grimond, David, 169, 220.
Grimond, James, 167, 169, 220.
Grimond, John, 169.
Grimond, Joseph, 220.
Grimond of Lornty, 219.
Guard House, The, 19, 174.
Guthrie, Dr., 97.
Gymnastic Club, 205.

H.

Haer Cairns, 77.
Haltown, 84.
Haremyre, 192.
Harris, Lily, 175.
Harris, Matthew, 175.
Hary, Daft, 176.
Harry, Blind, 33.
Hatton, 84, 262.
Hatton Hill, 13, 15, 236.
Haughs of Delvine, 25.
Haugh Park, 194, 204.
Haugh of Rattray, 14, 256.
Hays of Gourdie, 131.
Heathpark, 48, 231, 235.
Hebenton, Band-Sergt. William, 163, 251.
Hen, The, 195.
Henderson, Henry, 50.
Hering, James, 40.
Herring, Sir David, 84, 134.
Herons, The, 34, 84, 131.
Heron, Allan, 254.
Heughs of Mause, 15, 17, 21, 161, 232, 234, 236, 237.
Hey! an' How! 141.
Hicks and Charlewood, 71.
Highlands, 52, 55.
Highland Caterans, 35.
Highland Games, 160.
Highland Warfare, 36.
Highlanders, 42nd, 163, 248.
Highlanders, 75th, 251.
Highlanders, 92nd, 231.
Highlanders, 93rd, 163.
High Street, 17, 18, 67, 158, 172, 175, 179, 234, 244, 249, 263.
Hill of Blair, 14, 15, 16, 17, 18, 19, 47, 49, 51, 55, 94, 95, 146, 147, 161, 234, 249, 255.
Hill, Colour-Sergt. Adam, 163.
Hill Terrace, 234.
Hilltown, 45.
Hirchen Hill, 42, 79.
Hollymill Brae, 242.

INDEX.

Horse, The, 195.
Horticultural Society, 157.
Hour Glass, 262.
Howe of Strathmore, 11, 235, 242.
Hugh of Caledon. 80.
Hungus, King, 31.
Hurricane, A, 74.
Hymn Tune, "Blairgowrie," 251.

I.

Illuminated Clock, 255.
Implement Works, 20.
Improvements. 17, 125.
Improvement Act, 66.
Incense Cup, 78, 262.
Inchmartine. 229.
Inclosures, 124.
Inchtuthil. 14, 32.
Indigent Baronet, An, 103.
Inducement to Feuars, 255.
Industry and Invention, 265.
Infirmary. Royal, 157.
Instrument of Renunciation, 81.
Instrument of Tollerance, 81.
Instrumental Band, 55, 56, 57, 156, 162, 164, 250.
Interceptors, 73.
International Exhibition, 151.
Interesting Despatches, 257.
Interesting Notes, 255.
In the Jouggs, 104.
Invercauld, 186.
Inverness, 230.
Inverquiech. 133. 134.
Inverurie, 100.
Irons. Archie, 173, 187.
Iron Door Knocker, 262.
Iron Key. 262.
Iron Studs, 262.
Irvine. Jamie, 173.
Isla. River, 12, 134, 139, 185, 190, 191, 248.
Islands, 120.
Isle, The, 43, 120.
Isles. James, F.S.A., Scot., 69, 70, 78, 232, 255, 263.
Isles, William, 50.

J.

Jackson's Inn, 18.
Jackson, John, 179.
James I., 42, 83, 216.
James II., 83.
James IV., 216, 257.
James VI., 92. 216.
James VII., 85, 87, 92.
James Street, 18, 21, 57, 110, 245, 249, 255.
James Street House, 254, 263.
James Street Magazine, 158.
James Street School, 110.
Jardine, Sir Henry, 209.
Jessie Street, 20, 110.

Johann Hasting, 80.
John Street, 19, 21, 67, 109, 110, 249.
Johnstone, Jimmy, 172.
Johnstone, Robbie, 179.
Johnstone, Tammas, 75.
Johnstone, Thomas, 75.
Johnstone, William, 148, 173.
Josephus, 30.
Jouggs, The, 104, 241.
Justice of Peace, 52.

K.

Keay, Duncan, 50.
Keay, Street, 21.
Keepers of the Signet, 87.
Keith, The, 14, 43, 120, 186, 188, 233.
Keithbank, 233.
Kilry, 255.
Kincairney, 77.
Kinclaven. 33, 132, 133, 236, 262.
Kinclaven, Castle of, 132.
Kidd, David, 75.
King's Remembrancer, 209.
Kingoldrum, 214
Kinloch, 16, 68. 128, 131, 150, 151, 263.
Kinloch House, 239.
Kinloch Manse, 239.
Kinpurnie, 13, 234.
Kirk, The, 195
Kirke of Blair, 37, 44, 84.
Kirkwynd, 79.
Kirkyard, 46
Kirkmichael, 236, 239, 242.
Kirriemuir, 12, 17, 236, 242.
Kleice Kirn, 186
Kochredge, 82.
Knockie, 11, 44, 235.
Knockie Road, 235.
Knockie Quarry, 235.
Knock-ma-har, 11, 15, 17, 20, 22, 37, 78, 132, 234.
Knock-ma-har. Castle of, 132.
Knowehead, 45.
Knox, Mr, 26.
Kynballoch, 218, 219.
Kynoch. James, 232.

L.

Labour, 117.
Lady Lindsay's Castle, 133, 138.
Laighwood, 240.
Laird of Blair. 73, 85.
Laird, Jeems, 179.
Laird of Kinmonth, 217.
Laird, Sir William, 232, 264.
Lakes, 120.
Lamont, Colour-Sergt., 163.
Lands of Blair, 33, 85.
Lansdowne Golf Course, 204.
Lansdowne, Marquis of, 139, 210.
Larg & Keir, 160.
Lauder, William, 57.

Lawson, John, 94.
Legends, 44, 141.
Ledcrief, 84.
Leslie, James, 21, 75, 230.
Leslie of Kinrorie, 217.
Leslie, Mr, C.E., 64, 65, 189.
Leslie Street, 17, 19, 21, 67, 148, 150, 158, 202, 249.
Lethendy, 236, 237, 262.
Lethendy Tower, 84, 134, 241.
Lethnide, 84.
Letter from Chevalier, 254.
Lindsay, Col. William, 122.
Linnkeith House, 233.
"Lit.," The, 157.
Literary Societies, 157.
Little Blair, 33, 80.
Littleton of Rattray, 242.
Loch Blair, 34, 81, 141.
Loch Blair Castle, 135.
Loch Benachally, 63, 64, 65, 189, 190, 191.
Loch Bog, 77, 192, 195.
Lochend of Blair, 116.
Lochy, The, 18, 24, 47, 146.
Loch of the Leys, 192, 239.
Loch Leven, 184, 185.
Loch of the Lowes, 192, 240.
Lochy Terrace, 18, 193.
Lodbrog, the Dane, 31, 33.
Lodge, St John, 157.
Logie House, 140, 240.
Lomonds, The, 18.
Long Service Medals, 163.
Loon Braes, 69.
Lord of the Isles, 36.
Lords of the Treasury, 85, 87.
Lord Provost of Perth, 61.
Lornty, The, 15, 21, 49, 64, 78, 131, 168, 190, 233, 235.
Lornty Cottage, 47, 234.
Lornty House, 234.
Low, Abram, 179.
Low, Isaac, 181, 186.
Low, Jacob, 230.
Low, Private, 164.
Lower Mill Street, 49, 172, 233.
Lowrie's, John, 171.
Luke & Company, 169, 170.
Lunan Burn, 190, 192.
Lunan, Dr C. S., 173.
Lunan, Dr Robert, 75, 226, 227.
Lyall, James Durward, 232.
Lynedoch, Lord, 74, 211, 214.
Lyndsay, Sir David, 36.

M.

Magistrates, 60, 66, 67, 69, 70, 71, 73, 75, 225.
Makeden, 89.
Malcolm Canmore, 33.
Malcolm IV., 243
Malcolm filio Duncan, 80.
Malt Barns, 55.
Mann, Tammy, 175, 176.
Manchester Guardian, 62.

Manrent, Bond of, 37, 40.
Mansions, 129.
Manufactures, 121, 165, 187.
Map of Scotland, 81.
Marlee, 170, 191, 227, 228, 230, 232, 252, 262.
Marlee Hotel, 239.
Marlee House, 239.
Marlee Loch, 13, 184, 185, 192, 198, 236.
Markets, 124.
Market Cross, 82.
Marsh of Blair, 80.
Marshall, James, 98.
Mar Rebellion, 132.
Maryfield, 20, 231, 235.
Masonic Hall, 151.
Mause, 127, 237, 238, 253.
Mause, Ghost of, 43.
Mause, Mains of, 44.
Maybank, 263.
Mayriggs, 243.
Mayriggs Fossils, 23.
Meal Mill, 19.
Mechanics' Institute, 18, 80, 158, 175, 262.
Meethillock, 77.
Meigle, 12, 98, 135, 194, 201, 237, 242.
Meikle Blair, 33, 80.
Meikleour, 14, 30, 47, 48, 58, 61, 63, 78, 139, 209, 237, 241, 252, 263.
Meikleour Arms, 140.
Meikleour Cross, 241.
Meikleour Square, 241.
Melfort, 87, 88.
Memorial Tablet, 93.
Mercate Cross, 18, 37, 82.
Mercate Gate, 39, 51.
Mercate Green, 193.
Mercers of Meikleour, 209.
Mercers, Sir Andrew, Emily Jane, James, Sir Henry, Laurence, Sir Laurence, Col. William, 209.
Methods of Husbandry, 126.
Middle Mause, 43, 77.
Middleton, 68.
Millbank, 55, 69, 148, 229.
Millhole, 68.
Mill Street, 21.
Millwright Works, 170, 176, 233.
Mills on the Ericht, 121, 167.
Mills, 167.
 Ashbank, 166, 169.
 Blairgowrie, 166.
 Bramblebank, 162, 233.
 Brooklinn, 168, 220, 233.
 Carsie, 166.
 Haugh, 143.
 Keithbank, 233.
 Lornty, 168, 234.
 Meikle, 167, 169, 233.
 Oakbank, 167, 220.
 Plash, 170.
Miller, James, 174.
Miller, Jno. B., 69, 148.
Militia Act, 52.
Military Service, 50.
Milton of Clunie, 248.
Milton of Drumlochy, 77.

INDEX. 277

Minerals, 121.
Mineral Springs, 121.
Mineral Well, 121.
Ministers—
  Abbey, 98.
  Anderson, Robert, 263.
  Baxter, Dr John, 97, 221.
  Blair, Gilbert, 92.
  Blaire, Thomas, 92.
  Bowis, Robert, 263.
  Burton, John, 98.
  Butter, Laurence, 263.
  Carmont, Dr John, 99.
  Cowans, —., 96.
  Crumley, Thomas, 99.
  Davis, F. W. 98, 200, 251.
  Dobson, —., 100.
  Dow, William, 93, 263.
  Fraser, William, 93.
  Foyer, J. W., 255.
  Gray, James, 263.
  Grant, Peter, 100.
  Herdman, William, 162, 263.
  Hutchinson, Robert D., 96.
  Inch, Alex. S., 154.
  Jardine, John, 209.
  Johnstone, James, 90, 93, 114, 263.
  Kemp, Robert, 93, 157.
  Lyall, —., 100.
  Lyon, James, 93, 194, 263.
  Macdonald, Robert, 93.
  Marshall, John, 98.
  M'Crie, Charles G., 97.
  M'Culloch, Alex., 263.
  M'Rae, David, 157.
  Malcolm, John, 99.
  Mercer, James, 209.
  Miller, D. K., 154.
  Millar, George, 263.
  Miller, John, 100.
  M'Kay, James, 98.
  Muir, William, 97.
  Minniken, —., 98.
  Ogilvy, Alex., 263.
  Pringle, J. W., 154.
  Ramsay, John, 92, 98.
  Rattray, Silvester, 254.
  Richardson, —., 98.
  Ross, John, 92, 203, 204.
  Smith, —., 94.
  Stewart, Robert, 96.
  Stewart, William, 92.
  Tait, John, 100.
  Taylor, Robert, 97.
  Tennant, E. M., 100.
  White, Malcolm, 97.
  Willison, Alex. S., 96.
Mission House, 19.
Mitchell, David, 148.
Mitchell Square, 21, 179.
Mitchell, Thomas, 21, 55, 75, 231.
Moir, James, 232.
Moncur, James, 232.
Monkquhell, 89.
Monksmyre, 192.
Mons Grampius, 12, 17, 26.
Montrose, 14, 42, 43, 136, 255, 256.
Moorfield, 243.
Moray, Bishop of, 84.

Morganstone, 77.
Mortimer, Roger, 80.
Moulin, 239.
Mount Blair, 13, 234.
Mount Ericht, 140.
Mount Zion, 233.
Mowbray, Sir Robert, 103.
Muckle Mill, 49, 167, 169, 170, 233.
Muir of Blair, 14, 33, 34, 47, 49, 79, 80, 81, 82, 148, 175, 180, 204, 242.
Muir of Gormok, 77.
Muirton of Ardblair, 88, 236, 242, 254.
Muirton Ponds, 200.
Municipal Buildings, 266.
Munro, Alex., 162.
Murdoch, Alex., 161.
Murtoun, 88, 89.
Murthly, 92, 262, 263.
Murthly Castle, 135, 241, 252.
Murthly Stone, 23.
Mustard, William, 173.
Mydilbait, 88, 90.

Mc.

Macadam, Professor, 64, 65, 66.
M'Alpin, Kenneth, 31, 130.
M'Alpin's Warriors, 14.
MacCombie, Family of, 81.
Macdonald Fishways, 188.
Macdonald, George, 148.
Macdonald Hotel, 57.
Macdonald, J. A. R., 70.
Macdonald, Dr Robert, 93, 94, 96, 97.
MacFarlane, Professor, 232.
MacFarlane, William, 230.
M'Gregor, John, 172.
M'Gregor's Hotel, 57.
M'Intosh, Donald, 252.
M'Intosh, Donald, miller, 259.
M'Intosh, James, farmer, 260.
M'Intosh, James, violin maker, 259, 260.
M'Intosh, Hary, 176.
M'Intosh, Peter, 166, 169, 231.
M'Intosh, Robert, "Red Rob," 259.
M'Intosh, William, 260.
M'Intyre, W. A., 194.
M'Intyre & Co., 170.
Mackay, Mr (C. S. I.), 73.
Mackbeth, Judge of Gowrie, 80.
Makcomas, John, 81.
Mackenzie, Sir A. Muir, 140.
Mackenzie, Colin, 179.
Maclachlan, John, 179.
M'Lachlan, Thomas, 161.
M'Laggan, Thomas, T. 153, 232.
Maclaren, Daniel, 172.
Maclaren's Hotel, 55.
MacLaren, Lieut.-Col. G. G., M.D., 140, 231, 265.
Maclaren, James F., 231.
M'Levy, James, 262.
M'Nab's Ale House, 249.
M'Nab, James, 75.

M'Nab, John, 179.
M'Neskar, 38.
Macpherson of Blairgowrie, 73, 221.
Macpherson of Belleville, 221.
Macpherson of Cluny, 221.
Macpherson of Glentruim, 221.
Macpherson of Noid (Nuide), 221.
Macpherson of Philadelphia, 221.
Macpherson of Ralia, 221.
Macpherson, Alan, 72.
Macpherson, Alan D., 73.
Macpherson, Allan, 19, 55, 66, 67, 68, 71, 72, 82, 162, 222, 255.
Macpherson, Col. Allan, 21, 49, 51, 82, 122, 139, 168, 222, 248, 257.
Macpherson Fountain, 19, 71, 223.
Macpherson, Mrs E., 71, 72, 73.
Macpherson, Patrick, 50.
Macpherson, William, 51, 53, 82, 91, 222, 253.
M'Ritchie, D., F.S.A., Scot., 140.
M'Ritchie, John, 179.

N.

Nairne, Lady, 209.
Napoleon, 50.
National Gallery, 213.
National Museum of Antiquities, 261.
National Security Savings Bank, 148.
Neilsonian Cauliflower, 244.
Neilson, Dr James, 66, 75, 155, 223.
Neilson, Robert, 244.
Neill, Bandmaster, 251.
Nelson, Robert, 263.
Nether Aird, 46, 64, 77, 253.
Nether Clayquhat, 254.
News, Blairgowrie, 160.
Newtoun, 82, 83, 193, 206.
Newton of Blair, 38, 39, 81, 82, 84.
Newton Burn, 172.
Newton Castle, 14, 20, 21, 37, 42, 43, 47, 71, 136, 206, 211, 235, 236.
Newton House 128, 144, 249.
Newton Lane, 21.
Newton Street, 21, 159.
Newton Terrace, 18, 20, 97.
Newspaper, the First, 53.
New Schools, 110.
New Town Hall, 266.
Newtyle, 12, 168, 200, 201, 229.
Neylson, Henry, 89.
Nicholls, Piper & Co., 264.
No Session, 103.
North Inch, 74, 214.
North of Scotland Bank, 148.

O.

Oakbank, 19, 163, 167, 169, 220, 233, 236.
Ochils, The, 13.
Ogilvy Arms, 19.

Ogilvy Arms Inn, 263.
Ogilvy, James, 19, 67, 68, 140, 171, 232, 252.
Old Rhyme, 176.
Old Spittal, 229.
Old Worthies, 171.
Oliphant of Gask, 93, 130, 209.
Oliphant, Captain Blair, 200.
Oliphant, P. K. Blair, 200.
Opening of Railway, 53.
Operation, An Interesting, 248.
Operative Bodies, 59.
Orchar, Jamie, 176.
Ordnance Survey, 64.
Origin, 17, 115.
Origin of Street Names, 21.
Original Inhabitants, 76.
Orkney, Bishop of, 85.
Our Boys, 204.

P.

Page, Thomas, 89.
Paisley, 93.
Palace, The, 18.
Panbride, 85
Pandoo, 76.
Panton, John, 148, 149, 228, 229, 233.
Panton, William, farmer, 231.
Panton, William S., maltster, 20.
Panton, William, overseer, 228.
Parish Burying Ground, 20, 46.
Parish Church, 16, 18, 20, 37, 51, 57, 66, 79, 84, 91, 93, 94, 95, 96, 97, 144, 158, 230, 233, 234, 253, 254, 255.
Parish Church Literary Association, 157.
Parish Manse, 20, 42, 66, 79, 91, 122, 233, 234.
Parish School, 20, 67, 109, 110, 150, 220, 221, 225, 227, 228, 249, 262.
Parish Tokens, 90, 263.
Parkhead, 22, 48, 68, 232, 235, 254.
Parkhill, 229, 242.
Parkhill House, 139.
Parsonage, 20.
Paterson, Corpl., 164.
Paterson, Sergt., 164.
Patrick, Count of Dunbar, 80.
P'easant Hen, 17.
Pedigree of Drummonds, 83.
Penketh, Ensign, 162, 163.
Pennant the Traveller, 137, 246.
Pennycook, John, 172.
Paroche Kirke, 14, 37, 39.
Persie, 96, 97, 237, 238, 261.
Perth, 11, 12, 17, 36, 45, 53, 61, 74, 90, 92, 98, 99, 128, 210, 214, 216, 217, 228, 229, 230, 236, 241, 255, 256.
Perth Banking Company, 148.
Perth, Earl of, 85, 86, 87.
Perthshire Football, 204.
Perth Presbytery, 92, 93.
Perth Road, 236, 249.
Perth Savings Bank, 148.

INDEX. 279

Perthshire, 13, 43, 49, 61, 74, 82, 84, 95, 138, 139, 204, 212, 241, 248.
Perthshire, Regiment (90th), 214.
Perth Street, 17, 18.
Peters, David, 173.
Peters, James, 230.
Peter the Jailer, 172.
Phillip de Walloun, 80.
Photography, 98, 150, 151, 158.
Picts, The, 30.
Picts, King of, 31.
Pipe Band, 164, 251.
Piscatorial, 24.
Pitcairn, 77.
Pitcairn's Criminal Trials, 37.
Pitcarmik, 82, 230.
Pitlochrie, 237, 239.
Place of Repentance, 103.
Places of Interest, 236.
Plantations, 128.
Planting of Trees, 67.
Plash Mill, 19, 170, 233.
Playfair, John, 50.
Polcolk, 218.
Police Act, 52.
Pope Gregory, XI., 35, 81.
Population, 107, 114, 115.
Poor, 123.
Poor Rates Established, 107.
Porter, Robbie, 179.
Portsmouth Times, 230.
Post Heaps, 173.
Post Office, 159, 178.
Post Reid, 173, 178.
Powntrail, 186.
Preaching Station, 94.
Precepts, 85
President, The, 195.
Press, The, 52, 159.
Prices of Labour, 117.
Prices of Provisions, 117.
Priest's House, 254, 255.
Prince Charlie, 14, 18, 47.
Prince Charlie's Well, 234.
Printing Introduced, 52, 231.
Privy Council, 92.
Proclamation of the Estates, 92.
Produce, 125.
Professions, 114.
Propagation of the Eel, 184.
Provincial Curling Match, 199.
Province of Strathmore, 200, 201.
Provosts, 70, 74, 75, 225.
  Bridie, John, 75, 150.
  Chalmers, James, 21, 75, 231.
  Parker, 61.
  Stewart, James, 75, 232.
  Templeman, David, 75, 232.
  Yeaman, James, 153
Public Fêtes, 57, 58, 61.
Public Hall, 57, 58, 60, 70, 151, 156, 173, 201, 205.
Public Park, 69, 232, 266.
Public Schools, 18, 20, 66, 68, 96, 156.
Pullar, David, 81, 90.

Q.

Quarries, 22.

Queen, The, 14, 52, 54, 56, 69, 145, 161, 162, 184, 213, 219, 237, 245, 247, 265.
Queen Caroline, 208.
Queen Marie, 38.
Queen Mary's Summons, 38.
Queen of Scots, 38.
Queen's Hotel, 18, 57, 159, 227.
Queen's Visits, 14, 52, 54.
Quoad Sacra Parish, 95.
Quoit Club, 178.

R.

Rae Loch, 192, 239.
Railway Hotel, 19.
Railway Service, 14, 53, 168.
Railway Station, 17, 54, 55, 67, 73.
Raitt, William, 49.
Ramsay of Banff, 61.
Ramsay, James, 82.
Ramsay, Sir James, 94.
Ramsay, Keith, 245.
Ramsay, Sir William, 53.
Randale, Donald, 89.
Rattray, 12, 15, 43, 50, 55, 65, 67, 68, 69, 70, 82, 122, 136, 148, 150, 162, 186, 188, 193, 199, 221, 225, 234, 237, 242, 252, 254, 256, 261, 262, 263.
Rattray, Alanus de, 136.
Rattray Arms, 136.
Rattray, Bishop, 45, 83.
Rattray Churchyard, 215.
Rattray Curling Club, 200.
Rattray of Dalnoon, 218.
Rattray, Dr, 73.
Rattray Estates, 217.
Rattray, George, 84.
Rattray, James, 187.
Rattray, Sir J. Clerk, 74, 219, 258, 259, 264.
Rattray, John, of Coralbank, 162, 187.
Rattray of Persie, 218.
Rattray Public School, 205.
Rattray of Rattray and Craighall, 214, 256.
Rattray, Silvester, 254.
Recollections of the Past, 171.
Rectory, The, 200.
Red Brae, 250.
Rede, John, 89.
Reekie Linn, 249.
Reformation, 92, 131.
Reform Street, 17, 54, 95, 160, 243, 249.
Regality Court, 128.
Regiment, 90th, 74.
Register House, 81.
Reichip, 253.
Reid, John, Ogilvy Arms Inn, 263.
Relics, 262, 263.
Religious Persuasions, 115.
Rent, 115.
Rental Book, 88, 185.
Reservoir, 64.

INDEX.

Rest and be Thankful, 11, 265.
Revue de deux Mondes, 63.
Rifle Corps, 56, 59.
Rifle Range, 161, 194.
Rivers, 119, 189, 190.
Roads, 127.
Roaring Game, 199.
Robb, D. C., 225.
Robert I., 34, 80.
Robert II., 130.
Robert III., 35, 210.
Robert de Quinci, 80.
Robertson, Alex., Banker, 55, 147, 223.
Robertson, Donald, 88.
Robertson, Duncan, 172.
Robertson, George, Bailie, 75.
Robertson, George, Weaver, 50.
Robertson, John, Porter, 264.
Robertson, J. L., 161.
Robertson, Moreover, 174.
Robertson, Miss, 263.
Robertson, Robert, banker, 147, 223.
Robertson, Robert, schoolmaster, 25, 110, 147, 254.
Robertson, Thomas, 38.
Robertson, William, baker, 161, 232.
Robertson, William (cycle), 201.
Robertson, William, 75, 174, 179.
Roger of St Andrews, 80.
Rollock, Andro, 41.
Rollock, James, 41.
Rollock, Robert, 218.
Roman Camp, 32, 140, 241.
Roman Coins, 77.
Roman Catholic School, 19, 112.
Roman Pot, 78, 262.
Roman Remains, 77, 78.
Rory Street, 54.
Rory, William, 38.
Rosemount, 22, 48, 68, 204, 262.
Rosemount House, 135, 235.
Rosemount Station, 235, 243.
Rosemount Wood, 235.
Ross' Compendium, 53, 160, 231.
Ross, James, 53, 179, 231.
Rough Ford, The, 237.
Round the Golf Course, 235.
Round Knockmabar, 234.
Rowbowlis, 84
Rowchaille, 82.
Royal Arch Chapter, 157.
Royal Bank of Scotland, 148, 171, 179, 229.
Royal Caledonian Curling Club, 198.
Royal Hotel, 16, 18, 20, 55, 59, 179, 193.
Royal Infirmary, 14, 128, 207, 208.
Royal Insurance Society, 229.
Royal Route, 55, 237.
Royal Scotch Whisky, 264.
Royals, 21st, 54.
Russell, Earl, 14, 58, 59, 60, 61, 63.

S.

Sabbath Breach, 106.

Sabbath Shooting Match, 107.
Saddle, The, 195.
Saint Loch, 192.
Saunders, D. H., 154.
Saunders, George, 165, 231.
Saunders, John, 162, 245.
Saunders, Leezie, 174.
Scenery, 119.
Scheves, 40.
School Boards, 66, 156, 228.
Schools, 106, 108, 109, 122.
  Adventure, 112.
  Dames', 111.
  Episcopal, 111.
  James Street, 110.
  Parish, 108.
  New Public, 110.
  Roman Catholic, 112.
  William Street, 110.
Schoolmasters, 103, 108, 109, 110, 111, 112.
  Anderson, John, 109.
  Badenach, Alex., 109.
  Barbour, John, 110.
  Bell, W. Hamilton, 111.
  Binnie, —., 110.
  Blair, Thomas, 109.
  Burton, —., 111.
  Buttar, —., 112.
  Calderwood, D. S., 111.
  Campbell, —., 112.
  Douglas, James, 110.
  Dow, William, 109.
  Forbes, Peter, 109.
  Geddes, John, 110.
  Gelloch, William, 109.
  Grant, P., 112.
  Haly, Andrew, 109.
  Hislop, A., 110.
  Hunter, John, 112.
  Inch, John, 110.
  Johnstone, James, 112.
  Johnstone, Robert, 110, 254.
  Kermock, David, 109.
  Lothan, —., 111.
  Lowson, D. S., 111.
  M'Donald, A., 112.
  Macdonald, James, 110.
  Macfarlane, James, 112.
  MacGlashan, Thomas, 109.
  Malcolm, John, 110, 154.
  Ogilvy, David, 109.
  Oliphant, —., 109.
  Rae, Patrick, 109.
  Reid, John, 110.
  Robertson, Robert, 110, 147.
  Sinclair, Donald, 110.
  Soutar, Thomas, 253.
  Stoddart, Alex., 109.
  Sturrock, Peter, 110, 147.
  Wilkie, David, 110.
  Wyllie, —., 112
Schoolmistresses, 111, 112.
  Anderson, 111.
  Brodie, Amelia, 112.
  Brodie, Jeanie, 112.
  Chalmers, 112.
  Kennedy, 111.
  Lothan, 111.

INDEX.

Mackie, Jeanie, 112.
Murray, 112, 263.
Robertson, 112.
Thomson, 111.
Scone, 12, 33, 35, 80, 81, 92, 215, 216.
Scone, Commendator of, 84.
Scottish Antiquarian Society, 78.
Scottish Midland Junction Railway, 53.
Scotland, 55.
Scotsman, The, 62, 230.
Scots, The, 34.
Scots, The King of, 31.
Scots Magazine, The, 208.
Scott, James, 51, 75.
Scott of Westfields, 67.
Scott, Sir Walter, 14, 36, 138, 199.
Scrimgeour, Willie, 55.
Scutching Mill, 252.
Seals, 41, 83.
Seal of Commission, 70.
Seaton, Sergt., 162, 163.
See of Dunkeld, 99, 130.
Selling Aile, 101.
Severus, Emperor, 30.
Sewage System, 73.
Sextons—
   Blair, James, 113.
   Blair, John, 113.
   Curr, William, 113.
   Duncan, James, 113.
   M'Lachlan, John, 113.
   M'Lachlan, John (son of), 113, 173, 254.
   M'Lachlan, John (son of), 113, 254.
   Reid, Robert, 113.
   Rodger, Walter, 113.
Shawfield, 48.
Sharp, James D., 148, 195.
Shearer, Messrs, 81.
Shearing on Sabbath, 101.
Shee, The, 187.
Shepherds, A. O. F., 160.
Sheriff Court, 95.
Sheriff Depute, 84.
Sheriff of Perth, 34, 38, 48, 49, 81, 95, 217.
Shirra Muir, 251.
Sidey, George, 162.
Sidlaw Hills, 11, 12, 13.
Sim, Saddler, 172.
Simpson, Sergt., 163, 250.
Situation, 91, 116.
Skellies, 186.
Skermy Tree, 186.
Smiles, Samuel, LL.D., 264.
Smith, Archbishop, 99.
Smith, John, Painter, 160.
Smith, John, 151.
Smith Lamont, 178.
Smith, Robert, 38, 40.
Snaigow, 131.
Societies, 150.
   Blairgowrie and District Photographic Association, 150.
   Choral, 151.
   Dramatic, 152.
   Dundee, Blairgowrie, and District Association, 152.

Constitutional Club, 152.
Edinburgh Blairgowrie Club, 154.
Freemasonry, 156.
Horticultural, 157.
Literary, 157.
Shepherds', 160.
Soil, 21, 116.
Solemn League, 42.
Soo, The, 195.
Soutar, David, 43.
Soutar of Mause, 43, 45.
Soutar of Netheraird, 253.
Soutar, Peter, 187.
Soutar, Thomas, 88, 89, 253.
Soutar, W. S., 148, 149, 162, 183, 231.
South Free Church, 19, 20, 97, 255.
South Free School, 110.
Soveraine Lady, Our, 38.
Spate, The Great, 52.
Special Constables, 173.
Spens of Condy, 41.
Spittalfield, 193, 237, 241.
Spittal of Glenshee, 55, 238.
Spynie, 122.
Stage Coach, 52, 230.
Stamp Office, 117.
Standard, The London, 199.
Standing Stones, 76.
Stanley, 12.
Station Hotel, 18, 67.
Statistics, 114, 249.
Statistical Account, 93, 94, 98, 114.
Steed Stalls, 78
Stenton, 241.
Stenton Craig, 32, 241.
Steps of Cally, 238.
Steven, Thomas, 55, 57, 59, 60, 69, 70, 75, 232.
Stewart, Baron of Grandtully, 135.
Stewart, James, 67, 68, 70, 74, 75, 232.
Stewart, Thomas G., 155.
Stipend, 92.
Stirling, 229, 232.
Stirling Castle, 92.
Stobhall, 83.
Stock, 115, 209.
Stone Axe, 262.
Stone Cup, 262.
Stone Seal, 262.
Stores, Scottish Prison, 232.
Stormont, 25, 84, 191, 253.
Stormont Inn, 239.
Stormont Loch, 13, 24, 34, 77, 192, 199, 200, 235, 236.
Stormont Lodge, 20, 234.
Stormont, Lord, 152.
Strachan, Geordie, 187.
Straiton, Robert, 50.
Strathardle, 99, 189, 229, 238, 239.
Strathmore, 11, 12, 33, 96, 124, 127, 139, 229, 235, 242, 248.
Stron Calie, 82.
Strone Brig, 250.
St Andrews, 92, 93, 97, 225, 226.
St Benedict, 243.
St Catherine's, 98.
St Crux Well, 240.

INDEX.

St Fink, 253.
St Marie's Abbey, 33, 80, 209.
St Marie's Monastery, 33.
St Mary's Church, 19, 95, 224.
St Mary's Parish, 95.
St Ninian, 31.
St Ninian, Well of, 18, 31.
St Ninians, 78.
St Ninians, Provost of, 98.
St Salvador's College, 92.
St Stephen's Church, 98, 99, 109.
St Stephen's School, 112.
St Stephen's Union, 158.
Struth, James, 231.
Suetonius Paulinus, 25.
Sunk Wells, 63.
Superior, The, 49, 66, 82, 248.
Surface, 116.
Sutherland Fencibles, The, 53.
Survey of Mons Grampius, 30.
Swinton, John, 48, 49, 82.

T.

Tacitus the Historian, 25.
Tamson, Johnnie, 173.
Tannage Street, 18, 21, 67.
Tay District Board, 187, 188.
Tay, River, 12, 13, 25, 43, 78, 128, 132, 135, 139, 185, 191, 240, 241.
Temperature, 52.
Temperance Hotel, 19.
Templeman, Charles, 232.
Templeman, David, 75, 232.
Terminus Street, 17, 21.
Teuchat Knowe, The, 77.
Thom, James, 69.
Thomson, John, 89.
Thorn, The, 230.
Thorngreen, 230.
Tiend Sheaves, 88.
Tinder Box, 262.
Tod, David, 65.
Todd, William, 173.
Tornence, 38.
Torridone, 81.
Tower of Lethendy, 84, 134, 241.
Town Clerk, 223, 232, 246.
Town Council, 59, 72, 73, 225, 231.
Town Funds, 247.
Town Hall, 98, 156, 157.
Town House, 63, 82.
Town Park, 20.
Town Criers, 113.
  Law, Francis, 113.
  M'Lachlan, John, 113.
  M'Lachlan, John (son of), 113, 173, 254.
  M'Lachlan, John (son of), 113, 179, 254.
  Reid, Alex., 113, 173.
Traditions, 44.
Traquair, 80.
Tron, The, 241.
Trotter, Charles, 99.
Tulina, 30.
Tumuli, 76, 77.

Tullyduff, George, 38.
Tullyneddie, 240.
Tullyveolan, 14, 138, 160.
Tyrie, John, 18, 172, 173.
Tyrie, William, 248.

U.

Union Bank, 18, 148.
Union Street, 17, 18.
Upper Allan Street, 18, 19, 20, 108.
Upper Mill Street, 19.
Upper Stormont, 239.
Urns, 261.
Urrie, General, 43.

V.

Vespasian, 30.
Viconte de Mortain, 80.
Victoria Hotel, 19, 233.
Viewfield, 20.
Vikings, Danish, 32.
Village, 124.
Violin Maker, A Local, 259.
Voluntary Constables, 178.
Volunteers, 18, 50, 56, 57, 59, 63, 98, 161, 163, 184, 230, 232, 250, 257.
Volunteer Ammunition, 162.
Volunteer Armoury, 161.
Volunteer Band, 164.
Volunteer Camps, 163.
Volunteer Dress, 162, 163.
Volunteer Drill Hall, 164, 205.
Volunteer Instructors, 163.
Volunteer Long Service Medals, 163, 164.
Volunteer Magazine, 197.
Volunteer Oath of Allegiance, 162.
Volunteer Reviews, 162, 163.
Volunteer Rifle Range, 161, 194.
Volunteer Subscription Lists, 161.
Volunteers of 1804, 50, 161, 257.

W.

Waddell, Sandy, 173.
Wag-at-the-Wa', 263.
Walks and Drives, 233.
Wallace, Sir William, 33, 34, 133.
Walter, Justice of Scotland, 80.
Water Commission, 72, 73, 229.
Water Supply, 63.
Waterloo Heroes, 247.
"Wattery," 248.
Waulk Mill, 222.
Waverley, 138.
Webster, J. L., 264.
Weddell, Alex., 152, 153.
Weighhouse, 179, 262.
Weir, 49.
Wellmeadow, 17, 18, 19, 58, 67, 71, 72, 145, 147, 172, 202, 222, 223, 233, 249, 253.

INDEX.

Welltown, 17, 48, 50, 73, 116, 162, 179, 180, 186, 193, 230, 235, 236.
Welltown of Bamff, 68.
Welltown Brownies, 179.
Welltown Road, 18, 166.
Westfields, 187, 188, 189, 234.
Westfields Flute Band, 55.
Westfields Spinning Company, 229.
Wester Bog, 251.
Wester Cally, 238.
Westerly Cairns, 77.
West Gormack, 132.
Western Bank of Scotland, 147.
Whisky Roadie, 19, 172, 173, 178.
Whistlebare, 251.
White, Col.-Sergt., 163, 164.
White Loch, 13, 192.
Whitson, Bailie, 174.
Whitson, Captain C. Hill-, 139.
Whitson, Thomas, 75.
William de Cumyn, 80.
William of Glasgow, 80.
William the Lion, 33, 80, 136, 206, 209, 214.
William Street, 19, 110, 243.
William Street School, 110.
Wilson, Sergt.-Major, 163, 164.
Winter, 208.
Witness, The, 62.
Wolf of Badenoch, 35.
Wood, 23, 89, 90, 121, 241.
Woodhead, 43, 45, 161, 162.
Woodhill, 99, 190, 238.

Woodlands, 47, 48, 235.
Wood Plough Socket, 262.
Wood Rafter, 262.
Woodside, 12.
Wolseley, Lord, 74.
Working Men's Club, 158.
Wyntoun, 36.

X.

Xerxes, 12.

Y.

Yeaman, David, 50.
Yeaman, Provost, 153.
Ye Bailzies o' Blair, 144.
Young, James, 75, 161, 162.
Young, John, 247.
Young Men's Association, 203.
Young, William, 38.
Young Women's Literary, 158.

Z.

Zoology, 24.

LIST OF SUBSCRIBERS.

Anderson, James Chapman, of Aikenhead.
Anderson, Rev. James, Minister of Fortevoit.
Anderson, Dr William, Lynorne, New Rattray.
Anderson, David, Jeweller, Allan Street, Blairgowrie.
Anderson, George, Bootmaker, 10 Reform Street, Blairgowrie.
Aitken, James, Pattern Maker, 10 Tay Street, Edinburgh.
Ambrose, John, Abbeyhill Public School, Edinburgh.
Abercromby, John, Millwright, Edenbank, Newton Street, Blairgowrie.
Anderson, George, Halifax Commercial Bank, Brighouse, Yorks.

Blair-Cunynghame, R. J., of Cronan, 18 Rothesay Place, Edinburgh.
Barty, J. W., LL.D., Solicitor, Dunblane.
Baxter, John S., 12 St Mary Street, Brechin.
Bell, W. Hamilton, M.A., B.Sc., Headmaster, Public School, 1 George Street, Blairgowrie.
Bisset, George S., Ellenbank, New Rattray.
Butchart, John E., Litho. Writer, Reform Street, Dundee.
Brown, George, Coal Merchant, Commercial Street, Blairgowrie.
Beveridge, David, Stone Carver, 40 Watson Crescent, Edinburgh.
Brown, Allan, Butcher, High Street, Blairgowrie.
Bain, Alexander, Saddler, Bridgend, Blairgowrie.
Bell, Alexander, Crown Inn, Wellmeadow, Blairgowrie.
Bell, John, Baker, Balmoral Street, New Rattray.
Black, R. Robertson, Solicitor, Bank of Scotland, Blairgowrie.
Brown, Alexander, Bootmaker, 16 Wellmeadow, Blairgowrie.
Brough, Thomas, Joiner, Karsphairn Cottage, Blairgowrie.
Bell, Joseph, Plasterer, Allan Cottage, Blairgowrie.
B. J., Coupar Angus.
Beveridge, Thomas, Mason, 40 Watson Crescent, Edinburgh.

Cadenhead, W. M., Stationmaster, Caledonian Railway, Blairgowrie.
Chalmers, Rev. John, 2 Gladstone Place, Stirling.
Craigie, John, Advocate, 9 Wemyss Place, Edinburgh.
Cunnison, George, Burgh Surveyor, George Street, Blairgowrie.
Craig, Thomas, Roselea, Perth Road, Blairgowrie.
Craigie, Robert, Slater, High Street, Blairgowrie.
Culross, James, Bootmaker, 6 Allan Street, Blairgowrie.
Clark, Mungo, Clothier, Forneth Villa, Blairgowrie.
Crockart, William, Gunsmith, Parkside Villa, Blairgowrie.
Campbell, David, Bookseller, Wellmeadow, Blairgowrie.
Christie, Robert N., Cromwell Villa, Newton Street, Blairgowrie.
Collie, W. M., Watchmaker, High Street, Blairgowrie.

SUBSCRIBERS.

DUNCAN, G. S., F.S.A., Scot., Dunmore Villa, Newton Street, Blairgowrie (2).
DAVIE, WILLIAM, Woodbrae, Dunkeld.
DEWAR, JAMES, Dunkerton P. O., Iowa, U. S. A.
DUNCAN, ADAM R., Slater, Old Rattray.
DRUMMOND, WILLIAM, Public School Lodge, Blairgowrie.
DOIG, THOMAS, Joiner, New Rattray.
DONALD, GRAHAM, Newton Lane, Blairgowrie.
DUFF, WILLIAM, Butcher, Croft Lane, Blairgowrie.
DOUGLAS, D. B., Royal Bank, Pitt Street, Edinburgh.
DONALD, P. K., Painter, 26 Leslie Street, Blairgowrie.
DICK, JAMES, Westfield Cottage, New Rattray.
DUNCAN, A. B., Laurel Villa, New Rattray.
DUNCAN, THOMAS, Builder, Laurel Villa, New Rattray.
DRYERRE, HENRY, Bookseller, 10 High Street, Blairgowrie.

FINDLAY, JAMES, Architect, 33 Albert Square, Dundee.
FORD, JOHN L., Merchant, High Street, Blairgowrie.
FALCONER, W. D. M., James Street Cottage, Blairgowrie.
FELL, J. M.
FELL, Rev. WILLIAM P., Bridgend, Blairgowrie.
FELL, JOHN D., Butcher, Bridgend, Blairgowrie.
FELL, ALFRED M., Woodbine, New Rattray.
FLEMING, JAMES, Draper, 9 Wellmeadow, Blairgowrie.
FARQUHARSON, CHARLES, Farmer, Bank of Lethendy.
FERGUSON, Mrs JOHN, Fintry Inn, Fintry, Stirlingshire.

GRIMOND, ALEXANDER D., of Glenericht.
GEEKIE, ROBERT, of Rosemount.
GUNN, ROBERT, Royal Hotel, Blairgowrie.
GRANT, WILLIAM, Chemist, High Street, Blairgowrie.
GRANT, GEORGE, Farmer, Tullyneddie, Clunie.
GREWAR, ADAM, Corsehill, Blairgowrie.
GILRUTH, Mrs, Alma Villa, Newton Street, Blairgowrie.
GORRIE, THOMAS C., High Street, New Rattray.
GRANT, W. J. BREWSTER, Architect, Bengarth, Blairgowrie.

HUNTER, Rev. JOHN, M.A., B.D., F.S.A., Scot., Minister of Rattray.
HENDRY, Rev. CHARLES, M.A., Free Church, Kirkcaldy.
HOOD, Dr THOMAS H. F., Ivybank, New Rattray.
HODGE, JAMES M., Solicitor, Blairgowrie.
HILL, ADAM, Builder, Edina Cottage, Emma Street, Blairgowrie.
HENDRY, KENNEDY, Forester, Craighall.
HODGE, WILLIAM, Provost of Rattray.

ISLES, JAMES, J.P., F.S.A., Scot., Wine Merchant, St Ninians, Blairgowrie (3).
INCH, Rev. ALEX. S., M.A., Free High Manse, Dumbarton.

KEAY, JAMES W., Fernbank, Emma Terrace, Blairgowrie.
KEMP, Rev. ROBERT, M.A., Minister of Blairgowrie.
KING, Rev. ANGUS, 25 Kelvinhaugh Street, Glasgow.
KINLOCH, SIR JOHN G. S., Bart., M.P., Kinloch House, Meigle.
KIDD, GEORGE P., Plumber, Croft House, Blairgowrie.

SUBSCRIBERS.

KIDD, ROBERT. Plumber, 1 High Street, Blairgowrie.
KIRKWOOD, WILLIAM, Ironmonger, The Cross, Blairgowrie.
KYDD, JAMES, 10 Garland Place, Dundee.
KIDD, Mrs J. T., Mains of Errol, Errol.

LOW, Rev. GEORGE D., M.A., 27 Merchiston Avenue, Edinburgh.
LOCKHART, Mrs ROBERT A., Belleisle, 20. Polwarth Terrace, Edinburgh.
LUNAN, Dr CHARLES S., High Street, Blairgowrie.
LUNAN, ROBERT. High Street, Blairgowrie.
LOWE, ROBERT, Clerk of Works, Roselea, Blairgowrie.
LOWE, JAMES, C.E. and Architect, Roselea Cottage, Blairgowrie.
LAWSON, GEORGE, Horseshoer, Croft Lane, Blairgowrie.
LEITH, JAMES, Slater, Reform Street, Blairgowrie (2).
LAIRD, JAMES C., Plumber, Emma Street, Blairgowrie.
LOW, JAMES, Bookseller, High Street, Blairgowrie (2).
LEGGAT, JAMES, Joiner, Meikleour.

MACKENZIE, Sir ALEX. MUIR, Bart., Delvine House, Dunkeld.
MACPHERSON, Mrs E., Blairgowrie House, Blairgowrie.
MACDONALD, Rev. P., B.D., 2 Lorne Terrace, Abbeyhill, Edinburgh.
MACKINTOSH, ALEXANDER, Farr Lodge, Forfar.
MACRITCHIE. DAVID, C.A., F.S.A., Scot., Easter Logie (2).
MACDONALD, ALEXANDER, Camden Place, Dundee.
MALCOLM. Rev. JOHN, St Stephen's, Bank Street, Blairgowrie.
MONCUR, WILLIAM, Ironmonger, Allan Street, Blairgowrie.
MACLACHLAN, JOHN, Albert Institute Free Library, Dundee (3).
MILLER, JOHN B., Solicitor, North of Scotland Bank, Blairgowrie. ✓
MITCHELL, JAMES, Merchant, 34 Leslie Street, Blairgowrie.
MACLACHLAN, JOHN B., Saddler, Allan Street, Blairgowrie.
MACLAREN, Lieut.-Col. G. G., M.D., Falcon House, Blairgowrie.
MILNE, ALEX. C., Photographer, High Street, Blairgowrie.
MENZIES, JOHN, Butcher, Reform Street, Blairgowrie.
MITCHELL, WILLIAM C., Architect, Essendy.
MORRISON, HEW, Public Library, Edinburgh.
MACLAREN, R. D. G., 37 Bruntsfield Gardens, Edinburgh.
MACLENNAN, D. S., Sanitary Inspector, Cedar Mount, Rattray.
MACFARLANE, JAMES, jun., Letter Carrier, Brown Street, Blairgowrie.
MILLER, Rev. WILLIAM G., Blairhill U. P. Church, Coatbridge.
MILLER, Rev. DAVID K., M.A., U. P. Manse, Eyemouth.
MORRISON, Rev. J. H., M.A., Free Church Manse, Kirkmichael.
MILLER, Miss CHRISTINA, Music Teacher, Springbank, Newton Street, Blairgowrie.
MACDONALD, JOHN, Editor, "Forfar Review," Forfar.
MACINNES, Mrs A., Tullochcurran Farm, Kirkmichael.
MITCHELL, DAVID, Ardmhor, Hill Street, Blairgowrie.
M'LAREN, JOHN, Merchant, 65 High Street, Blairgowrie.
MONRO, GEORGE, Old Rattray.
MONCUR, ALEX. H., Manufacturer, Dundee.
M'KENZIE, THOMAS, Draper, Perth Street, Blairgowrie.
MUIR, Rev. WILLIAM, B.D., B.L., First Free Manse, Blairgowrie.
MILLS, W. B., Bookseller, "Observer Office," Kirriemuir.
MONCUR, JAMES, Westgarth, Colinton, Edinburgh.
MONAIR, D. G., Reporter, Elmbank, Blairgowrie.

SUBSCRIBERS.

Moir, James, 20 Ann Street, Hillhead, Glasgow.
Macfarlane, George, Bootmaker, High Street, Blairgowrie.
Murray, W. A. M., Cabinetmaker, George Street, Blairgowrie.
Marshall, W. M., Milton Cottage, Ann Street.
M'Ritchie, David, Joiner, Mitchell Square, Blairgowrie.
M'Lae, Miss J., 71 Watson Street, Dundee.
Macdonald, George, jun., Joiner, Trades Lane, Coupar Angus.
M'Levy, James, Librarian, 14 Newton Street, Blairgowrie.
M'Dougall, John, Butcher, 17 Perth Street, Blairgowrie.
Mitchell, William, Fish Merchant, Westfields.
M'Donald, James M., Farmer, Welltown.
Macpherson, Thomas, Solicitor, 3 Charlotte Street, Perth.
M'Intyre, Douglas William, Blairview, Rattray.
Mitchell, P. B., Retired Factor, 6 Union Street, Coupar Angus.
Mechanics' Institute Library, High Street (J. B. Maclachlan, Convener).
Mackay, Robert, Architect, 23 Barossa Place, Perth.

Neilson, Alex. J. R., Inspector of Poor, Wellmeadow, Blairgowrie.
Nelson, J. Sidey, Solicitor, Bank Buildings, Blairgowrie.
Nelson, Robert, Solicitor, Bank Buildings, Blairgowrie.

Ogilvy, James, Brewer, Mount Ericht, Rattray.

Panton, William, Maltster, Stormont Lodge, Blairgowrie (2).
Panton, William, The Feu, Newton Street, Blairgowrie.
Petrie, J. D., Chemist, High Street, Blairgowrie.

Rattray, Lieut.-Gen. Sir James Clerk, K.C.B., of Craighall, Rattray.
Robertson, Dr J. Anderson, M.A., M.B., 6 St James Terrace, Hillhead, Glasgow.
Robertson, R. A., University, St Andrews.
Richardson, James, Baker, High Street, Blairgowrie.
Reid, Andrew, 17 Petershill Road, Springburn, Glasgow.
Robertson, John, Manufacturer, Elmslea, Dundee (4).
Reid, James, Allan House, Newton Street, Blairgowrie.
Reid, Alex., Lime Villa, Newton Street, Blairgowrie.
Reid, John, Ogilvy Arms Inn, Wellmeadow, Blairgowrie (4).
Robertson, Robert H., Clothier, High Street, Blairgowrie.
Reid, Alexander, Enochdhu, Kirkmichael.
Robertson, Miss, Apna Cottage, Blairgowrie.
Robertson, Robert, Solicitor, Bank of Scotland, Blairgowrie (4).
Robertson, Alex. P., 2 and 6 Cathedral Street, Glasgow.
Robertson, James, "Liverpool Evening Express."
Robertson, Patrick, Merchant, 61 High Street, Blairgowrie.
Robertson, William, Engineer, 32 William Street, Blairgowrie.
Robertson, W. T., Joiner, Victoria Place, Blairgowrie.
Robertson, Miss, James Street House, Blairgowrie.
Robertson, Alex., Merchant, Post Office, Old Rattray.
Robertson, W., Draper, Lenzie.

Smith, James A., Bishop of Dunkeld, 29 Magdalen Yard Road, Dundee.
Smith, A. Davidson, C.A., Secy. R. C. C. C., 4A York Place, Edinburgh.
Stewart, Miss Margaret, 41 High Street, Blairgowrie.

STEWART, LADY GRAINGER, 17 Charlotte Square, Edinburgh.
SOMERVILLE, JAMES, Cabinetmaker, High Street, Blairgowrie.
STEVEN, WILLIAM, Joiner, Newton Place, Blairgowrie.
SCOTT, ROBERT J., Commercial Bank, Selkirk.
STEWART, Mrs, 20 Osnaburg Street, Forfar.
STEVEN, THOMAS, Joiner, Newton Place, Blairgowrie.
STEWART, WILLIAM, Merchant, Leslie Street, Blairgowrie.
SMAIL, ROBERT, Knoweside, Craigie, Perth.
SOUTAR, GEORGE, Moulder. Bankhead, Blairgowrie.
SHAW, DR P. W., High Street, Blairgowrie.
SMITH, JOHN, Painter, High Street, Blairgowrie.
STRACHAN, JAMES, Jeweller, Allan Street, Blairgowrie.
STEWART, JOHN, Merchant, Stanley Cottage, Blairgowrie.
SCOTT, CHARLES, Headmaster, Schoolhouse, Rattray.
STEWART, Rev. ROBERT, St Mary's Manse, Blairgowrie.
SHARP, JAMES D., Banker, Union Bank of Scotland, Blairgowrie.
STRAIN, WILLIAM, Daniel Stewart's College, Edinburgh.
STEWART, JOHN, Farmer, St Fink.
SMALL, THOMAS, Hagg Crescent, Johnstone, Renfrew.
STRAIN, GEORGE W. F., M.A., Public School, Coupar Angus.
STEVEN, JOHN, Merchant, 1 Reform Street, Blairgowrie..
STEVEN, ALEXANDER, Hairdresser, 16 Allan Street, Blairgowrie.
SPALDING, DAVID, Joiner, Boat Brae, Rattray.
SANDEMAN PUBLIC LIBRARY, Perth. (Per John Christie, Bookseller,
    32 St John Street.)
STIRTON, ADAM, Hostler, Queen's Hotel, Blairgowrie.

TEMPLEMAN, DAVID, Flaxspinner, Provost of Blairgowrie.
TEMPLEMAN, Dr CHARLES, M.D., West Bell Street, Dundee.
TYRIE, W. B., 23 Patrick Street, Cork.
TULLY, Rev. THOMAS, M.A., Free Church Manse, Rattray.
TERRACE, ANDREW, Manager, Gas Works House, Blairgowrie.
TENNANT, Rev. E. MARSHALL, Congregational Manse, Blairgowrie.
THOMSON, JAMES B., 10 Panmure Street, Dundee.

WHITSON, Capt. CHARLES HILL, of Parkhill, Rattray.
WISHART, ALEX. R., 14 Greenhill Terrace, Edinburgh.
WHITE, Rev. MALCOLM, M.A., Free South Manse, Blairgowrie.
WILSON, Miss JESSIE, 12 Newton Street, Blairgowrie.
WILSON, ROBERT C., 37 Hollybank Terrace, Edinburgh.
WYLLIE, GEORGE, Road Surveyor, Rosebank, Rattray.
WADDELL, FORBES, Manager, Gas Works, Forfar.